THE
BOOK OF
WHY

Understanding Your Soul's Journey

Judy Hall

FLYING HORSE BOOKS

Published in 2010 by
Flying Horse Publications
an imprint of
The Wessex Astrologer Ltd
4A Woodside Road
Bournemouth
BH5 2AZ
England

www.wessexastrologer.com

ISBN 9781902405483

A catalogue record of this book is available at The British Library

Cover design by Dave at Creative Byte, Poole, Dorset

Acknowledgements

I would like to thank all the people who so willingly gave permission for me to use their stories so that other people could benefit. I would particularly like to thank Julie Chimes, Simon Jacobs and Mario Reading for their contributions and courage. The rest of you know who you are so I will not name you and break confidentiality but I would like to say to all my astrology clients, workshop participants and regressees that, if you were not approached for permission, then the case history, although it may resonate strongly with you and have echoes of your own experience, is not your personal story. I chose the story precisely because it was so ubiquitous and names have been changed for the sake of confidentiality unless a surname is used. I thank you all because without you I couldn't have explored karmic interaction so widely. I would also like to give thanks to the late Edgar Cayce, Christine Hartley and others on whose published work I have drawn. Special thanks go to Margaret Cahill and Paul Newman who took a rough, unfinished draft and turned the book around in record time. Any mistakes are my own, the improvements are theirs. As always discussions with Margaret and her partner Stephen Gawtry added considerably to my understanding of the ramifications of the concepts discussed in this book. They (gently!) pushed me to where I needed to go.

For Rosie

With love

Contents

They said of old the Soul had human shape,
But smaller, subtler than the fleshly self,
So wandered forth for airing when it pleased.
And see! beside her cherub-face there floats
A pale-lipped form aerial whispering
Its promptings in that little shell her ear.

Now is there civil war within the soul:
Resolve is thrust from off the sacred throne
By clamorous Needs, and Pride the grand-vizier
Makes humble compact, plays the supple part
Of envoy and deft-tongued apologist
For hungry rebels.

Our deeds still travel with us from afar,
And what we have been makes us what we are.

Full souls are double mirrors, making still
An endless vista of fair things before,
Repeating things behind.

Hath she her faults? I would you had them too.
They are the fruity must of soundest wine;
Or say, they are regenerating fire
Such as hath turned the dense black element
Into a crystal pathway for the sun.

George Eliot, Middlemarch

Definitions

Akashic Record: the record of all that has been or will be containing all potentials and possibilities (rather similar to the quantum field idea) which can be read to ascertain past lives and soul purpose.

Flashback: a spontaneous remembering of a past life. It may come out of the blue or be triggered by a place (déjà vu), person or object or by touching the part of the body involved in the memory.

Higher self: the part of the soul that exists at a higher vibration and, not being so mired in the physical level of incarnation, can take an overall view of the soul's progress and which can communicate information from other lives as it knows the whole history of the soul and its overall plan for evolution.

Interlife: the holding space the soul inhabits between physical incarnations. Often initially experienced according to cultural or religious beliefs, the interlife has many dimensions and planes of experience. Not all souls are instantly reborn into a physical body. Those who are not occupy a less dense 'body' in a space not located on earth – although it may have a similar appearance. To the soul, this space is solid and tangible. It may be called, Heaven or Hell, the Bardo, the Otherworld, the Afterlife, karmaloca, purgatory, the Summerland and so on. Healing and reframing can easily be carried out in the interlife and the soul's purpose ascertained. Souls spend an indefinite period in this space until ready to return to earth when a 'planning meeting' takes place to prepare for the new life.

Karma: dynamic, continuous process of learning and meeting the credits and deficits of previous actions, and what is being set in motion now.

Karmic: experiences or lessons arising from or appertaining to a past incarnation. Debts, beliefs and emotions such as guilt are carried over into the present life and create dis-ease but past life credits and wisdom are available to heal these.

Karmic enmeshment: entanglement with another soul that has its roots in past lives in which karma or actions are repeated over and over again.

Life Reading: an impression of past lives and karmic causes received by a psychic when tuning into the person concerned or reading the Akashic Record.

Other lives/past lives: the previous lives that a soul has lived upon the earth and in other planes of existence.

Past life therapy: being guided to a time before birth in the present life, that is into another life, to uncover and heal the causes of problems and blockages that have arisen in the present life or to the interlife to identify soul contracts and the soul's plan for the present incarnation.

Reframing: changing the lifescript for a particular incarnation. It may entail a change of scenario, replaying it with a different outcome. It may need to be seen from a different perspective or with forgiveness or compassionate witnessing. Changing the past in this way changes the present life experience.

Reincarnation: successive lives lived in different bodies. Reincarnation postulates that someone now living, previously inhabited a different physical body and then died but the soul continued in another dimension and was (at some stage) incarnated in a new physical body.

Soul: the vessel which passes from life to life and which is a vehicle for karma or evolution and also a carrier for the eternal Spirit. The soul is capable of fragmenting and reuniting across different lifetimes.

Soul contract: an agreement willingly made in the interlife before the present incarnation that one soul would interact with another in a specific way. Or: an agreement that is carried over from a previous life or a previous interlife but which has not been reconsidered before incarnation. Soul contracts can be positive and constructive, or destructive and soul contracts that are not completed in one life may be unwittingly carried over to another.

Soul group: people with whom we have travelled throughout time, over many incarnations and interacted with in all possible combinations. Not all members of a soul group are in incarnation at one time, but those people who help us to learn the hardest lessons in life are usually members of our primary soul group – soul groups can split into 'sub-sets'. A resonance frequency may be established between souls who have taken part in a particular soul drama so that the participants are pulled back into incarnation at approximately the same time to rework or reframe some of the outstanding karma from that life.

Soul hologram: a record from the original core soul essence 'pool' which splits off to form individual souls and is carried by each particle of that soul essence as it enters incarnation. Each and every part of a soul hologram contains the whole and can communicate with the other parts, feeding back experience or receiving information itself.

Soul imperatives/overlays: deeply ingrained patterns or intentions laid down over many lifetimes which may have been outgrown but not shed by the soul and which compel certain behaviour no matter how much the soul may wish to override them. Such scripts are made up of all the 'oughts, shoulds and musts', conditional responses and expectations arising from the past, whenever that might be. Changing a soul imperative can bring about a profound level of healing.

Soulplan: the soul's intention for the present life formulated in the interlife before incarnation.

Soul purpose: the soul's intention for the present life which may be part of a greater pattern either of the soul or the soul group.

Soul retrieval: identifying and reintegrating parts of the soul that have been left in other lives or at traumatic moments in the present life.

Spirit: the eternal spark

Introduction: why is this happening to me?

It is conceivable that I might well be reborn as a Chinese coolie. In such a case I should lodge a protest.

Winston Churchill

eople often ask me: 'Why is this happening?' The question of 'why' is something that is around us all the time: 'why am I ill?', 'why have I lost my job?', 'why did someone die so young?', 'why is there this war, that disaster or that tragedy?' 'why did I meet that person' and so on. It repeats again and again. People ask me because I'm a karmic counsellor, someone who looks at past life patterns in the birthchart to discern the purpose and soulplan for the current incarnation – and who uses psychic 'far memory' to read past life causes or interlife choices. In other words, I examine the credits and deficits on a soul's spiritual bank account – and how the present life is going to contribute to their growth or diminishment.

Knowing why can help to guide us through difficult times but nevertheless, even with the understanding I have, there are moments when everything seemingly goes wrong and I feel let down and I instantly revert to my Gnostic past. The Gnostics believed that this earth is ruled by an 'evil' demiurge who takes great pleasure in tormenting the souls incarcerated on earth and that the 'good' demiurge is only to be found outside incarnation in the spiritual world. In those moments I perceive that this universe is ruled by a malicious, cruel-hearted being with a black sense of humour who delights in thwarting my plans and playing cosmic jokes. The trickster at the heart of the universe. This is what I call a soul overlay. Some ingrained soul overlays are particularly hard to shift, especially when events seem to support the belief encapsulated within them.

It doesn't take long though before I start to ask 'why has this happened?' and to look for the gift or learning in the situation, which admittedly is sometimes hard to find. Given time, it usually becomes clear that either something better was waiting or that I was stuck in an old pattern that simply had to go. Nevertheless, that moment of railing at fate or whatever, still occurs. No doubt it does to you too. It is all too easy to intellectually understand, logically with our head, the necessity for change but it is much harder to emotionally understand and embrace this with our hearts.

Deep down, I am convinced that facing this necessity for change is all part of a soulplan I laid out before I was born and that part of that soulplan was to one day be able to face those moments with equanimity and without flipping into my old beliefs. That I no longer flip into them for days, weeks, months, years even lifetimes is progress. I now try to compassionately witness what I am going through without beating myself up and with forgiveness for myself and my slips in my heart. My latest slip reminded me to put this paragraph into this book – I often recycle my life and my experiences to provide examples as I would not want my readers to think 'it's alright for you, everything is fine in your life'. It isn't, but I'm getting there and this book contains insights that have helped me to find my way and which I hope will help you to find yours.

A question I am frequently asked is: 'Why do people need to know about their past lives and interlife choices? What possible value can it have?' Just a few of its benefits are:

- dramatic change in how we view life and death and our family
- elimination of guilt and anxiety
- or overcoming irrational fears
- insight into the cause of chronic health problems
- understanding the dynamics of family and relationship dysfunction
- unlocking potential or latent talents and abilities
- changing ingrained habits and core beliefs
- dealing with the cause not the symptoms
- integrating all facets of the soul
- pinpointing where a soul is punishing itself or others

- getting to the bottom of sexual difficulties, addictions or eating disorders
- shedding outworn emotional or doctrinal conditioning
- creating better understanding of others
- developing compassion, empathy and forgiveness
- recognising that the past can be reframed
- learning that a person who seemingly hates us may actually love us enough to provide an apparently horrendous learning situation – and the reasons behind it
- revealing our soul purpose and the reason for incarnating in the first place.
- setting positive change in motion

Above all, it can show that you are not a victim of circumstance but are experiencing a carefully planned path of soul evolution. You learn that you are an immortal soul who happens to be on a human journey at this moment but who is capable of multi-faceted experience in different dimensions.

I've had a long (exceedingly long if you take other lives into account) training to do this work, including conducting hundreds of regressions, reading well over a thousand maps of the soul's plan – the birthchart – and talking to many 'higher selves' who have a much broader view than is possible from here on earth. I've accompanied numerous people into the interlife, attending the planning meeting at which they broadly map out the purpose and path of the present incarnation and the soul contracts that may go with it. I've also been to the life review that follows death to see how far that purpose was achieved.

At one time I believed that, when it is viewed as purposeful, self-generated and subject to free-will, the *process* of reincarnation resolved all the great questions of life: providing a reason for 'suffering', the 'fairness" or otherwise of a situation a person finds him or herself in, and the apparent unjustness of one short life – plus recognising that current life actions will have consequences.

Nevertheless, I had always thought that, while war for instance is caused by greed and man's inhumanity to man, it could be part of a collective karma in which individual souls could be swept up. Now I recognise that there are other aspects to the life we lead. Soul choices made in the interlife are powerful and may override even the most compelling karma or soul overlay if the intention or need is great enough, although this is not always the case and the reverse may occur.

Soul overlays that contain old soul contracts well past their sell-by date but not yet rescinded can have a powerful effect on the present life. These soul overlays present as an ingrained, repeating pattern over many lifetimes that, while it may have its roots in karma, has little to do with consequences – being more like an old gramophone needle stuck in a groove of 'must do' that needs to be shed by the soul.

Distinguishing between present life soul purpose and past life soul overlays that have carried over into the present life is challenging – and has occupied much of my time over the last thirty-five years. They trip up many a soul's evolutionary intent as deeply ingrained imperatives often seem to be determined to play out at all costs and can take a great deal of disentangling and renegotiation – which can spread out over a surprisingly long period of time as the layers peel back. It can be difficult as we start out on our journey to distinguish between our karmic consequences, the soul contracts we have made and the purpose we have incarnated to fulfil.

However, even I am continually surprised by how the unfolding of what appears, on the surface, to be karmic or an overwhelming catastrophic event that is beyond personal karma may well be a soul decision to grow through exceedingly difficult circumstances not from karmic compulsion, but from a soul choice.

Rather than a dire event being karmic retribution, reparation or restitution, what seems to be a collective disaster may be a set of circumstances specially chosen by the soul as an opportunity for learning, or for service to humanity or compassionate witnessing of our plight. Compassionate witnessing is a somewhat pretentious term for an unconditional, non-judgmental observation of ourselves and others. I will never forget working to facilitate a group soul rescue at the site of one of the most horrendous death camps. As the souls were freed and passed through a portal of light, they each turned to help the next soul up, forming a long chain. It mattered not on which side the soul had fought, or that before passing through the portal they had appeared to be mortal enemies for all time. An internee would turn to help a guard and, after passing through the portal, they would embrace and go on their way together. When I asked about this, I was told that this particular group had incarnated knowing what would happen and hoping that, by allowing the world to witness the worst horrors one race could perpetrate on another, it was hoped that it would never happen again. Although that was the overriding group soul intention, within that group many individual souls were expanding their own soul learning. Author Robert Schwartz has extensively explored the interlife experience and concludes:

> *I have realized that each of us has a divine purpose, a reason for being here, that includes but goes well beyond our own learning. That is, we plan life challenges not only to remember who we really are, but also to share ourselves, our unique essence, with one another.*[1]

Two souls may respond to similar situations in very different ways depending on their karma, their soul overlays and their intention for the present life. I knew two men for instance who had severe scoliosis of the spine. One was gentle and kind with great compassion for everyone, especially those who were in difficult circumstances. He never passed a beggar without giving a gift or an old person without offering a smile. His soul intention was to learn humility and to empathise with the suffering of others. The other man, who expressed his resentment constantly, appeared to be a deeply twisted and angry individual carrying a huge chip on his shoulder. And yet he had the voice of an angel and could give enormous pleasure to people. As he hadn't asked me to look at his karma, I can make no conclusion as to what his intentions were when he incarnated or whether his scoliosis was an example of attitudinal karma, but it could well have been.

Understanding of situations like these cannot be made without intimate contact with the person's soul and their intention for the present life. Time after time, I have seen that a soul not only has freewill but also freedom of choice and that the pathway through life is not fixed and static, it unfolds according to choices the soul made both in and out of incarnation. Yes, certain things may be pre-ordained but they are usually consciously planned and 'seeded' into the soulplan and certain triggers are arranged. It is only when a soul is being particularly obtuse or stubborn, or when soul overlays run very deep indeed, that apparent 'fate' or karmic restitution intervenes and, even then, there is the possibility of progress and soul evolution as, at any moment, the soul can wake up to what is going on and find the gifts and learning in the situation.

Some people assume – or presume – that they know why things are happening to others: seeing it through a warped and restricted view of karma, a judgemental punishment for past deeds. A day or two before I sat down to write this introduction, an acquaintance said to me: 'that wife and daughter must have burned people as heretics in past life or been arsonists or something like that and the husband suffered back then and now's he's got his own back'. She was talking about a woman and her daughter who had been shot by the husband before he set fire to their house, the man himself then perishing in the fire. There was no indication from her of what William Bloom calls 'compassionate witnessing' either for someone else's journey or, indeed, for her own. This same acquaintance had said some years previously; 'well, she must have been a witch ducker or something like that' when there was only one fatality amongst 246 people caught up in a ferry disaster. This person sees karma only from the biblical 'eye for an eye, tooth for a tooth' perspective. She has a conviction that a soul must make reparation or suffer retribution but, as Shakespeare said in one of his sonnets: 'The offender's sorrow brings but small relief to him who wears the strong offence's cross'.

Let's pause for a moment and consider what sort of satisfaction would the 'offender' flagellating him or herself in a present or future life bring to someone who had borne the brunt of an ill-judged action in a previous life. Would it give karmic satisfaction or bring about karmic balance, or would it set up a 'tit for tat' seesawing between two extremes? That person, let's call him Dave, may not even remember the past life cause but may carry a powerful sense of having been ill-used or a resentment that attaches to no particular cause in the present life. Dave could be carrying the karma of suffering, having an expectation of victimhood even though he had been offended against and might perhaps be expected to be on the receiving end of a rebalancing life. Supposing however, the offender in the next life, let's call him Bob, freely performed an act of service for Dave his former 'victim'. This might change Dave's attitude. As could 'the victim' becoming the misuser in another life so that Dave could understand how it occurs in the first place. But if that attitude of 'I've been hard done by' is deeply ingrained, then attitudinal karma could attach and have karmic consequences that manifest physically in Dave's body. However, if Dave learned to freely forgive and let go through a soul choice then the karma of grace could operate on both souls.

We'll be looking at all these kinds of karma and karmic and soul growth possibilities throughout the book but let's take a look now at just how many possibilities there can be within one scenario. I have come to recognise that karma is much wider than the restricted view – and that there is karma and then there is soul choice and freewill. There is also dharma: the work or service that your soul has come to do. It is with soul choice and dharma that we will be concerned later in this book.

Last night I was talking with friends when one of them mentioned a local railway bridge from which many people cast themselves in front of trains. The bridge was opposite a home for the mentally disturbed and it attracted those with suicidal tendencies like a magnet. We were discussing how the possibility of interlife choices changes how you look at situations and whether the driver of the train could have agreed in the interlife to be an 'agent of death' for a soul that felt it simply could not live any longer.

From the kismet or fated point of view, it would be pure fate that that driver, let's call him Ted, happened to be driving that particular train at the precise moment when Jane, our suicide, felt she simply could not go on. In the kismet scenario, it would be her fate to jump at that moment in front of that train. She could do nothing else but follow her fate. All well and good but that takes no account of Jane's freewill nor does it give any consideration to why Ted should be called upon by fate to have that traumatic experience. Both would merely be passive victims of something implacable and outside of themselves.

From the karmic point of view, and particularly from the highly judgemental and personal retributive karmic perspective, Ted could perhaps have killed Jane in a former life by chopping her with a sword or driving his carriage over her and now Jane is exacting retribution. But is it this simple? Experience leads me to say an emphatic no. For instance, Ted might possibly have thoughtlessly or even joyfully killed many people in other lives, but not actually killed Jane. He could, in a very extreme way, be weighing all that killing against what seems to be a random involuntary act, but which in fact brings home to him what it means to take a life – however accidentally. Equally, however, he could have held an extremely strong pacifist view point that created a bigot who narrow-mindedly judged those who killed others as beyond the pale, and so his higher self arranged a random killing to clear out that extreme attitude. Or, Jane could have hated Ted for something in another life and chosen this as a way of punishing him *even though she wasn't aware of who he now was*. I know it all sounds far fetched, and agree it is unlikely, but such things can occur and by including these possibilities I simply want to widen out your viewpoint. You'll need to stretch your mind as we journey through this book.

From a soul perspective, Jane could, in the interlife, have planned that her next life was going to be extremely challenging and traumatic, so much so that she might not be able to handle it and could potentially use the karma of grace to get out. The karma of grace says that when you have dealt with a situation to the best of your ability, you can get out without further karma accruing. Many people assume that suicides will inevitably be severely punished or placed in hell 'forever' but, from regression work I have found this is not the case – although many suicidal souls or soul fragments can still be wandering near their body if it was buried outside consecrated ground and so their belief system told them that they would be consigned to hell, for instance. Part of the healing work in regression may be to collect this shade, or soul fragment, and return it to the overall soul for forgiveness, healing and integration. But I digress.

Let's return to Jane and Ted and to the preplanning meeting in the interlife. At that planning meeting Jane could have asked a member of her soul group to act as 'an agent of my death' as it was put at one such meeting. This meant that she had a guaranteed way out if she needed it – and that the soul who took on this role would not necessarily accrue karma in so doing. It would all depend on how the soul responded afterwards. We tend to forget when in incarnation the tasks we have taken on and can set new karma in motion through our actions or our feelings. If, for instance, Ted had a tendency to martyrdom, he could see such an occurrence as 'all my fault' and he could go on 'punishing' himself for a very long time without realising what the core problem was. This is an extremely common reaction. Someone who was involved in a motorbike accident for which he was entirely blameless but in which a young man died, for example, later had four of his dogs killed on the road one after another. He became obsessed with finding a safe place for his pet to live, getting into debt in the process, but failed to see that it was his own hidden guilt that created this situation again and again. The way out was to forgive himself and let go, then wherever he and his dog lived they would be safe. If he had been able to accept that he was playing his part, rather than feeling that it was cruel fate, his passage through life would have been considerably eased.

As we will see, it takes a soul who loves us deeply and unconditionally to take on a traumatic task and so a member of our immediate soul group often volunteers as an act of service. This may also fit in with issues such as martyrdom or guilt which that soul wants, for their own soul reasons, to explore and this gives them an opportunity. There is no contradiction between service and karmic learning. So our volunteer Ted could have either agreed from pure altruism or for his own reasons which will rarely be clear unless contact is made with the original plan – and even that could have become distorted by either Ted or Jane's ingrained soul overlay that subtly subverted the original intention. One thing is certain, we cannot judge the outcome from the perspective of our earthly selves.

Other people's karmic imaginings on our behalf can be cruel. An elderly woman was told at a psychic fair that her inability to have children in her present life was because she had killed her children in a former life. As can be imagined, this woman was deeply distressed by such a suggestion – which was made accusatorily with no sense of compassion or understanding. Nor did it look to the wider picture. Desdemona is a writer who has birthed many books, plays and poems. She has learned throughout a long life to be creative in a different way and according to her astrological chart her soulplan does not include children this time around. But Desdemona's life experience did include the searing grief of losing a child by miscarriage several times over so that her soul was scoured. This gave her a deep understanding of loss that she has communicated to others through her writing. It leads me to wonder how anyone who knows nothing of a life – or lives – can make such a bald and hurtful statement without understanding the breadth of past lives and interlife choices – and indeed as to whether karma is inadvertently brought into being by such a statement.

In regression, I have occasionally come across people who have had to kill or offer up to be killed a child for one reason or another in a past life, as a religious sacrifice, for instance, or to keep a baby quiet when it was in danger of giving away the position of a group of hunted people, as well as those who have, inadvertently or otherwise, killed a child. Some people have been forced by circumstances to give up a child. Or, a wealthy woman may have followed the fashion of the day and left her child with servants. For all such people there followed an almost unbearable period of grief that needed healing in the interlife, but they rarely felt they had to punish themselves by not having children in another life – although there may have been difficulties or delays that helped them to value the child more when it finally came into incarnation.

When a person has been through this kind of experience there may be a deeply embedded decision not to put their soul through that kind of pain again. Souls who have had to make such sacrifices may deprive themselves again and again but not in the 'eye for an eye' way that either ensures their child is not born at all, dies young or is disabled. The soul is more creative than that and such a situation may come about for reasons of soul scouring, soul growth or service to humanity as we shall see. Many people, as with Desdemona, chose not to have children so that they can move beyond biological creativity and into a wider exploration of what creativity could mean for them.

What does seem to hold good is that, apart from glimpses of other lives, on the whole most people forget about their previous incarnations and their soulplans once they are clothed in a physical body again. (The ancient Greeks referred to this as being bathed in the River of Forgetfulness before birth). They become aware of their deeper purpose as and when appropriate. After all, for many people, if they knew intellectually what it was they were here to do they would do it – but this would be from the head not from the heart and the soul would not grow. At some point, however, their soul might chose to give them a nudge and that is where people like me come in, as do near death experiences, grievous loss, accidents, terminal illness, soulmate meetings and other such wake-up calls.

The most beneficial way to deal with all such possible manifestations of karma, dharma or soul cultivation is to witness with infinite compassion what is going on within your life and that of those around you, refraining from making a judgement about what is or could be, not beating yourself up about it, and simply being with what is. This compassionate witnessing comes from building a deep connection with your higher self, creating a quiet central point around which the ebbs and flows of incarnated life can whirl and be experienced without being overwhelmed or drawn in. So that you receive soul guidance as appropriate and move gently forward as you cultivate your soul.

As so many of the words used when referring to reincarnation are open to different understandings and misinterpretations, I have included Definitions that I hope will make perfectly clear to what I am referring. I hadn't intended to cover areas I have visited before, but as my reincarnation books are out of print and many people have said how useful it is to have all the information in one place, I have included detailed material on the history of karma and reincarnation in religion on my website www.judyhall.co.uk. If you are new to the concept of karma and reincarnation, you'll find that and the first two sections of this book enlightening and it will provide a useful reference even if this is familiar territory. But, as it covers areas I have visited before, although with new case histories and further insights, if you fully understand the karmic process, you might like to turn to Part 3 first which contains new material on soul contracts, interlife planning and soul choice.

Part 1

The Process of Reincarnation

It is no more surprising to be born twice than it is to be born once.

Voltaire

eincarnation is an ancient belief. The idea of rebirth occurs all over the archaic world with surprising consistency as to the circumstances not only of a new life on earth but also the post-death state. In some views of the post-death state the soul, or consciousness, appears to be housed in a less dense but none-the-less tangible body, in others it is pure energy but in virtually all views the soul retains awareness and memory – something supported by the regression experience of literally thousands of people. In numerous ancient myths souls go into the cauldron of rebirth. Whilst there is little written evidence available, mythology and early grave artefacts give strong hints at a belief right at the start of history in the continuance of life, and it is a particularly enduring idea notwithstanding many attempts to wipe it out.

The idea of rebirth in the East is subtle and complex, souls reincarnate to fulfil or pay-off their karma, and to pursue enlightenment. Karma, which means reaping the results of previous actions, is, for the East, the driving force behind rebirth. There is little volition or freewill. It is an automatic process that ends with enlightenment and reintegration into the divine. In Western thought, although karma is part of the equation, freewill has a place. This gives the soul the opportunity to move beyond karma by its present-life actions. The soul is regarded as being on a path of growth and development, the object of which is reintegration with the divine. How the process of reincarnation works is a perennial question, especially from sceptics who insist that, when the body dies, there is nothing left to reincarnate. But, virtually all religions teach that we have a soul that moves out of the body after death. Where the arguments start is what happens to this soul after death.

In the traditional Christian view, for instance, the soul is in a state of suspension, awaiting the resurrection of its old physical body at the last trump – something rarely supported by regression experiences unless the soul was stuck for another reason. These days, if you're a Christian, you're more likely to believe that you'll be abiding in heaven or hell – purgatory having been officially abolished – but you may also be waiting for the Rapture to fall upon the earth so that the chosen few can inherit the earth or ascend to sit at God's right hand.

If you're a traditional Buddhist, you may believe that your essence scatters into several parts which might then, confusingly, rebirth themselves in various bodies – something only rarely supported by regression evidence although the idea of the holographic soul can be seen as perhaps equating to this view as can 'accidental' soul splits or fragmentation. As a Hindu you'd believe you received a new body according to your past karma. (You can find out more about religious beliefs governing reincarnation on my website).

Regression experience over the past hundred years or so certainly supports the idea of an on-going soul with individual memories and awareness and for anyone who has had a near death experience (NDE) there is no doubt that consciousness survives death. Despite what sceptical neuroscientists might say, even when death has been pronounced, awareness lives on and there are some enlightened researchers who support the idea of continuing consciousness after death.[1]

Having had an NDE or two myself I can report that I was very much alive, functioning in several dimensions at once in a subtle energy body, aware of a least one past life in which I had died in similar circumstances, and was more than ready to move onto another dimension but returned to my present body instead when told I'd have to repeat everything I'd endured up to that stage in my life, in a future life.

For most modern, not necessarily religious, believers in reincarnation the belief is that the soul, having left a physical body at death, will, sooner or later, seek out a new physical body. Where further evidence is coming to light is in how much of the choice of a new life is ruled by karma and soul overlays, and how much by the soul's purpose or intention set out in the interlife or, indeed, during an NDE.

Sir Arthur Conan Doyle, the creator of Sherlock Holmes, was an ardent reincarnationist. In his *History of Spiritualism* he gives a classic exposition of the continuous existence of the soul:

> *When the question is asked, 'Where were we before we were born?" we have a definite answer in the system of slow development by incarnation, with long intervals at spirit rest between, while otherwise we have no answer. Existence afterwards seems to postulate existence before.*
>
> *As to the natural question, 'Why, then, do we not remember such existences?' we may point out that such remembrance would enormously complicate our present life, and that such existences may well form a cycle which is all clear to us when we have come to the end of it, when perhaps we may see a whole rosary of lives threaded upon your personality.*

I'm not so sure I'd agree with the 'long rests' in spirit that Conan Doyle suggests occur in between times, which implies a linear progression. Regression shows that reincarnation is neither linear nor at specific allotted intervals, and time is by no means a continuous line. Some people reincarnate *from the view of earth* quickly and others take longer. People might *appear* to have reincarnated quickly in terms of timespan and yet in the spiritual dimensions it would have seemed that aeons had passed before they returned. And, we must remember, there are many dimensions beyond this world in which people can reincarnate and have experiences that contribute to soul growth.

For the vast majority of modern believers, reincarnation is a 'pathway to evolution'. It provides an answer to the modern spiritual hunger for meaning – and causes. Reincarnation, in most contemporary Western teaching, is based on the theosophical idea of an on-going learning process. A seemingly lowly or difficult life, which would be seen as the result of negative karma in the East, may in the Western view have been taken on for the soul's growth or as a service to humanity rather than as punishment or reparation.

Reincarnation memories do not have to be earth shattering. Not all of them are of important people who stalked the field of history. At its simplest level, the sense of something clicking into place, throwing light onto the previously inexplicable can be a great relief and can assist in understanding otherwise incomprehensive day-to-day feelings. So, for example, a woman regressed to being a much loved only child. She was a real 'daddy's girl'. Given a pony for her birthday, she was ecstatically happy. She leapt onto the pony, which promptly bolted and she was thrown and killed. Asked what the connection was with her present life, she replied that whenever she was happy she would suffer from inexplicable anxiety. There was always a deep sense of dread. She associated being happy with fear and loss. Having been killed in that moment of supreme happiness in her past life made sense of her present life fear. It was a simple matter to rewind the memory, re-vision it so that she had an ecstatic ride and continue on through a happy life. Her anxiety ceased and she was able to enjoy life fully for the first time in the present incarnation. Your inexplicable worries may stem from the same kind of simple experience in another life.

The Soul's Path

> I remember now,
> I was in the pottery studio, clay and water are mixing
> A new body being made, which is
> Another workshop, another studio, my new home.
>
> Rumi

So, here you are a soul that is waiting to incarnate, to set out on a great journey. What exactly are you? Where are you? How are you going to come back? And are you 'all of a piece' or are some parts of your soul stuck in other incarnations or dimensions?

Let's start with the soul itself. The soul has been defined as 'the immaterial part of man', 'the moral and emotional portion of man', or 'the intellectual part of man'. Not very helpful definitions as far as I am concerned. In some views, the soul is immortal, in others divine. It may be a vessel for divine spirit or a part of the universal mind. All very boring and nothing like the reality that emerges from personal experience of this state of being. It is clear from regressions, near death or out of body experiences, spontaneous rememberings and communications from beyond death that the most singular characteristic of a soul is its aliveness and, at the level of vibration nearest to the earth, its individuality. It is conscious and aware, capable of movement and choice, and it has a cohesive identify. The last thing the soul is, is 'dead'. It is also clear that the soul may inhabit many different dimensions and timeframes *all at the same time*.

So, how did it become 'a soul'? Well, in modern esoteric belief, the soul has 'split off' from a pool of spiritual essence and moves through increasingly heavy vibrations until it takes on solid form and resides in a physical body. In the process, it may split from or form part of a larger soul group or group soul several times. It may fragment and reintegrate. I wish the process was simply to describe, it would make writing about it so much easier. But unfortunately, the more experience I have, the more complex the process seems to become. However, what I do find useful is the concept that the soul and the universe are essentially and energetically holographic – and can therefore reflect and experience all the other parts of itself when it has fragmented as, like a holograph, it will contain the whole. As it is energetic rather than physical, it only takes a small leap to say that a hologram is the sum of its parts and can communicate with and receive experiences from its many fragmentations (something we'll look at later).

We can put this another way. Several years ago now I asked a question about consciousness, what exactly was it? The answer that came to me was that consciousness was interstellar dust and interstellar dust was consciousness or soul. This interstellar dust interpenetrated everything, including us and the planet we stand upon. Robert Bauval says that we are star material that has become conscious, part of the first particle that expanded and became many. For him the answer to who we are is that we are star material learning who it is. Which is very similar to an answer I received when asking why the original pool of spiritual essence – or spirit – had fragmented into so many souls. I was told 'spirit wants to know itself'. For Robert, as for me, this means that we are an integral part of the universe and our planet. Our bodies are made from the same material. But what about our souls? Well, most of the universe, as with our bodies, is 'empty space' filled with energy. So, for me our souls are carriers of that energy. Having been back to witness the 'big bang', I don't happen to think that consciousness started with the event that seemingly began our universe, but that's another story for a different book. But it was all part of the same process of expansion and evolution that the soul undertakes (see soul group or group soul below).

In my view, the soul is the carrier for the spark of original spirit – but, like a hologram that spirit permeates through the soul and the physical body, it is not separate. So it can be everywhere at once, along with its energetic vessel the soul, or be carried in soul fragments. I also believe that we have a 'small self' down here in incarnation at the densest level of being: the physical. But we also have a 'higher self' that is not fully in incarnation and which has access to other realms of being and is therefore much wiser than the 'me-down-here'. (I use 'up' and 'down' in terms of vibratory levels as this helps me to navigate through complex dimensions). This higher self too is holographic and knows what soul contracts have been made, the full extent of the soulplan for the present incarnation and where it fits into the soul's overall evolutionary plan as well as the soul's history. It also keeps track of incarnatory experiences and guides the soul towards understanding and fulfilment. My higher self is what I use to contact both the Akashic Record (which holds the imprint of all that has been or will be) and a client's higher self when undertaking karmic readings or regressions.

Why on earth would the soul want to go through all that, I can hear you ask. Well, the purpose seems to be evolution of the greater whole with individual souls taking their learning back to the bigger group and, ultimately, to consciousness as a whole. As that guide once put it 'soul wants to know itself'. But we will explore this further as we go through the book. As to the where the soul is after death, as the same guide said to me 'we haven't *gone* anywhere, we've just moved to a higher vibration that interweaves with your world'. Apparently in terms of distance, they were close by but in terms of resonance, they could be a very long way away indeed as the dimensions expanded and the vibrations lightened. However, it has to be said that while many souls report being located on far away planets beyond our solar system during the interlife all have to return close to the earth to begin the journey or reincarnation back into a physical body if they are to incarnate again on this planet.

Soul group or group soul?

At some times we hear about a group soul and at others about a soul group. This is not just a question of semantics or thoughtless use of language (although people may not realise this). There is a definite difference between the two. In a group soul, the soul is shared by several people or has a kind of 'oversoul' that pulls the strings for its puppets in incarnation. The way the group soul operates often sounds like a kind of holographic control freak that allows little freewill. It manipulates the 'puppet souls' into situations that are suitable for growth and the 'puppets' send information back to the puppet master – the oversoul.[2]

But not everyone looks at the oversoul in this way. It is sometimes seen as a higher entity that encompasses the whole. The philosopher Ralph Waldo Emerson said:

We live in succession, in division, in parts, in particles. Meantime within man is the soul of the whole; the wise silence; the universal beauty, to which every part and particle is equally related, the eternal ONE. And this deep power in which we exist and whose beatitude is all accessible to us, is not only self-sufficing and perfect in every hour, but the act of seeing and the thing seen, the seer and the spectacles, the subject and the object, are one. We see the work piece by piece, as the sun, the moon, the animal, the tree; but the whole of which these are shining particles is the soul.[3]

In this view the oversoul is rather like the pool of spiritual essence from which the souls emerged and it incorporates all levels and layers of being – or Robert Bauval's 'star material'. So, a soul could have experience as a crystal, an animal, a human or even a mountain or a cloud and 'send back' its experience to the whole, although it wouldn't need to 'send it back' because the whole would be instantly aware of what every particle was experiencing just as the hologram encompasses each and every part of itself.

In a group soul, everyone works together, rather like bees in a hive although often nowhere near as harmoniously. In a soul group, each person has its own individual soul but is part of a group that has travelled together throughout many lives and may have been a greater soul – or hologram – at one time. A group soul may also have the intention of learning through the different parts of the soul in incarnation so that the whole may benefit and share what it has learnt.

A soul group is somewhat looser. It too is a group of souls who have travelled together throughout time but which may change or interweave as necessary for the overall or individual experience. Members of a soul group share the same essence but have much more freewill as to how they experience things.

As people tend to travel with the same group of souls or interact with several soul groups, reincarnation memories often include recognition of family members, close friends or enemies, or people on the periphery of the current or previous life. It is unlikely that someone will look exactly the same – although something about the eyes tends to remain the same. The other person may have taken on a different gender and a completely different role, or the roles may remain the same: parent and child, husband and wife and so on according to the karma and the soulplan being played out.

Soul splits, soul retrieval and the like

Shamanic practitioners and many regression therapists take it for granted that the soul is not 'all of a piece'. That is to say, a soul is not an indivisible entity. It can combine and recombine with other members of a soul group, for instance, but it can also fragment to remain behind in a traumatic incarnation – or a particularly joyful one. Thinking of the soul as a hologram helps in understanding this process. A hologram can be both here and there, split and yet still cohesive. Gathering up pieces of the soul so that it can reintegrate has been practised by soul retrieval practitioners throughout aeons of time and it can be extremely helpful in cases where someone does not feel fully present or in some psychiatric illnesses.[4] Pieces of a soul may be left earlier in the present life, or in other lives and it is part of past life therapy to retrieve and reintegrate these fragments as appropriate.

One of my clients, for instance, came for a follow up session after having explored a particular life in great detail in a workshop. Sarah initially 'thought it had been dealt with' because it had given her great insight into her present position but it became clear that there was more to do.

> I'm back in that house again. I feel a bit funny. I keep walking round but no one will talk to me, no one seems to see me. I'm moving around a lot, I don't seem to walk there. One minute I'm in one room, then I'm somewhere else entirely. I can't find my room, everyone looks different... I don't know what I'm doing here, I'm so lost.

It became clear that she'd gone back to a time after she had died in the house, but before she moved on. Certain things kept her attached. She was rather like a ghost, but she had conscious awareness. Asked if there was anyone in the interlife to help Sarah said:

My guide's come to find me. He's taking me up into this light. It's very
bright. It's nice here. I like it better. I'm being healed. He says I have
to go forward in time. That I've got left behind. We're moving forward
extremely quickly. Oh, there's another me waiting. It's me before I was
born. She's coming forward to give me a hug. [Her physical body jerked
as though from an electric shock]. Oh, that's better, we're one now.
Now I can be born. I'll be whole again. We're going into the womb.

Sarah commented later that she'd always felt like she had a piece
missing and that it had now come back to her. Interestingly, a friend
of hers had actually picked up a 'ghost' at the house. Following the
regression, the 'ghost' disappeared and was not seen again. In another
regression a taxi was waiting for her which rushed the soul part to her
just as she was being born into her present life and so yet another piece
was reintegrated.

Soul splits can also be created by widely differing past lives. One
common 'either end of the spectrum saga' centres around the sexuality-
spirituality axis. If someone has taken a vow of celibacy in a previous
life, and not rescinded it, it can be re-activated either through a past life
remembering (which may be spontaneous or through regression) or be
borne deep in the soul as a spiritual unease that finds it really difficult to
commit to intimacy with another person.

So, for example, a man spontaneously reconnected to several lives
where he had been celibate and deeply spiritual – and others where he
had been, as he expressed it, deeply debauched and carnal. In his present
life Paddy was married and following a spiritual pathway. After the
spontaneous memories surfaced, he felt that he could no longer follow
his spiritual path and remain married. He turned away from his wife,
excluding her from his life and accusing her of sabotaging his spirituality.
His astrological chart indicated that his purpose in incarnating this time
around had been to learn to be both spiritual and sexual at the same
time. Paddy had an opportunity to heal a deep soul split but as it was he
continued to live out the warring factions within himself. He turned to
prostitutes and porn to fulfil the side of himself that he had thought so
shameful and fought so hard to overcome when a celibate monk – but
then spent long nights in his present life scourging himself of the guilt
and thereby repeating an old pattern. Interlife work could have helped

him reconcile these two facets of himself but he wasn't yet ready to make that integration.

Sometimes, however, a soul 'splits' and comes into incarnation in two separate bodies. This is often because 'one half' is to assist or facilitate the 'other half' in a specific task. I was once very surprised to find myself talking to the 'other half' of a 'new age guru'. This 'other half' was closely involved in bringing the guru's work to the public through the media. The two guys looked alike, had the same energy, and shared similar interests. Rather like non-identical twins or perhaps more properly put, identical twins that had been born to different mothers. However, soul splits can occur for more traumatic reasons and it is part of past life therapy to uncover and resolve the core issue. Some 'soul splits' reintegrate after death, but others continue as separate souls.

Higher selves

Our higher self is the part of ourself that is not fully in incarnation and therefore has a much clearer picture of why we are here. It carries the memory of our previous lives, our soulplan – and our soul overlays. It is obvious to me both from my own experience and that of clients in regression that our 'higher self' acts as guide, mentor and information assistant to the soul in incarnation – and may be behind some of the triggers that prod the incarnated soul along the planned road to evolution. If you stray too far off this path, the higher self will instigate a series of events that – gently or otherwise – push you back onto your path. It can prod you into attending an event at which you meet an important person for that journey and bring about 'serendipitous synchronicities' that move you on your way. The more you talk to your higher self, the clearer the plan and the path become.

Exercise: meeting your higher self

The following exercise can be memorised but it could also be taped, with appropriate pauses, or be read aloud by a friend giving you plenty of time to carry out each instruction. Holding a Selenite crystal in your hand aids the process and you will have the crystal as a tangible reminder of your connection to your higher self.

Settle yourself quietly in a chair in a place where you will be undisturbed. Let your physical body relax and settle. Breathe gently and bring your attention into yourself. If you have any thoughts that do not belong to this work, let them drift past. Do not focus on them.

Take your attention to the top of your head and allow yourself to mentally reach up to the highest possible level. You may feel that you are being pulled up by a piece of string attached to the top of your head. If your head spins, take your attention down to the base of your spine and open the energy centre there – you will feel it pulsating and holding you in incarnation. Then take your mind back up to the top of your head. When you have reached up to the highest possible vibration, ask your higher self to make itself known to you in whichever way is appropriate for you...

Watch out for any unexplained feelings in or around your body – tingling, touch, movement of air, etc. You may receive a mind picture of your higher self or have a sense of someone with you.

Spend as long as you need getting comfortable with your higher self and find a way to attune more strongly to the guidance it gives you.

When you have completed the exercise, bring your attention back down to the top of your head and imagine flower petals closing over it. Then slowly bring your attention back into the room.

Take a deeper breath, open your eyes, wiggle your fingers and toes and stand up making a strong connection with the earth.

Practise this exercise every day for a week to strengthen your awareness of your higher self. Be alert for the clues and triggers it sends to you.

Who was I?

As we shall see, a better question might be 'why was I?' It is the experiences, soul contracts and attitudes that you had in the past that are important to understand rather than the particular persona you adopted – and this is especially so if you feel you might have been 'someone of importance'. If you do believe you were an important historical figure or have experienced being one in regression, it is more than possible that you are plugging into an archetypal figure or a soul hologram rather than your own true memories *but it is still reflecting your soul's story.* Everyone doing past life work has met our share of Cleopatras, Napoleons, Egyptian pharaohs, John the Baptists, ancient Atlanteans and so on and, if we are wise, we explore with our clients why they are attracted to these particular figures. Yes, it may be illusion or egocentricity, but it also may be the soul's history clothed in a different disguise, one that is perhaps easier to resonate with – although as we shall see the historical figure is not always immediately identifiable as 'desirable' or a good role model. As Dr Ron Jue an American past life therapist says:

> I have discovered that the value of past life images does not lie in the literal understanding of the images but more in the metaphorical aspects. For example, if someone says, "My past life was Cleopatra", that's very interesting but what can you do with it? But if I look at Cleopatra as a metaphor for that person, then it's a metaphor for issues of vanity, power, control, seductiveness.[5]

Dr. Jue was part of a group who journeyed down the Nile and had the ubiquitous experience of reliving a part of history, Ramses II and his court in this case. He commented that it wasn't important whether he was Ramses II or some other pharaoh, the important thing was what it meant for his group to be together in Egypt doing rituals and initiations from that time. His group was by no means the first, or the last, to have exactly those same experiences. Maybe the very nature of Egypt, where magic and ritual is impregnated in every stone, means that anyone who goes there who is in the least sensitive and attuned to the past will experience something of that past. I certainly did – and wrote a novel based on my experiences.[6]

Egyptian pharaohs and the like are very romantic but what about the seemingly less desirable figures from the past? I've personally met three people who believed they were Judas, for example, and know of five or six others through different regression therapists in various countries. But I've met others who regressed to Judas but did not believe it was their own incarnation and therefore reframed it as a release of collective karma. However, all of these souls told the same story, one which contradicts the biblical account. These people were all exploring the friendship and betrayal theme. They may well have been connecting to the Akashic Record but they could equally be holograms of the soul that was Judas and then split.

We also meet people who have severe trauma or unfinished business that their soul is skirting around and so they use an historical personage as distraction or 'fantasy in fancy dress' but it will still have elements of their story. As thoughts are very powerful, identification with an historical figure or a strong fear that the same kind of thing can happen that happened to this historical figure can play its part in who we think we were. The mind doesn't differentiate between what is happening in the outer and inner worlds and each becomes imprinted on the Akashic Record or the soul hologram as 'my experience'. So, I've regressed people who went back into what they feared would happen rather than what actually happened, people who went into fantasy lives of what could have been if only... the possibilities are endless.

So, not all remembered past lives are true?

Decidedly not! Past lives can be an ego-trip, wishful thinking, deeply symbolic, the result of vivid imagination, a fantasy in fancy dress, a compensation for deep feelings of inadequacy and so on. As we've seen, people can sample the Akashic Record and tap into an experience that wasn't personally undergone. But these 'memories' reflect either their soul's story or knowledge that they need for the present life so they should not be dismissed as mere delusion. They are extremely useful in understanding the journey of a soul and there are many past lives that are, seemingly, supportive of the idea of individual reincarnation memories.

But we must remember that when reading someone else's past lives, it is all too easy to pluck an historical story out of the overall hologram. Even someone like Edgar Cayce may have plugged into the Akashic Record or into his own subconscious beliefs to find an example. He often cites his clients as being 'at the foot of the Cross' or 'in the Holy Land when the Saviour walked the earth'. So many people were told this that it would have been a very tight fit indeed if everyone were there, but that doesn't mean we should dismiss it, as something else might be going on – soul splits and the like could account for these ubiquitous experiences, as could the Akashic Record and the hologram within our soul.

At a very deep, collective level we share the same past. Archetypes and classic scenarios abound but it has been suggested that there are in total only a handful of stories which humankind is repeating over and over. So in the case of Judas, for instance, the archetype or hologram of the betrayer is being plugged into because it is what the soul resonates with. Dolores Cannon, another very experienced practitioner of regression and far seeing supports the imprinting theory that says if you've missed out on an experience but need it for the present incarnation, then you'll go to the Akashic Record before incarnation or, I would suggest, into your own inner hologram that is connected to the whole while in incarnation and during regression.

Over-identification with an historical figure is yet another explanation. If someone has been strongly identified, either in a past life or the present, with an historical figure such as Gandhi or a pop star like Jimi Hendrix, for instance, they make that experience their own and it gets regurgitated in regression sometimes with all the emotions that go with it *even though it may or may not feel like 'my experience'*, although usually without the fine detail. The American seer Edgar Cayce stated quite categorically that he wouldn't be reincarnating until 2300 and something, and yet there is a claim on the internet that he is back and writing books. We can ask, did he change his mind? Or did someone identify so strongly with his work that he sincerely believes he is that soul returned? And does it matter?

Some 'reliving' can be immediately recognised as metaphoric or symbolic, containing parallels with the present life. I regressed a present-day monk to apparently being a family man somewhere in the East who longed to go into the solitude of the desert. However, his family responsibilities prevented this. Although all the detail was there, a certain emotional charge was missing. I noted that his arm was twitching so his body was responding to the images. Asked what the arm represented Edmund answered that it was expressing his ambivalence between sexuality and emotions, an inner conflict he was experiencing in his present life. As Edmund was an experienced therapist, we were able to look at that life as a mirror image of what was happening to him now. It contained several of the same issues and paradoxes. Having been a teacher-monk for twenty years (something he knew was a compulsion from a past life), Edmund had a dramatic change in his life when 'The Rule' by which his order lived was relaxed. He became much freer. His order happily paid for courses in hypnotherapy and counselling. But, training in another country, Edmund unexpectedly fell in love. The woman was younger and wanted children but he did not feel these were a priority with him as, he said, he would be 'old before they are grown'. He did not feel he had the energy for both a family and the kind of counselling work he envisaged. So Edmund chose to remain a monk. In being celibate, he felt that he could give more of himself to the work he was called to do. Whereas in the 'other life' he had resisted the call and put the demands of his family first. In living the symbolic life, Edmund could experience the other opposite extreme *as though he had lived it at the time.*

Symbolic or compensatory lives often surface when the issues are ones of self-doubt, self-sabotage or betrayal, and when there are karmic patterns that are being lived out strongly in the present life. It is often enough to recognise the pattern, or the underlying feeling, so that it can be reframed rather than having all the details. Indeed, if our soul has become enmeshed with a group who have been pulled back together by a resonance frequency – such as betrayal – to rework the past, it may be better not to know the details of the past and so an allegorical life is presented in symbol and metaphor instead.

The Rebirth Process

Now if it be true that the living come from the dead, then our souls must exist in the other world, for, if not how could they have been born again?
                                                               Socrates

The process of reincarnation starts with a death. In order to have a rebirth, the soul must leave a body it currently occupies, whether physical or subtle, taking its memories and lessons with it. In Buddhism these memories are believed to scatter as there is no individuality to hold them together. In Western esoteric thought, which takes more account of individuality, the soul moves through successive spiritual planes, gradually letting go of subtle bodies. After the body dies, the subtle etheric bodies separate from the physical and pass to a Life Review where situations and emotions are re-experienced and then drop away with the emotional body. The soul is then housed in an astral body in which it experiences its unlived-out desires. It goes on to detach from the ego and the desire nature. From here it moves into the mental body where it reviews its ideas, beliefs and constructs. When the mental body is let go, the soul can receive higher spiritual teachings. Finally, the soul moves into a spiritual body where it is freed from karmic patterns. This is not a new view, death at the emotional, mental and sensory level was set out in the two thousand year old *Hermitica*, a compendium of Graeco-Roman and Egyptian thought circulating at the time Christianity began.

Regression experience broadly supports the western esoteric idea and the *Hermetica*, although stages may be condensed or missed out altogether, particularly as some souls never progress very far from the dense vibrations of the physical realm it has just left – such souls are usually trapped by desires and unfinished business and that will affect how, why and when the soul reincarnates.

The Stages of Death

1. Subtle bodies leave the physical.
2. Pass through a tunnel of light.
3. Detach from the physical.
4. Life Review – re-experience old emotions and assess how far the soulplan was achieved and lessons learned.
5. Detach from emotional body.
6. Move into astral body. Live out unexperienced desires. Personality falls away.
7. Detach from desires.
8. Move into mental body. Review ideas, beliefs and constructs.
9. Detach from beliefs and ideals. Receive 'higher mind' teachings.
10. Move into spiritual body. Make decisions that are not simply a repetition of karmic patterns and receive further teachings or experiences on the spiritual planes before considering reincarnating.

From regressions to the interlife and reports on near death experiences, it appears that the soul can reincarnate again at any of these stages. If it is pulled quickly back into incarnation by unfinished business or unfulfilled desires, it will take its old emotions and unlived-out desires with it and will almost certainly have a strong soul overlay. Such an incarnation may not be purposeful other than to repeat the old pattern. If the soul moves to the higher spiritual planes first, then the incarnation is more likely to be better planned and purposeful, with a new soul intention set in motion, although old vows and promises may pull it back to be with another soul again or to work on unfinished business.

Choosing a New Incarnation

Explanations about how the body comes back into incarnation, whether the choice is made by the soul or, seemingly, forced upon it, and the decisions concerning what is to happen, varies in religious teaching and in regression experiences. The decision may arise from an unfulfilled desire on the soul's part or prodding from the higher self to evolve. From past life work, it would seem that most souls have at least a modicum of choice, although there are some people who do not progress far enough in the interlife to make an informed choice. They simply 'bounce back' into incarnation because of a strong desire to be in a physical body again, to be with a particular person, or ingrained patterns, addictions or old promises or vows that have not been rescinded.

The major challenge for the present life may be to break the habits of lifetimes or to release someone – or oneself – from an outdated promise or soul contract. It is people who incarnate without plan or preparation but who carry a strong soul overlay that could be said to be 'fated' and to experience life as an implacable 'hand of God' steering them into situations.

Alternatively, someone who may appear to be 'fated' because of trauma, illness or difficult life situations may have actually prepared most carefully for the incarnation and will have a profound reason for making that choice. It may be for personal growth and learning, to work out karma or develop a new attribute, or to assist other people in their lessons or intentions.

If too much is left to chance and someone skips over or ignores the stage of planning the next incarnation, things can go awry. The soul may arrange to meet up with someone for a specific task but somehow doesn't get around to the details so misunderstandings and karmic enmeshments arise. There may be a vague, unfulfilled feeling that the soul should be doing something but is not sure what. People can incarnate into inappropriate bodies or settings for what they want to do. So, the interlife planning stage is extremely important.

The planning meeting
Under regression, most people who are in the interlife considering their options for the next incarnation visit what I call the planning department. They meet with their higher self, members of their soul group, guides and other advisers and are shown what they have already learned, or failed to learn, in other lives. This meeting frequently presents just like a board meeting with people sitting around a table

with audio visual/multi-media equipment ready to review the past and explore possibilities for the future. Discussions are held with those with whom we intend to incarnate once again. If a soul needs to learn a hard lesson or to immerse itself in a particular ambience, mistaken beliefs or toxic emotional states, for the sake of understanding or reframing, then this is when someone from the soul group may volunteer to provide the difficult circumstances which will allow us to develop insight.

A 'resonance frequency', in other words a similar and familiar vibration, may have been set up over several lives within a soul group who all had roles in the soul drama that unfolded and this may draw a soul group back together, willingly or otherwise, so that the saga can be reworked or framed. If the soul group is conscious and aware of the pattern, then this will be discussed at the planning meeting but if it is not aware, then the 'resonance frequency' will act like an imperative soul overlay pulling the participants together to re-enact the story once again. If only one soul has become conscious of the saga, this may be enough to break the pattern – provided awareness is retained or reactivated during the current life.

At the planning meeting too we programme in the illnesses, diseases and seeming disasters that will focus us back on what we intend to be doing with our life to grow our soul and we may chose a genetic inheritance that contains that potential. Of course, once in incarnation we forget that there is a soul who loves us enough to help us learn that lesson and who has offered us the gift, or that we made that particular choice. It feels like fate or the hand of God intervening. Insight may only come at the last possible minute.

So, for instance, if we have an old soul overlay that says 'I don't deserve love', we will tend to take on experiences where we lack love to such an extent that we simply have to find this for and within our own self. A woman who came on one of my workshops listened with great interest when I spoke about this but said nothing. The next day she came to the workshop and told us that she had been estranged from her mother for a long time. As she left the workshop she had received word that her mother was in hospital in a coma and not expected to live. She went to the hospital and sat by the side of her mother's bed. 'Well mother' she said, 'if we incarnated together for you to teach me what it's like not to have been loved, to have been overlooked while others were favoured even to the extent of a child brought in from outside the family being loved while I wasn't, to have been abused and misused and to have felt so small that I wanted to extinguish myself then you did well. You completely snuffed out my sense of being a person and helped me to live out my 'I don't deserve love' script. You did it so well that I simply had to find out who I was for myself and to love myself as I was, so I thank you for a job well done and I forgive you and myself'.

Her mother opened her eyes 'That's alright dear', she said, 'that was what I was here for. I love you'. With that she closed her eyes and died.

Despite her grief, the daughter came to the workshop the next day to tell us what had happened because she was so in awe of the timing. 'If we hadn't had that conversation yesterday', she said, 'She would have died and I would have gone on hating her and feeling unloved. As it is, I know she was playing her part in my drama'. In the workshop we carried out a ceremony to thank and forgive the mother's soul for playing her part so well and help her on her way.

The genetic, environmental and belief system possibilities for a new family are also explored in the interlife. Sometimes there will be one option but at other times there will be several, all of which have to be weighed up to see which is most appropriate. This process is universal and is reflected in the most ancient of scriptures although choice is less of a factor here. This may reflect the soul's evolution and assumption of more responsibility as it matures.

Incarnating souls often make use of the genetic nature of certain chronic illnesses in order to experience what they need to go through for their growth – and to fulfil their soul purpose. A client of mine suffered from a very rare, apparently incurable genetically carried disease which had passed through many generations of her family. She was determined to find a way of healing the condition and set up a foundation to look into alternative therapies, genetic medication and the like. She found a way to dramatically lessen the effects which gave hope to future generations.

In addition to physical genetic factors, families are chosen because of certain attitudes that prevail and for the skills that may be held within the ancestral inheritance. On the radio today a man was describing how he got into making sundials. A friend showed him an antique one he was taking to auction and he was instantly hooked. By evening he had made his first sundial despite lacking training in the complex mathematics and cosmological concepts involved. He now makes sundials that are in demand around the world. He'd known about a famous sundial maker from a few centuries ago through a scientific institution to which he belonged. What he didn't know until recently was that the man was one of his own great-grandfathers through the maternal line. Whether we look on him as a physical reincarnation of his old self, or as embodying the ancestral inheritance doesn't really matter. That innate understanding of the complexities of sundials – and the passion for them – was there.

However, no matter how carefully we may plan, everyone has freewill and others involved in our drama may choose to go their own way. Say we have been souls who were too closely bound in another life and agreed to go our separate ways in the current life. But one person forgot that when in incarnation and clung on desperately while the other strove to be free. The resulting struggle may take many lifetimes to resolve.

So, at the 'planning meeting' guides and teachers help the soul to assess what progress it has made, to identify the conditions needed for new growth and any reparation that may be required, and to find appropriate parents to provide the genetic and cultural inheritance, emotional ambience and environmental influences needed for the new incarnation or to create a completely new script, one that is created to serve another stage in their growth (see Beyond Karma).

The soulplan

The soulplan created at the planning meeting includes the soul's spiritual purpose in incarnating and also brings in opportunities to confront repeating patterns or ingrained attitudes that the soul wishes to change. If the soul has unfinished business, either as karma or as promises or contracts that have been made in other lives, the soul may also plan to deal with this in the present incarnation or these may lie undetected as soul overlays that will unconsciously influence the soul once it has incarnated again.

To me this soulplan is laid out in the astrological chart as the soul carefully chooses a moment to be born that reflects all the issues and potentials and soul intentions. This soulplan is not rigid, however. It is an outline rather than a line by line account of how the life will go. It is adaptable but it does have structure. The soul chooses a family situation, for example, which will reiterate attitudes, experiences or lessons from the past which the soul wants to confront. The soulplan will have 'key moments' and trigger events mapped out so that karmic meetings or fateful decisions occur. It may also incorporate a point when previous life memories will become conscious once more to aid the soul in its evolution. For the most part, the soul does not carry a conscious awareness of past lives, although these can take the form of vivid dreams or memories almost from birth. Such memories usually occur when the last death has been violent and premature and there is a 'break through' of the memories because the membrane between the lives is very thin.

Exercise: Attending your planning meeting

This exercise uses visual imagery but you don't have to actually 'see' anything to access your soulplan. Some people are clairauditory rather than visual – that is they hear or sense a voice telling them the information. Other people 'just get a sense' or 'know'. Not expecting things to happen a certain way allows your inner knowing to communicate with you in the most appropriate way. However, looking up to the spot above and between your eyebrows ('the third eye') can help images to form as can deep relaxation.

Choose a time to do this exercise when you will not be disturbed, turn off the phone and find a comfortable place to sit or lie. You may find it helpful to record this script or have a friend read it to you with appropriate pauses to allow time for the information to surface. If you have images or a way of accessing the information that is different to the script, go with your own knowing but be sure to come back fully into your body at the end:

> Close your eyes and breathe gently, setting up a slow, unforced rhythm. Bring your attention deep into yourself and let any thoughts that are not relevant to the answers you seek to simply float past and go on their way.
>
> Picture yourself in a sunny meadow, let yourself feel the grass beneath your feet, smell the flowers, feel a gentle breeze on your face. Enjoy this lovely place for a few minutes and then let your feet take you across the meadow to a building you can see in the distance.
>
> As you open the door to this building, you will see a lift in front of you. Step into this lift and allow the doors to close. You will see a button marked 'the planning department'. Press this button and allow the lift to take you swiftly up to the level you need.

As the doors open, your higher self will be standing waiting to greet you. Spend a few moments greeting your higher self.

Your higher self will then conduct you to the planning meeting and explain things to you if necessary.

Sitting around a large table you will see all the people with whom you intended to incarnate and the guides and helpers who will assist the process.

Take time to look at each person. Listen to what they have to say, the contributions they made to the planning, and check out the role they will have in your life.

Ask your higher self to reveal to you the soulplan you formulated for your present incarnation and to show you the reasons for your choices where appropriate. (If you need to change anything agree this with your higher self.)

Ask also that you be shown outdated and outgrown soul overlays that may trip you up when putting your soulplan into action. Allow these overlays to dissolve or to be reframed into something more positive and appropriate to your current stage of life.

Before you leave, ensure that you clearly know the soulplan you are working to and the part that people are to play. Thank those people for the task they have taken on.

Ask too whether you have agreed to specific roles and, if these are no longer appropriate, adjust or reframe them.

When you are ready to return, your higher self will take you back to the lift. The doors will be open, waiting for you. If appropriate your higher self will step into the lift with you. Press the button for the ground floor.

When you step out you will be back in the building that leads out onto the meadow. If your higher self has joined you in the lift, ask that it will be available any time you come back to the meadow.

Walk back to the centre of the meadow.

Then breathe a little deeper, move your hands and feet, and open your eyes. Take time to adjust to being back in your physical body. Then get up and stand with your feet firmly on the ground, feeling your connection with the earth. Have a warm drink and then write down your experience.

It may sometimes take several sessions to be able to fully experience the planning process and to access your soulplan. If this is so, ask your higher self to assist you by sending clues and triggers into your everyday life to remind you.

Stages of Reincarnating

No matter how long is, or is not, spent in the interlife, eventually the soul will make the decision to return or will be persuaded by the higher self and guides that it is time. This process follows a broadly similar path for every soul:

1. Decision to return.
2. Attend the planning meeting and formulate soulplan.
3. Choose parents, ancestral patterns, environment, birthchart, etc.
4. Leave the higher spiritual realms, taking the spiritual imprint and karmic blueprint in the form of a soul hologram.
5. Move into the mental body. Receive 'higher teachings' that will be needed.
6. Conception.
7. Move into the astral body. Reconnect to old skills and emotions.
8. Move into the etheric body. Organise the new physical body from karmic blueprint and the soul hologram.
9. The soul takes up residence in the new physical body ready for birth.
10. Inter-uterine experience re-activates old emotional and mental patterns.
11. Birth into new incarnation.

Some souls find the process of re-incarnation difficult. They have to be persuaded into an incarnation which will help them to grow rather than repeat old patterns. Others resist the incarnation, despite having made an intellectual decision to return. Even when the soul has agreed, as it nears earth it can still be reluctant to incarnate as memory is lost of the reasons for the incarnation and many regressees report difficulty in coming into another body, just as some people who go through near death experiences do not want to return but have to nevertheless.

I still vividly remember one of the earliest regressions I facilitated. At the planning meeting following a particularly traumatic and mismanaged life, the soul reluctantly decided to return to have another try. On the way 'down' into incarnation however, as the vibrations became denser, the soul changed its mind and started to protest vehemently. To my surprise, the guides and helpers who had been present at the planning meeting began to push the soul down towards conception, one of them literally standing on top of the energetic soulbody – explaining as they did so that the incarnation had to be there and then. The timing was crucial and didn't allow for a change of mind.

How I sympathised with that reluctant soul. Sometime previously, when I'd undergone hypnotic regression to conception, I'd experienced something similar. My first sensation was being loosely attached to a developing foetus following conception but, as a soul, free to come and go as I pleased retaining contact with the spirit world. The uterine environment was highly toxic, my mother fraught with anxiety at it was wartime and I quickly opted out – much to the surprise of the hypnotherapist conducting the session.

However, he then facilitated my going back to the planning revision meeting (something he hadn't considered before) that followed my 'escape'. There I met with guides who pointed out that I had known exactly how toxic the womb would be and had chosen it for that very reason, along with the family patterns that went with it. It was part of the learning situation I had set up for myself. I agreed to have another try.

This time was very different. I immediately shrank to the size of a tiny dot pinned into the wall of the uterus and there I stayed for ten and a half long months. I was desperate to get out, my mother determined to hold onto me. Her best friend had given birth to a stillborn boy halfway through my mother's pregnancy and she felt guilty about having a live birth. That struggle is precisely and eloquently mapped in my birthchart and it, along with my past and present life experiences, betrays a long intimacy with death as part of the process of birth. I chose both a moment to be born that reflected that pattern and a womb that would reinforce it and assist with imprinting it neurologically on my developing physical body.

Why choose a toxic womb?

From the moment of conception, the experience in the womb shapes the brain and lays the groundwork for personality, emotional temperament and the power of higher thought.[8]

Years ago, when I was teaching astrology with Howard Sasportas, Howard used to wax lyrical about Neptune and the oneness of the watery, inter-uterine environment from which we all emerged, and how wonderful that was and how so many people longed to return. At this point I'd start fidgeting and clearing my throat (if you've read the above you'll realise why) and he'd say, 'Oh yes, of course, there are five star wombs and then there are no star wombs. Why is that do you think?'

Well, karma aside, Neptune is amongst other things the planet of illusion – and of delusion and deception and the most profound mystical union. I wonder how many people if they went back to pre-birth would find that they were in a five star womb and how many a no star, or the stages in between? If my clients are anything to go by – and they are of course a self-selected group who have good reason for wanting to explore the roots of their current life traumas and dramas – the spread is about the same as it would be with hotels, a few five stars and a proliferation of one or no stars. It's rather like the question a guy (whose name I have forgotten) asked at the start of a rebirthing workshop many years ago: 'did you come from a big bang or a damp squib?' He went on to explain that conception and the emotions surrounding it had a profound effect on how the foetus and the child would develop.

I have often asked myself exactly why I chose such a toxic womb. When I first revisited the interlife planning meeting, I was only told that I'd chosen it because I needed the experience and that it fitted into the Hades Moon pattern in my birthchart – a reiteration of the rejection, abandonment, alienation and deep mothering karma from other lives. Even though I had had that very graphic reliving of the toxic womb, I hadn't fully realised the depth of its impact on my unfolding life. I had always glibly said that our early experience resets and reinforces the karmic pattern but thought that I was referring to the emotional environment in which a young child was immersed after birth rather than the actual physical womb – there is considerable research to show that genetic mechanisms are switched on or off by the growing child's *and the parents'* response to environmental and emotional factors, a form of social adaptation. As Bruce Lipton put it 'the fundamental behaviour, beliefs, and attitudes we observe in our parents become "hard wired" as synaptic pathways in our subconscious mind'.[9] Recently however I've come to realise what a profound impact the womb, be it five or no star, has on the growing foetus and how it sets the mental and emotional pattern for the life to come.[10] A loving conception and a five star womb leaves a child feeling safe, nourished and loved, setting the scene for confidence and abundance to grow throughout life. Even if a child who has had a five star womb experience encounters setbacks, they are unlikely to crumble under the adversity. This will reflect previous life experiences where positive, beneficial qualities such as self-reliance and self-worth were cultivated and then reinforced in the five star womb.

But, pre-birth researchers now recognise concepts such as 'core starvation' and the 'umbilical effect'. 'Core starvation' occurs because, after conception, the minute cluster of cells that will eventually implant in the wall of the uterus and become a foetus initially has to travel down the fallopian tube, which takes about a week and can be a fairly smooth transition or an exceptionally difficult voyage depending on whether the fallopian tube is healthy and cooperative. As Juliet Yelverton puts it, 'it is a perilous journey and can leave a cellular imprint of 'core starvation'.[11] Even when the foetus has implanted and is starting to be nourished via the placenta and umbilical cord, the trauma may not stop there. If there is a 'toxic onslaught' via the umbilical cord to the baby, whether emotional anxiety – which sets up noxious chemicals in the blood – or environmental poisons, then the foetus will attempt to keep the toxic soup from reaching its developing brain. It will contract to shut down the umbilical cord transportation of nutrients, as the maternal blood also includes the poison, thus enhancing the 'core starvation' pattern – this can lead to poverty consciousness and the feeling that 'there will never be enough'. A variety of other coping strategies are also employed, which are then replicated later in life. A toxic onslaught sets up physiological and psychological patterns such as depression, high blood pressure, diabetes, addictions, eating disorders and craving of all kinds. The foetus moves from a cellular experience that is somatised (made physical) by being hardwired into the neurological systems of the body.

If the foetus doesn't feel safe in the womb, the child will feel unsafe and unsupported in the world. If we aren't able to receive nourishment via the umbilical cord, we will find it impossible to give or receive nurturing or reassurance. If we feel that we are 'in the wrong place' as a developing embryo, then we will feel subtly 'wrong' and displaced in the outer world. Our emotions and sensations in the toxic womb will be mirrored as the world around us fulfils our expectations and replicates our prebirth experience. As we create our reality by being programmed to notice what we expect, this core programming is constantly reinforced throughout life until consciously amended and reprogrammed.

I vividly recall the intense sense of suffocation as I attempted to exit the toxic soup but was repeatedly held back. Accordingly to Karlton Terry, one of the foetus's strategies is to contract the respiratory diaphragm – which has been one of my weak points since childhood. It can lead to asthma, chronic obstructive disease and other problems with breathing. A respiratory weakness shows up in my birthchart and has led to several bouts of pneumonia and near death experiences – from which I have received many insights. So, it would seem to be all part of my soul plan.

It would also seem to have been part of my soulplan to learn as much about psychic protection as possible – initially from screening out that toxic soup but from many experiences later in life.[12] Reading Bruce Lipton brought another aspect of this to light. He says that if the father leaves and the mother questions her ability to survive, it profoundly changes the interaction between the growing foetus and the mother. In my own case, my mother was also questioning my father's ability to survive every time he went back from leave – the average span between joining the RAF in those days and dying was about six weeks. She once told me that she had a child so she'd have something to remember him by, so she was clearly anticipating his death. This was what led to her stress and to the threatening uterine environment in which I found myself. As Lipton points out 'stress hormones prepare the body to engage in a protection response'. Once they cross the placental barrier between mother and child – which normally keeps a child 'safe' – the stress hormones trigger in the foetus exactly the same 'flight or fight' response. No wonder I have written almost as many psychic protection books as I have on crystals, one of my favourite means of protection.

Bruce Lipton has also written about 'resilient wonders'. Children who survive such deprived experiences as abandonment in orphanages (we will meet one such person in Part 3). He suggests that this may be based on a better pre- and peri-natal nurturing environment. However, many of the children in the Rumanian orphanages he is speaking about were abandoned at birth by desperate mothers and would have experienced the same toxic womb scenario. So, I have another suggestion. These are children whose soul planning included immersion in a toxic environment but who, in other lives, may have learned resilience and self-nurturing and who wanted, for their soul's own reasons, to experience the opposite and to overcome its effects. Or, who had experienced such a depth of noxious abandonment that the soul plan was to finally overcome it by being so immersed in it that the only way was to break out.

So the answer to why we might choose a toxic womb may be that we wanted to experience the crippling sense of lack that arises from core starvation and which either echoes our past life experiences or is the polar opposite. We might have felt vulnerable and unprotected against the noxious tide or variations on the poisoned interuterine theme. The toxic womb may be one of the tools our soul deliberately chooses to put a developmental plan into action (see Part 3), as is the actual birth experience itself. So, no blame attaches to the maternal womb, it is perfect as it is. The soul knew what it was going into prior to conception – and it also knew how the birth process would assist the imprinting. As Dr Frederick Leboyer said about birth:

> It is futility to believe that so great a cataclysm will not leave its mark. Its traces are everywhere – in the skin, in the bones, in the stomach, in the back. In all our human folly.[13]

And, I would suggest, in the lives of us all. But all is not lost, the effects can be re-patterned – once we have recognised the soul lesson we set for ourselves or overcome the karma behind our toxic beliefs. And while we are still experiencing the somatic effects, watching ourselves with compassion and unconditional love can go a long way towards healing any feelings of not being good enough, or of being downright 'wrong'.

Exercise: Revisioning the toxic womb

Give yourself plenty of time for this exercise and repeat it as often as appropriate until the healing is complete – it may take several sessions spaced out over several days or weeks. It can be extremely helpful to have a perceptive friend – the kind who doesn't panic but who gently urges you through – with you as you do this exercise. If you have any qualms at all about doing this exercise then do find an experienced person to help you through.

The breathing is deep, rhythmical and slow and should not be forced. Allow your body to find its own rhythm. In the initial stages it is quite common to cough violently and to feel as though you are choking, but persevere and breathe your way through. Gently massaging your diaphragm and the solar plexus helps it to relax (pure, natural rose oil is particularly good for this). People occasionally feel that they need to vomit all the toxins out. If this occurs then afterwards gently message the base and sacral chakras and then up to your solar plexus and return to the rhythmic breathing.

Make sure that you choose a time when you will not be disturbed, take the phone off the hook and close the door. If there are other people around, warn them that you may cough violently and ask them not to interrupt the process.

Once you have cleared out the toxins, the process reframes any toxic or negative thoughts you carried by putting in the positive thought. To find the positive, simply think about the polar opposite. So, if you think 'I can't possibly survive this, it'll annihilate me', tell yourself 'I am a strong eternal spirit who lives freely with power to create whatever I wish for'. If you feel unsafe or afraid, assure yourself 'I am safe, confident and brave'. The process also puts new energy into the places where all the toxicity was held as it is essential to replace negative energy with positive as otherwise more toxic energy floods in to fill the vacuum.

Wrapping yourself tightly in blankets or pillows can assist this exercise. The 'dot' visualisation helps your brain to move into the brainwave pattern that is most conducive to regression. If the womb was particularly toxic, you may need to break the exercise down into small manageable pieces, working for fifteen to twenty minutes at a time. If you do this, remember to go to the final stage (see further on in this exercise)* before coming out of the process to prevent toxic energy from flooding back in. Holding a Rose Quartz or Mangano Calcite crystal can assist you in putting healing light and unconditional love into all the places from which you have released the old energy.

Lie down comfortably and close your eyes. Breathe deeply right down into your belly, hold it for as long as comfortably possible, then breathe out pulling your abdominal muscles back and up completely emptying your lungs. Continue this breathing establishing your own rhythm.

When you feel totally relaxed, picture in your mind's eye writing your name in dots, followed by the word 'relax'. Take several more breaths.

Now allow yourself to drift gently back through time towards your birth, don't force it, simply allow time to move around you as though a film were running backwards. If you notice any traumas and dramas on the way, be a compassionate witness, simply forgive all those involved including yourself and let yourself continue drifting back to your birth.

When you reach your birth, allow yourself to continue moving backwards until you are a tiny foetus and then back to your conception. At the point where you are about to be conceived remind yourself that you chose these parents and the waiting womb and allow yourself to know why. Once conception has taken place, time begins to run forwards once again. Allow yourself to feel all the feelings you have as you develop, to experience how it was to float in the waters of the womb. Wrap yourself in the pink light of love and forgiveness.

Notice what thoughts come into your mind, the messages you give yourself. Notice how the environment feels, what you can hear and sense around you. Notice how your body reacts to noise and to your mother's feelings. Don't criticise or blame, be a compassionate witness to the process you are both going through.

If it begins to feel like you are floating in toxic soup, deepen your breathing, pulling the breath right down into the base of your spine into the base chakra and on down into your toes. Let all the toxins be pulled into that airstream. Pull your belly back and up, letting the breath out in a big whoosh until your lungs are empty. Let all the toxins go out with your breath, and then breathe in clean pure air pulling it right down to your toes. Feel it energising and healing all the spaces where the toxins were. If you need to cough, let it all out, cough out the toxins and stale air. Notice what thoughts accompany this process. Then begin your rhythmic breathing again. You may be able to feel the empty spaces where the toxic energy has left your body, if so let them be empty for a moment and notice how much lighter it feels.

Continue breathing until your body feels pure and clean all over. Relax your diaphragm and imagine that you are breathing in healing light that gently adjusts your inner patterning and dissolves any dis-ease in your body, mind, emotions or spirit. This healing light fills all the empty spaces. (If you are using a crystal place this over the appropriate places and breathe in its energy).

Now think about those thoughts that came to you. If they were negative, find the opposite, positive statement to make and repeat it three times – if you have a friend assisting you, ask that they tap very gently on the top of your head as you repeat your statements.

Ask your soul or higher self to tell you all that you have learned from the toxic womb and its repercussions. Listen for an inner voice or simply be open to the answers coming to you in the way and time which is appropriate. Embrace the lessons it gave you fully, take the positive insights and put them to work in your life so that your soul plan can proceed.

Become aware that you are floating in a womb of unconditional love, forgiveness and compassion. Know that the gestation and birth that were right for you have now changed to be even more perfect. A new pattern has been set, the dis-ease dissolved, your soul plan can move forward.

*Final Stage. Wrap yourself in pink light, let the love and forgiveness it contains percolate through every pore of your being, filling up any empty spaces. Keeping yourself wrapped in this light move forward in time floating gently through the birth process so that it becomes as perfect as can be. Then come forward through time, still wrapped in the pink light of love, forgiveness and compassion, passing effortlessly through to the present moment.

Take a few moments to breathe gently, becoming aware of your body once more. Feel your diaphragm and lungs moving as you breathe. Wriggle your fingers and toes. If you have been wrapped in blankets, push them aside, emerging from your cocoon as a butterfly does when it is reborn and flies free. When you feel ready, sit up slowly. Put your feet firmly on the floor and anchor yourself in the present moment and onto the earth. Wrap pink light all around yourself.

Repeat the exercise until there is no more toxicity, the womb feels warm, welcoming and embracing, full of nurturing and unconditional love, and your body feels whole and healed.

If you have used a crystal in this process remember to cleanse it thoroughly under running water before and after each session and then place it in sunlight to recharge for a few hours.

Healing the mother-child bond

Our children come to us to make-up for indiscretions in past lives. They
are hold-overs from lifetimes we have not solved.
Martin Sheen

If reading about the toxic womb has made you feel sad or guilty because
you were a mother who went through a difficult pregnancy, then the
bond can be gently healed with the use of flower essences and crystals
if this was on your soul plan and healing is part of the soul intention. This
method can also work well if you are a child who has become aware of
having had a toxic womb experience and it is very helpful if a parent or
child has passed on.

To heal the bond and repattern the ancestral line: Drop Bush
Essence Boab or Green Man Focus Fixes onto a crystal Brandenberg or
clear Quartz point placed on a photo of the parent or child with whom
you want to heal the bond. Continue dropping the essence on daily until
you feel a shift in yourself or see a difference in your own life and that of
the other person if they are still around. Before you begin, hold the crystal
and ask that the work will be for the highest good of all concerned and
in accord with the soul intention of everyone concerned. Brandenberg
crystals are particularly useful for this work because they take the soul
back to the original 'perfect' blueprint, or hologram, before anything
negative became imprinted and then bring balance and harmony down
through both the soul and the ancestral line into the present and out into
the future.

There are many other tools available and you can work with yourself
or with the other person – it is even possible to use yourself as a surrogate
on behalf of another person *if this is part of your soul contract and if you*
heal yourself at the same time (you cannot 'do it for someone else' without
shifting your own attitude or where it is not part of the original soul
contract unless this can be renegotiated). One of the most useful ways of
working on yourself is with Crystal EFT (see *Good Vibrations*) or with a
system such as Psych-K® which rewrites the subconscious belief system
from the present or any other life in the same way that you can erase a re-
recordable CD and overwrite something else on the disc. Psych-K®works
on a principle set down by the Stoic philosopher Marcus Aurelius almost
two thousand years ago:

If you are distressed by anything external, the pain is not due to the thing itself, but to your estimate of it, and this you have the power to revoke at any moment.

An example of how Pych-K® can work and help you to understand the subtle ramifications of the mother-child bond was given to me by Liz Rowe-French[14] who went back into the womb and discovered that all was not as she had always believed. Part of her soul contract with her mother was that she would help her mother to heal a long standing pattern around pregnancy, which would in turn prepare Liz for her vocation as a healer – reactivating her already existing skills whilst still in the womb:

My mother had two existing sons, she'd worked out that when she was older they wouldn't take care of her – this was her theory – so she wanted a girl to take care of her. Her first husband was in the Army during the war. After the war was finished he went over with the Army of Occupation and returned with a German girlfriend. My mother was apoplectic, steaming doesn't begin to describe it. She'd lost a lot of her possessions and been seriously affected by the war – she felt it was very personal. She'd actually been machine gunned as she was walking down the road with one of my brothers in the pram, so she really didn't take kindly to the Germans and certainly not to her husband establishing a relationship with one. She then met my father who was actually a war hero and she thought that was good because he'd been in the navy. She didn't take into account post traumatic stress syndrome but that's another story.

So she was with a different guy, still believing that although she had three men in her life they weren't going to take care of her when she was old. She'd always wanted a daughter and had been deeply disappointed when her second child turned out to be a boy.

In a new relationship, and living in Devon with my father and the two boys who adored him, she didn't tell anybody what she'd done but she stopped using contraception and became pregnant. My father was furious about her pregnancy because he was perfectly happy with his two step-sons. They were running a 30-acre farm and a guest house so someone taking time out to look after babies was not sensible. There was a big scene when she told him she was pregnant. She had been warned by her obstetrician never to have another child because if she did it would kill her. The doctor said her body would not support a pregnancy never mind a labour (which was what I was also told some years later).

So we can see that there was a family pattern operating here.

She was a rule breaker by nature and decided she was going to get pregnant and have this daughter. So she did. She made sure through exercise, nutrition and other things that I stayed very small so I was only four pounds when I was born, yet I was three weeks overdue. She wanted to stay small so that nobody would know. She waited till she was five months pregnant, presented herself to her obstetrician and when he said 'you know what I would have done', she said 'yes but it's too late now'.

From my angle, as a mother and her daughter, she had me and I celebrate the fact that she gave birth to me. While I admired her courage she could at times be too full of character and take on too many fights – in my opinion.

So this was how I went into the Psych-K® life bonding, still thinking on lots of levels: a) she really deeply offended my father and b) it did cause havoc in everybody's lives and c) yes she could be a bit rebellious. I'd done rebirthing and all sorts of other things over the years so I wasn't approaching this as a novice; it was a different level of experience, believe me.

During the Psych-K® the conception aspect was fine, getting further involved with the pregnancy was fine too. It was a very warm, cosy, secure place to be which, if you'd asked my conscious mind, I wouldn't have thought would be the case. I did recall the conflict at the time when she explained what was happening to my father, but it was as though none of it mattered and externally I would have put that down to her pigheadedness and her deciding that all was going to be well. As I went deeper into the Psych-K® breathing the birth was fine, although there was a mad dash for blood because she needed eight pints. She very nearly did pop it but that was only a problem to the other people involved. I knew there never was a risk. There was no risk because she and I were accommodating each other the whole of those ten months, I was acting as her internal healer and I was chosen for that experience because I had been a healer in previous lives. I finally understood that my mother knew there was no risk – regardless of everybody else's fear.

I was specially chosen – and we must have all chosen each other – for that miracle to happen and it was paving the way for a lot more miracle babies. We forget that a baby is an old soul and is bringing old energy in and could be healing the mother. The contract that we make when we decide to be born, when we have sat down with the council and consciously made that decision is then unconsciously stored. We are therefore as much a part of the contract as the mother, it's what we have chosen and maybe I owed her that, maybe I owed her that healing.

I also did do a lot of healing with her before she died, using crystals and all sorts of things to give her an amazing passing. Her doctor said that with her condition he'd never seen anybody depart so peacefully, he couldn't believe it. He sat by her bedside for half an hour because the peace in the room was something else.

So you see the healing that started pre-birth carried right on until death, so that must have been a contract and a very deep and rewarding one. The first reading I had with a psychic after my mother had passed over, he said 'goodness me, doesn't she talk, she's going on and on. What she's telling me is that everything that's wrong in your life now, emanates not from you, but from things she didn't understand. Stand back, trust her and let her work – she will smooth the path for you'.

So, my judgemental attitude towards my mother and the risks that she'd taken completely floated out of the window, there was no risk, there never was going to be one. My whole internal structure was healed and whole and since I did that Psych-K® work I haven't had the emotional highs and lows I used to have, I don't need them. It's unlocked something so huge in me I really would not have believed how cool and calm and collected I've been since then. It's not that life hasn't thrown as many issues at me, it has, but I just haven't gone along with it, I haven't behaved as I would have done with my judgemental self. So that's what has altered.

Having been kept very small and invisible during that pregnancy Liz certainly makes up for it now. She may still be short in stature but she has a huge energy that radiates out all around her – and her blonde-streaked-with-shocking-pink hair and wacky, brightly coloured clothes ensure that she will never be overlooked again, as does her lifework of healing and assisting her clients in reprogramming the subconscious mind.

Timing of Incarnations

Since the soul is not in linear time, the soul views a lifetime as very brief, something that is here and gone, like a clap of thunder.

Robert Schwartz

People often ask about why a specific time is chosen for an incarnation. My reply is that it's usually because the circumstances are right – or because they are caught on a karmic treadmill that recognises a particular issue and goes for an incarnation where that will be repeated. A friend of mine who lives in a fundamentalist Islamic country and who has the gift of reading people's past lives wrote to me asking:

How often do we break the mould and have a life that is completely different? What's the ratio?

He observed that:

Being a pilgrim father or hardline Jew one life then a bearded muzzein the next isn't much different. It's just more hardline religion and you incarnate wherever and whenever the conditions allow the hardline religion to thrive. So zealots and the intolerant would have been drawn to lives in the Middle East over the past 20-30-40 years. Perfect conditions – the ideal time to incarnate – hence the cyclical nature of things as history repeats itself.

Here he was pinpointing the karmic treadmill, and he also wondered if there was a balancing effect:

Could all those Buddhist monks in Thailand have had past lives as hardliners? They seem so serene. Could a life there be used to balance one as a zealot?

The answer, from my point of view, is of course they could but there might be more to it. He went on to say that he had noticed certain characteristics suggestive of previous lives:

I am struck by the number of bods here (me included) who have had significant past lives as Jews. Two guys on the bus – both wear glasses and one studies all the time – he even walks across the road reading a book – he has a special torch in his pen. His shoulders are very rigid – I was trying to recall your little book with the yellow/orange cover.[15]

Then it occurred to me that the rigidity in his case comes from the Jewish thing of rocking back and forwards?

The other only needs sidelocks and he'd be perfect. His glasses are so thick – he's very short-sighted and can't even drive – wow! This is very karmic stuff indeed – I can see him with his black velvet cap on – so both have physical characteristics that stem from past life causes.

My reply was that, from my experience, there was no fixed number of incarnations, or of timing, and neither was there a set rule at all where reincarnation is involved and yes, people do carry certain characteristics with them. Some people live the same kind of life over and over again – as in the examples given above – or bounce between the two extremes so how can we say they are living a different incarnation? What they are doing is living one or two lives over and over again. It's rather like asking the question 'have you been a teacher for thirty years or have you taught one thing for thirty years?' In other words, has there been growth and expansion based on insights gained or merely a repetition. There may be an unconscious soul overlay that repeats a pattern or tries to complete unfinished business or soul purpose from one life in the next, or a karmic reaction that bounces between two extremes for many lifetimes. So many factors operate. People move out of the cycle of the karmic round as and when their soul is ready.

But, much as I'd like it to be, that is not necessarily the end of incarnating. They may put their karma on hold to help someone else, or they may call on the karma of grace to let a pattern dissolve. But they may have soul lessons or a path of soul evolution that they want to follow – especially if they have been stuck in one of those karmic rounds of fundamentalism or hardliners. Religious zealots are everywhere, some are just more cunningly disguised; fundamentalism is an attitude of mind that shows itself in many forms.

Many religions assigned fixed time periods to rebirth – for the Egyptians 3,000 years or so apparently passed between births, for example. However, it is clear from past life regression that the soul chooses a moment to be born that fits the experiences needed and that rigid time plays little part in the cycle of rebirth – which may be almost instantaneous, or can take hundreds of years of earth-time. Indeed, time itself does not appear to operate outside the earth plane. Many children remember having been in a family previously but having to leave precipitously through an accident or illness and so decide to return what appears to be almost immediately.

Incarnation may even entail returning with an overlap between the last life and the present life. Spontaneous memories have arisen where the soul has seemingly gone back in time to incarnate; or has taken over a body immediately prior to or at some time after birth. When linear time is taken out of the argument, it gives the soul greater opportunity for incarnation. When the time is right, or when an important moment occurs in the evolution of the process, the soul will return.

The River of Forgetfulness

It is nature's kindness that we do not remember past births. Where is the good either of knowing in detail the numberless births we have gone through? Life would be a burden if we carried such a tremendous load of memories. A wise man deliberately forgets many things.

Mahatma Gandhi[16]

Many people wonder why they don't remember their incarnations. Well, for one thing, the soul cannot bring the full weight of memories back into incarnation. It would be swamped and unable to deal with it all.

Most philosophies envisage a 'river of forgetfulness' in which souls are immersed prior to death. In the Gnostic text *The Pistis Sophia*, Jesus speaks of the soul drinking from a cup filled with the water of forgetfulness before undertaking the journey back into physical incarnation. The ancient Greeks believed that souls were dipped into the Lethe, the river of forgetfulness, before being reborn. Many people in regression find that the waters of the uterus act exactly like the Lethe wiping memories – although the American psychiatrist Stanislav Grof discovered during holotropic breathwork regression to birth that with every uterine contraction (which momentarily cuts off the oxygen supply to the emerging foetus) a significant previous life memory would be recalled and, as we have seen, tendencies and negative self-beliefs can be re-imprinted in the womb. Some young children do, of course, have very vivid memories of their past lives although this tends to fade as they grow older. A past life memory can also be repressed or forgotten again after birth only to surface from the subconscious mind as unresolved emotional or spiritual traumas in later life.[17]

Male or female?

In some views, the soul retains one gender throughout all its lives. The Jewish Kabbalah, however, warns that a man who behaves badly will be punished by returning in the body of a woman and Plato was of the same opinion. Yet it is clear from reincarnation memories and regression to the between-life state that souls are essentially genderless and can inhabit different-gender bodies according to the lessons and purpose of the incarnation. The soul may have a preferred gender to which it returns after death but many people during regression speak of having little sexual identity, especially when having been in the interlife for a long period and moved far from the vibrations of earth.

As with so much in reincarnation, the gender of the body to be inhabited appears at least in part to be dependent on what progress the soul has made since death of the last body as well as the lessons to be learned. If the soul 'bounces back' quickly, then it may be into the first available body – male or female. The same happens where there is considerable karma or the soul is attracted to a family with whom karma is ingrained or which will provide it with appropriate circumstances for specific learning. On the other hand, the soul may be inexorably drawn to a body of the same sex because that is what it has always known. Where the soul has evolved further, it chooses a body with more care. Even so, it is apparent from regressions that 'accidents' do happen and the soul may find itself in a body that is, apparently, 'the wrong gender'. This can be an explanation for someone who feels that they were 'born with the wrong body' as so many transsexuals express it. It could be that, in the interlife a decision may have been taken to experience a different gender, and yet the soul finds it difficult to adapt without remembering the reason why.

Some souls may choose to adopt only one gender for many lifetimes to escape from or deny an experience in a differently gendered body. I learned this early on in my regression work when I encountered a man who said he remembered hundreds of lives, all lived as a man and all strung together with little historical time between. When I asked him about possible lives as a woman he indignantly replied that he had never been a woman. It struck me that he had bounced so quickly and determinedly back into incarnation to avoid having to think through a decision to change gender. I asked if I could regress him.

During the regression he curled in on himself like a foetus with one arm and hand covering his ears and mouth and the other protecting his solar plexus (the site of old emotional angst). He muttered that he wasn't going to let me know what was happening – but continued to give a running commentary. He went back several millennia to being a young Greek girl who was raped by a gang of soldiers. As she died she swore vehemently that she would never incarnate as a woman again. He had kept that promise for over 3000 years. In the interlife we were able to do some healing work and renegotiate that contract he had made with himself never to incarnate as a woman again. We left open the possibility that, in a future incarnation, he could choose to incarnate as a woman. However, he wasn't yet ready to look at why he might have had that experience and, as he failed to keep an appointment to do so at a later date, it may be that he will reconsider in the next interlife planning meeting.

Animal, mineral or human?

Throughout the ages, teaching has varied as to whether humans can take up incarnation within a plant, animal, insect, and so on. The Druids were said by Julius Caesar to believe that the souls of the dead could transmigrate into animals and many tribal people still share this belief – as do more 'modern' souls. In several ancient texts souls are punished for misdemeanours by being banished to the bodies of animals. In India, devout Jains wear a mask so that they do not inadvertently breathe in an insect that could be the soul of a deceased human, and they would not swat a fly for the same reason.

Other people believe that the evolutionary chain goes from mineral, through insects and animals and then to human who, having reached that level of soul evolution, continue as human. Two of my friends are convinced that their beloved dog will be their human partner in the next life. For the Sufi poet Rumi, founder of the Mevlevi dervish sect, rebirth was part of a great cycle of spiritual evolution through multiple realms:

I died as mineral and became a plant
I died as plant and rose to animal,
I died as animal and I was man.
Why should I fear? When was I less by dying?
Yet once more I shall die as man, to soar
With angels blest; but even from angelhood
I must pass on.

I have, however, only conducted a handful of regressions out of more than a thousand where someone 'regressed' to being a crystal or an animal – my method of regression is deliberately non-directional so that I do not insert any ideas or potential 'lives' into the session. In the case of a crystal it is philosophically difficult to determine exactly when a crystal 'dies' in order to be reborn although many crystals do go through stages of decomposition and regrowth that could be viewed as a death; of course, consciousness could remain in the crystal and take form elsewhere, but this concept is difficult to conceive with our limited human minds. In meditation, many of us experience unity consciousness in which we are both the whole and then an individual again. As crystal healers will tell you, crystals retain a being within them even after being mined. Continuation of awareness could lead us into a fascinatingly complex discussion about time and the duration of consciousness that cannot be pursued here (I freely admit I do not understand all the implications and ramifications myself but I left this in to stimulate your own thoughts).

In the case of becoming an animal, I see no reason why soul consciousness should not choose an incarnation which taught it particular skills or a way of seeing only available through that body. But it could turn out to be a replay of a shamanic ally journey in which consciousness entered the shaman's power animal and journeyed in that body. Shaman Alberto Villoldo vividly describes in one of his books how, in his present life, he climbed down an incredibly steep cliff by merging with a jaguar. He wasn't quite sure how he managed it as he was still a 'trainee shaman' as it were. I would say that he was calling on skills he had already learned in another life. In that particular case, he took his physical body with him too, an impressive feat of shamanism, but a great deal depends on the views and expectations of the person conducting the regression session. Back in the 1980s I spoke to hypnotherapist

John Richardson who 'always took clients back to see what animal they had been' and, of course, neither he nor they were disappointed. They inevitably experienced an animal incarnation. Other regression therapists have never had a client become other than human while some have had clients who were 'star people' or angelic beings who happened at this time to be in physical incarnation within a human body.

In regression therapy the greatest number of memories are almost certainly of human lives, although as I said, I have known a few people to live out wondrously long and bright lives as crystals, or brief lives as animals in which they learned a particular skill such as cunning or developed the olfactory senses. It is all part of a continuum of the learning experiences that fuels their soul's evolution. However, we must bear in mind that when the physical body dies it returns to its constituent minerals so, in a sense, there is a mineral incarnation, although one without the soul unless it leaves a hologram there to experience the reunion with the earth.

If we look at the oversoul idea of Ralph Waldo Emerson (see page 9), then *because we are an integral part of the whole* we can all experience each and every aspect of consciousness through the oversoul or, as I would put it, through the soul hologram.

Etheric impressions
The etheric body is the organising field of the physical body, comprising different subtle energetic layers such as the astral, emotional and mental which carry impressions at those levels. The etheric body is visible to psychics – it is often called the aura – and many psychics report seeing the etheric body leave the physical body at death. As we will see, one of the explanations for how past life memories can transfer into a new body is that the etheric body, or layers of it, dies or dissolves as it progresses beyond physical death and experiences death on other levels of being – but the experiences are transferred through the subtle energy field. I call this the karmic blueprint that does not dissolve (see the karma of dis-ease in Part 2). The etheric body can also be looked on as a holograph containing all the information from past lives that will be carried into future lives.

To me the most helpful concept is if we think of the soul and the karmic blueprint as also containing a hologram of all that is. We can see that the soul might choose to shine the light of awareness through another part of the pattern, which would reflect a different attitude of mind and give the soul a whole new perspective on an old issue or open up new areas to be explored.

The Akashic Record

The Akashic Record is said to hold the imprint of everything that has been or will be – functioning rather like a super-computer or an original hologram for the universe and beyond. That the Record holds an imprint of what will be implies that the universe is fated but exploration of the Akashic Record shows that it functions rather like a virtual reality, multi-possibility, parallel-universes projector. In other words, it encompasses all that could be as well as all that was. If someone in regression goes 'back' to a previous life and changes the script or reframes it in the interlife, the effects register on the Akashic Record and 'move forward through time', changing the outcome in the present or future lives. The author Richard Bach wrote about how he piloted his plane through parallel realities, following each thread to a different conclusion according to the choices that had been made. But, he emphasised, all this was going on at once. It wasn't an either/or scenario. It was a multiple universe in which the consequences of each thought and action were taken through to their conclusion *all at the same time* although apparently as separate lives. I personally believe that this is why progressions to future lives – which tend in my experience to reflect the person conducting the progression's own beliefs as to what will be – can show various possibilities and why it is possible to heal the past by stepping onto a different pathway in the present life.

At a planning meeting during a regression, one of my clients suddenly asked if he could be allowed to see his future lives. He felt that it would help him to make some difficult choices in his present life. He was told by his higher self and the guides that were with him that he could see the future. He was taken to read the Akashic Record for his soul. He was shown three widely different scenarios, only one of which was the 'living on a blighted earth' disaster scenario that features so strongly in published works on future lives. Another possibility was living on an evolved multi-dimensional earth that had shed its chrysalis and metamorphosed into a fully conscious entity along with evolved human beings. The third was midway between the two. He was told that each outcome depended on a choice he would make and on how his consciousness developed. It was emphasised that through his personal choices and soul evolution he would be influencing the outcome for the collective. If we use the holographic soul analogy, this is where one part of the hologram, his incarnated soul, could feed back to the original hologram and thereby share insights with the whole and potentially influence the overall outcome. He commented that it seemed an awesome responsibility but that his choice was to cultivate his soul and serve humanity.

When we discussed this later, he said that the impression he had gained was that, no matter what he did, those three possibilities would be played out in different dimensions but that he, in the individual consciousness of his present life, could choose to step onto whichever timeline was appropriate for the outcome he instinctively felt was most desirable or most attainable. If he chose to be pessimistic, he could enter the blighted earth scenario. If he chose to be optimistic *and to put certain thoughts and actions into practice*, then he could choose the evolved earth scenario. If he went on as he had been doing, then the middle course was the most likely outcome.

This is perhaps a sobering thought for all those people who are caught up in the end-of-the-world disaster scenario of 2012 or in the notion of ascended beings whose consciousness has evolved so that they can leave behind the dense vibration of earth to live in the fifth dimension while still on this planet. I recall the contents of a website in which the, allegedly, ascended person was saying 'well, that's it, we've done it, we're safely through into another dimension, the door has shut on all those others who haven't attained our level of consciousness and so they are written off'. She then went on to say that many adjustments still had to be made and the fact that her group were finding themselves without partners, lacking visible means of support and basically living a pretty awful life was just temporary until the necessary adjustments had been made. That might be so in her world view – and she may well have created such a scenario with her powerful thoughts. But it sounds to me like yet another potential example of escapism or delusion. And somehow I can't help feeling that mentally consigning most of the world's population to oblivion might just generate a great deal of karmic consequences. As does, of course, the enormous fear around the notion of 2012 and the end times – not a new phenomenon, it was exactly the same two thousand years ago at the start of the Christian era. Time will, of course, tell. The teaching I have received is that this is a time of changing consciousness, shifting our awareness higher and opening our perceptions much wider and deeper and, as the astrological Age of Aquarius is being ushered in, of being concerned about our fellow human beings and our connection to the whole. This is at least one strand of the Akashic Record and I'd like it to be the timeline that I stand on.

The Akashic Record has another function. Rather like a cosmic internet, it can be accessed from any point in time, space or consciousness. So, if a particular experience is required for the next incarnation that the soul has not yet had, plugging into the Akashic Record can transfer all that is required via another soul's experience. It doesn't matter that the 'memory' is not of the soul's own previous lives. Some years ago I did a karmic reading for a well known healer. I saw him sampling the lives of great healers of the past and plugging into the knowledge and abilities of people like Paracelsus, Imhotep, Hildegard of Bingen and the like to prepare him for his healing mission this time around. He hadn't needed to fully live those lives himself, and he didn't have time in the present life to learn all he needed, so he could benefit from the souls who had. I suspect this kind of thing happens rather more frequently than most regression therapists or researchers realise.

It is a very different experience to that of a woman who in regression had been an extremely talented but uneducated healer who simply laid hands on her patients and they recovered. She commented that in her present life although she very much wanted to heal, her abilities were nowhere near as strong. In the interlife, however, she had said that she wanted to understand what she was doing. In the present life she studied hard but lacked the spontaneity of her past life approach to the work. She was struggling to regain her skill because her mind wanted to be involved. Once she realised this was why, she was much more relaxed about the whole thing and called on her past life self for assistance as and when needed, which raised the efficiency of her healing to a much greater level.

Exercise: reading the Akashic Record
This is a method I was taught by my mentor Christine Hartley almost forty years ago. I have adapted Christine's basic method, concentrated

withdrawal onto the inner planes and focusing the third eye, to incorporate asking your higher self to guide you to the right chapter of the Record, as it were. Do not attempt to read the Record for someone for whom you don't have permission whether from the person themselves or their higher self. Once you become practised you can adapt the method to suit yourself and the information you are seeking.

When you first begin, you'll probably have 'practice runs'. That is, you'll get glimpses but they may not make much sense. This is rather like tuning in one of those old-fashioned television sets. You get a lot of static and a few glimpses of images that move on quickly before you can fix them in place, and then gradually you can tune into an image, hold it and have the scene move on slowly enough to understand what you are seeing. Because moments of great emotional trauma and soul dramas seem to make the biggest impression on the record, these are what tend to be seen first and it is possible to tune into a specific historical event without actually having been there. If you find a scene distressing, remember that you are seeing it objectively at a distance, not reliving or embodying it. The scene can be reframed into a different outcome if it needs healing, and the same goes for if you are seeking to see the future rather than the past. You can attune to the various potential futures that exist in each moment – every one the outcome of a different choice. This also works well if you want to see the potential outcomes of choices you or someone else has to make in the present life.

It is useful to have a trusted companion with you when you first try this. Obviously it is helpful if the companion is psychically aware, but it is more important that he or she possesses common sense – and a few instructions such as 'don't try to yank me out suddenly if you think I'm contacting a traumatic scene', 'treat me gently and only intervene if I ask you' (you can arrange a signal such as lifting your arm to indicate you need help). What is essential is that this companion is appraised of the way to bring you back safely should you wander too far or get lost in a scene. Please familiarise yourself – and your facilitator – with this return process before you set out on the journey to read the Akashic Record. It won't make total sense to you at this stage – you won't know what the lift signifies for instance, but you do need to pay attention to the return process *before you need it* – it is repeated at the end of the reading the record exercise in a slightly different form to ensure your safe return. If you have become lost in a scene your facilitator – or your higher self if you are doing the process alone – should say:

Withdraw your attention from that scene and disconnect your energies and awareness*. Make your way back to the lift, asking your higher self to accompany you. Step into the lift and press the button for 'everyday reality'. The lift will bring you down through the vibrations until you reach the place you started from. Step out of the lift and be aware of leaving the past (or the future) behind. Cross the meadow until you reach your starting place.

Slowly return your awareness to the room, come into the present moment [if appropriate state the date and time]. Take a few deep breaths and then slowly open your eyes. Wiggle your fingers and toes and make sure your feet make a strong connection to the earth.

*If there is any hesitancy about returning, your companion should ask if there is any unfinished business that needs attention and then find a creative way to deal with it if there is – higher selves are usually all too willing to offer assistance with this. Tea and a biscuit usually completes the process of return to everyday awareness.

To read the record
Settle yourself comfortably in a quiet place where you will not be disturbed. Turn off the phone. Close your eyes and place yourself in a pyramid of protection. Open your base chakra and let it hold you safely and gently so that you can bring the information down to earth.

Breathing rhythmically and easily, withdraw your attention from the outside world. If any thoughts pass through your mind that do not relate to this work, let them pass on by. Focus your attention on your third eye (above and between your eyebrows) and allow your inner sight to open.

Now see yourself in a beautiful meadow. Feel the ground beneath your feet, smell the air and enjoy being in this beautiful place. Let your feet take you over to a small building that is away to one side.

When you reach the building, open the door and go in. In front of you you will see a lift with its doors standing open waiting for you. Inside the lift are several buttons. One is marked 'Akashic Records'. Press the button and let the lift take you up through the dimensions to where the Record is housed.

As the lift doors open, your higher self steps forward to meet you to conduct you through the multi-media experience that is the Akashic Record. Your higher self may take out the Book of your Life for you to read, or hand you a DVD to play. It may show you the many rooms and dimensions of the Record. Simply let the experience unfold before you with your higher self guiding the process for your highest good. If you have any specific questions, put them before your higher self and ask to be shown the answers as and when appropriate.

...

When you have completed your Akashic session, disconnect your energies from the scene, thank your higher self and ask it to accompany you back to the lift.*

    Step into the lift and press the button for 'everyday present reality'. The lift will bring you down through the vibrations until you reach the place you started from. Step out of the lift and be aware of leaving the past (or the future) behind. Cross the meadow until you reach your starting place.

    Disconnect from the scene and slowly return your awareness to the room. Take a few deep breaths and then slowly open your eyes. Move your fingers and toes and make sure your feet make a strong connection to the earth. Have a drink and a biscuit.

*If there is any hesitancy about returning, ask your higher self if there is unfinished business that needs attention and then find a creative way to deal with it if there is – higher selves are usually willing to offer assistance with this.

Printer's Pie?

Unless we have lived before, or the grotesque incongruities of life are to be explained in some way unknown to us, our present existence, to my mind, resembles nothing so much as a handful of what is known as "printer's pie" cast together at hazard and struck off for the reader to interpret as he will or can.

Rider Haggard, 'On Religion'.

A year or so ago I researched Rider Haggard extensively before talking to the Rider Haggard Society as the theme of reincarnation runs throughout his work. I was particularly struck by the disparate criticisms of his books, which some people saw as 'typical colonialist and racist spiel'. However, as other commentators pointed out, his books do have a considerable, and totally natural, unforced sympathy with native peoples and the plight they find themselves in and his writings were some of the first that brought this to the attention of the public – something that was well before his time but which was to become part of the zeitgeist of the twenty-first century, as was the concept of reincarnation. In his writing on reincarnation, Haggard seeded into the collective or mass consciousness ideas that would flower over a century later – including that of soul contracts and karmic consequences. Haggard was also able to effortlessly take himself back into a deep sense of place and immerse himself in the ambience of the time. Was this part of his soul plan I wondered? I'm including him here because he pondered on many of the questions that the concept of reincarnation and remembrance of past lives evokes.

In many ways H. Rider Haggard was a typical Victorian country gentleman, erudite, inquisitive, eclectic and creative – and a convinced Christian. His writing is full of reincarnation themes and in *She*, the story of an immortal woman who waits for millennia for the return of her soulmate and the fulfilment of a soul contract between them, his heroine states:

> *'I wait now for one I loved to be born again'*... *'Following the law that is stronger than any human plan, he shall find me here, where once he knew me'*.[18]

In a forward to *She*, Stuart Cloete says that Haggard 'lifted the garment of an Africa that was then virgin, and in fictional adventure-romances described events and scenes which have since been proved to be historical reality'.[19] In this, Haggard appears to have displayed prescient knowledge of both the past and the future. He had, for instance, never heard of the Zimbabawe ruins (they'd been lost to history for a thousand years and not yet rediscovered) nor could he have known that diamonds would be found outside Kimberley, but he put such things in his books and they were later substantiated. My suggestion is that he, as with Joan Grant, Barbara Erskine, Annya Seton, myself and many other writers, incorporated his own past life memories and an ability to read the Akashic Record and travel outside time into his books. His nephew Godfrey Haggard has stated that 'Rider believed that he had lived before' and his great grandchildren have no problem believing that he knew at least some of his past lives.[20]

Author Shirley Addey, a long time member of the Rider Haggard Society, puts Haggard's ability to engage so fully in the time and place down to well-developed intuition and the ability to step into the atmosphere of a period – to read the collective record (the Akashic Record). But, in his piece 'On Religion', written in 1912 on board a ship off Aden when he was 56, Haggard sets out what from my viewpoint is a clear indication that, although he was a devout Christian, he also believed that souls could take on new bodies: in other words, souls could reincarnate. Haggard states that, in his private opinion:

> Some of us already have individually gone through this process of coming into active Being and departing out of Being, more than once – perhaps very often indeed – though not necessarily in this world with which we are acquainted.., I am strongly inclined to believe that the Personality which animates each of us is immeasurably ancient, having been forged in so many fires, and that, as its past is immeasurable, so will its future be.

He goes on to give a list of indications which may be said to support reincarnation:

- 'vague memories',
- 'affinities with certain lands and races',
- 'irresistible attractions and repulsions, at times amounting in the former case to intimacies of the soul so strong that they appear to be already well established, such as have drawn me so close to certain friends, and notably to one friend recently departed.'

At the same time Haggard qualifies this with the observation that, and I quote, 'none of this is proof – like everything else that has to do with spirit' – something that both writers and regression therapists would support. But he refers to 'that strong conviction of immemorial age which haunts the hearts of some of us.' I love the imagery he uses to encompass the long process of reincarnation:

a great ball-room wherein a Puck-like Death acts as Master of Ceremonies. Here the highly born, the gifted and the successful are welcomed with shouts of praise, while the plain, the poorly dressed, the halt, are trodden underfoot; here partners, chosen at hazard, often enough seem to be dancing to a different time and step, till they are snatched asunder to meet no more; here, one by one the revellers of all degrees are touched upon the shoulder by the Puck-like Death who calls the tune, and drop down, down into an impenetrable darkness, while others who knew them not, are called to take their places.

But if we admit that every one of these has lived before, and danced in other rooms, and will live again and dance in other rooms, then meaning informs the meaningless.

Then those casual meetings and swift farewells, those loves and hatings, are not of chance; then those partners are not chosen at hazard after all.

Then the dancers who in turn must swoon away beneath that awful, mocking touch, do not drop into darkness but into some new well of the water of Life.'

However what we behold, continues Haggard, is but:

a few threads, apparently so tangled, that go to weave the Sphinx's seamless veil, or some stupendous tapestry that enwraps the whole Universe of Creation which, when seen at last, will picture forth the Truth in all its splendour, and with it the wondrous story and the meaning of our lives.

It may be that Haggard's acceptance of the belief of the return of the soul was something which grew over time although he was clearly well versed in the concept when, at age 30, he wrote *She*. His description of the writing of *She* is one that will be familiar to many novelists, the sense of being taken over by the story as though you were merely a channel for it or, as Kipling called it, a telephone wire. As Kipling put it to Haggard: 'You didn't write *She*, you know, something wrote it through you'. As Haggard describes it:

the whole romance was completed in a little over six weeks. Moreover, it was never rewritten, and the manuscript carries but few corrections. The fact is that it was written at white heat, almost without rest, and that is the best way to compose.

I find myself identifying with Haggard, for this is the way most of my novel *Torn Clouds* was written. The first five thousand words or so were scribbled down in less than an hour in Luxor during a sandstorm that triggered memories for me. One memory was being stretched out full length in front of a statue of the goddess Sekhmet with my skin being flayed by stinging sand. In my present life I can't imagine making this kind of obeisance to anyone, but when I went to her temple the next day, it was all I could do to refrain from throwing myself out in front of her. The remaining 90,000 or so words of my novel were written in three weeks, when the character of Megan took over. She was not a past life persona but rather a creative construct who wanted to tell her story and who incorporated many of my own past life rememberings into the tale. My experience accords with Haggard who says:

> I remember that when I sat down to the task my ideas as to its development were of the vaguest. The only clear notion that I had in my head was that of an immortal woman inspired by an immortal love. All the rest shaped itself round this figure. And it came – faster than my poor aching hand could set it down.

In 1924 when at Karnak Temple, my own favourite place in the whole of Egypt, Haggard wrote in his diary:

> It is not difficult for the imagination to repeople those pillared halls and courts with the thousands of priests and priestesses who filled their sacred offices in them for uncounted generations.
> It is impossible to refrain from wondering where these are today, and, if they live, with what feelings they look upon their desecrated fanes. Are they angry – or just contemptuous – having learned the truth and thereby acquired charity?'

Haggard is presumably suggesting here that they might have reincarnated and be able to see what has happened to their temple, or that they can view it from the spirit world. I certainly find myself both going back in time to a place I knew intimately and enjoying the reconstruction work that has gone on since Haggard's time in my recent visits to Egypt. It feels like my old home is being re-created. Haggard was a freemason and a close friend of the Egyptologist Wallis Budge, who, if Haggard and others are to be believed, was well acquainted with fortune tellers and astrologers in Victorian Egypt as well as having an intimate knowledge of the past. Another good friend Andrew Lang, to whom *She* was dedicated, was president of the Society for Psychical Research in 1911 and had an extensive knowledge of reincarnation and all matters psychic. Lang was one of the friends with whom Haggard said he was in 'supreme sympathy' and it was Lang who suggested to Haggard that, 'I might have been a monk of Ely and you might have flayed me and composed a saga at first hand. It would have been a good saga but I could not stand being flayed.' In other words, he was suggesting that they might have shared a previous incarnation some thousand years previously and were part of the same soul group.

Haggard tantalisingly tells us that 'someone' – sadly he doesn't give a name – told him about three of his incarnations after the launch of *She* in 1887. In his autobiography, after informing us that he'd been fascinated with ancient Egypt from boyhood, Haggard says:

> A friend of mine who is a mystic of the first water amused me very much not long ago by forwarding to me a list of my previous incarnations, or rather of three of them, which had been revealed to him in some mysterious way. Two of these were Egyptian, one as a noble in the time of Pepi II who lived somewhere about 4000 BC and the second as one of the minor Pharaohs. In the third according to him I was a Norseman of the seventh century, who was one of the first to sail to the Nile, he returned but to die in sight of his old home. After that, saith the prophet, I slumbered for twelve hundred years until my present life.

It sounds to me as though his mystic friend read the Akashic Record on his behalf. Haggard goes on to say at that time:

> it is a fact that some men have a strong affinity for certain lands and periods of history, which of course, may be explained by the circumstances that their direct ancestors dwelt in those lands and at those periods. Thus I love the Norse people of the saga and pre-saga times. But I have good reason to believe that my forefathers were Danes. I am however unable to trace any Egyptian ancestor... [but] with the old Norse and the old Egyptians I am at home. I can enter into their thoughts and feelings. I can even understand their theologies...
>
> Whatever the reason, I seem to myself to understand the Norse

fold of anywhere about 800 AD and the Egyptians from Menes down to the Ptolemaic period, much better than I understand the people of the age in which I live. They are more familiar to me... I positively loathe the Georgian period... on the other hand I have the greatest sympathy with savages. Zulus, for instance, with whom I always get on extremely well. Perhaps my mystical friend has left a savage incarnation out of his list.

In this he's expressing feelings and dilemmas that are common today. A fascination with certain places is seen as one of the indications of having possibly lived there previously, as is a revulsion against a place. If Haggard were one of my clients I'd suggest he'd had a difficult Georgian life, the memory of which his soul had tried to wipe from the record as 'a loathesome period'.

Haggard himself questioned where his 'memories' came from. Ancestral memory, which Haggard mentions with regard to his Norse connections, is one of the explanations put forward for alleged past life memories and, of course, it is difficult to rule it out. But it is equally difficult to say that it is the only explanation. It's the same with crypto-amnesia or para-amnesia – a kind of false remembering built out of what has been read or heard before – and Haggard certainly read his share of Egyptology from a very young age. Ancestral memory was something Haggard would put forward as a possible explanation when writing his autobiography in 1912 together with other explanations, as we'll see – one of which was that he was relaying pictures of his own incarnations. To quote Haggard in 1912 yet again:

As I am touching on mystical subjects, probably for the last time, I will instance here a series of imaginings which developed themselves in my mind at intervals over a period of several months early in the present year. I noted them down at the time and, except for an addendum to No. 4, give them without alteration, as I think it best not to interfere with the original words, on which, perhaps unconsciously, I might attempt to improve. Indeed it would be easy to make a story out of each of these mind-pictures. At the head of them I have stated the alternative explanations which occur to me. Personally I favour – indeed I might almost say that I accept – the last [– subconscious invention].

What he describes are images that are typical in the hypnopompic state – the state between sleeping and waking – which some people believe can access the collective unconscious or the Akashic Record.

During the past few months there have come to me, generally between sleeping and waking, or so it seemed, certain pictures. These pictures, it would appear, might be attributed to either of the three following causes:
(1) Memories of some central incident that occurred in a previous incarnation.
(2) Racial memories of events that had happened to forefathers.
(3) Subconscious imagination and invention.

Probably the last of these alternatives is the one which most people would accept, since it must be remembered that there is nothing in any one of these tableaux vivants which I could not have imagined – say as an incident of a romance.

Now, before I forget them, I will describe the pictures as well as I can.

1. A kind of bay in a thicket formed of such woods as are common in England today, especially hazel, as they would appear towards the end of June, in full leaf but still very green. A stream somewhere near. At back, in a tall bank, something like the Bath Hills, the mouth of a cavern. About thirty feet from this a rough hut made of poles meeting on a central ridge (I have forgotten how it was thatched). In front of the hut a fire burning, and an idea of something being cooked by a skin-clad woman, I standing by, a youngish man, tall; children playing round, and notably a boy of about ten standing on the hither side of the fire, his nakedness half covered by the pelt of some animal, his skin, as he lifts his arms, very white. A general sense of something about to happen.

2. A round hut, surrounded by a fence, standing on a grassy knoll, no trees about. A black woman moving within the fence and, I think, some children; myself there also, as a black man. An alarm below, which causes me to take a spear and run out. A fight with attackers; attackers driven off, but I receive a spear-thrust right through the middle below the breast, and stagger up the slope mortally wounded back into the enclosure round the hut, where I fall into the arms of the woman and die.

3. A great palace built in the Egyptian style. Myself, a man of about thirty, in quaint and beautiful robes wound rather tightly round the body, walking at night up and down some half-enclosed and splendid chamber through which the air flows freely. A beautiful young woman with violet eyes creeps into the place like one who is afraid of being seen, creeps up to me, who starts at seeing her and appear to indicate that she should go. Thereon the woman draws herself up and, instead of going, throws herself straight into the man's arms.

4. An idea of boundless snows and great cold. Then the interior of a timber-built hall, say forty feet or more in length, a table by a doorway and on it three or four large dark-coloured trout, such as might come from a big lake. Wooden vessels about, brightly painted. A fire burning in the centre of the hall, with no chimney. On the farther side of the fire a bench, and on the bench a young woman of not more than two – or three-and-twenty, apparently the same woman as she of the Egyptian picture, or very like her, with the identical large violet eyes, although rather taller. She is clothed in a tight-fitting grey dress, quite plain and without ornament, made of some rough frieze and showing the outline of the figure beneath. The hair is fair, but I cannot remember exactly how it was arranged. The woman is evidently in great grief. She sits, her elbow resting on her knee, her chin in her hand, and stares hopelessly into the fire. Presently something attracts her attention, for she looks towards the door by the table, which opens and admits through it a tall man, who, I know, is myself, wearing armour, for I catch the sheen of it in the firelight. The woman springs from the bench, runs round the fire, apparently screaming, and throws herself on to the breast of the man.

The general impression left is that she had believed him to be dead when he, probably her husband, appeared alive and well.

Haggard later added an addendum:

Some months later I was favoured with an impression of another scene set in the same surroundings. In this picture postscript, if I may call it so, the identical man and woman, now persons of early middle age, were standing together in bitter sorrow over the doubled-up and fully-dressed body of a beautiful lad of about eighteen years of age. Although I saw no wet upon his clothes I think that he had been drowned.

5. The mouth of a tunnel or mine-adit running into a bare hillside strewn with rocks and debris. Standing outside the tunnel a short, little woman of about twenty-five, with black hair, brown eyes, and brownish but not black skin, lightly clad in some nondescript kind of garment. Resting on her, his arms about her shoulders, an elderly man, very thin and short, with a sad, finely-cut face and sparse grizzled beard, wearing a dingy loin-cloth. The man's right foot covered with blood, and so badly crushed that one of the bones projects from the instep.

Today, in the 21st century, using past-life-regression therapy we'd look very carefully at, and reframe, such an incident, since past life carry-overs of injuries such as this, appear to cause a weakness in the present life. Haggard for example suffered from gout which may have had its roots in a crushed foot in another life. Haggard goes on,

The woman weeping. By his side on the ground a kind of basket filled with lumps of ore, designed to be carried on the back and fitted with two flat loops of hide, with a breast-strap connecting them, something on the principle of children's toy reins. Growing near by a plant of the aloe tribe, the bottom leaves dead, and some of those above scratched in their fleshy substance, as though for amusement.

Walking up the slope towards the pair a coarse, strong, vigorous, black-bearded man with projecting eyes. He is clothed in white robes and wears a queer-shaped hat or cap, I think with a point to it. From an ornamented belt about his middle hangs a short sword in a scabbard, with a yellowish handle ending in a knob shaped like to the head of a lion. He carries over his head a painted umbrella or sunshade that will not shut up, and is made either of thin strips of wood or of some kind of canvas stretched on a wooden frame.

Haggard notes that:

[The] general idea connected with the 'dream' is that this man is an overseer of slaves who is about to kill the injured person as useless and take the woman for himself. She might be the daughter of the injured man, or possibly a wife a good deal younger than he. In any case she is intimately connected with him. Further idea. That the injured man was once an individual of consequence who has been reduced to slavery by some invading and more powerful race. The characteristics of the site of the picture remind me of Cyprus.

These are classic 'past life memory snapshots' and Haggard goes on to describe the well-known Spiritualist Sir Oliver Lodge's reaction to these pictures:

> *I described these tableaux to Sir Oliver Lodge when I met him in the Athenaeum not long ago, and asked him his opinion concerning them. He was interested, but replied that if they had appeared to him he would have thought more of them than he did as they had appeared to me, because he said that he lacked imagination. The curious little details such as that of the dark-coloured trout on the table in No. 4, and that of the scratchings on the aloe leaves in No. 5, seemed to strike him very much, as did the fact that all the scenes were such as might very well, and indeed doubtless have occurred again and again in the course of our long human history, from the time of the cave-dwellers onwards. Probably if we could trace our ancestors back to the beginning, we should find that on one occasion or another they have happened to some of them. I may add that by far the prettiest and most idyllic of these pictures was that of the primitive family in the midst of its green setting of hazel boughs by the mouth of the cave. Only over it, as I have said, like a thunder-cloud brooded the sense of something terrible that was about to happen. I wonder what it was.*

Experiences such as these will be very familiar to people who experience déjà vu – a sense of having being in a place or event in another time, or who undergo spontaneous regression experiences to what appear to be their own past lives, or who are seemingly born with knowledge of their past lives. Such experiences carry a clarity of detail, like Haggard's 'scratches on an aloe leaf', that is not usually available in ordinary 'imaginings'. During hypnopompic imagery, such details quickly fade as waking consciousness takes over so it sounds to me that something more could be happening here, a breaking through of past life memories or an accessing of the Akashic Record. I prefer to think that he was incorporating his own memories into the journey of his soul.

Part 2

The Karmic Path

Genius is experience. Some seem to think that it is a gift or talent, but it is the fruit of long experience in many lives.

Henry Ford

*S*o, if you're wondering why certain things have happened to you or why you have a specific talent, the key to your present life experiences may lie in other lives – your karma – or in the choices that you made in the interlife. Indeed, this is the part of the book where you may develop a nasty case of karmic hypochondria, when you decide you must have had every kind of karma possible because so many karmas fit your situation.

Most people who follow the way of karma believe that their present life is created, wholly or partly, from their prior actions and in this section we'll explore what those karmas mean – and whether it's a question of fate or if freewill has its place. But karma is not just the result of direct action. It also arises from ingrained attitudes, thoughts, desires – and actions that have not been taken when they perhaps could have been. In other words, the things that ought to have been done but have not. But where does that 'ought' come from? The answer lies not only in the soul and its choices, but also in the mind.

Thought is a powerful manifestor of karma, particularly if it arises from ingrained habit. The thoughts and beliefs of yesterday are the soul imperatives and the physical reality of today. Someone who has a habitual attitude of resentment, for instance, can create physical illness or circumstances for themselves which gives them something tangible to resent such as poverty or betrayal. Equally, their soul imperative might be that they have to get even (with whom they are not quite sure) or that the world owes them a living. Last thoughts before death in a previous life are particularly potent. Someone who dies believing 'there will never be enough' is likely to be born again with the propensity for addiction, for instance, although that may be focused on a substance or a person or a sensation.

On the other hand, when you begin to think about your karma you may go into total denial: 'Oh, no, that can't possibly be true'. In my experience what cannot possibly be true usually is, and the rest is often an example of 'mea culpa'. You think 'I must have sinned' because so much religious teaching instils a sense of guilt and sin – and guilt may be a strong soul overlay from another life. Somehow, people seem to prefer to focus on the 'bad karma' – surprisingly often used as an excuse for continuing the situation in which people find themselves – rather than the 'good karma' they have generated. Indeed, many people are still stuck in a karmic round of endless repeats of the same life, or else bounce between two extremes.

So, keep an open mind, do not jump to conclusions until all the evidence is in. Reserve judgement. Better still, put it aside entirely. Judgement is never a good idea as we know so little from the perspective of our earthly selves. It is our higher selves – that part that is not fully incarnated and which can therefore see so much further because it is connected to past life memories and to the soul's plan for the present life that was created in the interlife – that holds the answers and assist us in the life review following death and prior to reincarnation.

Karmic Process

I saw how beings vanish and come to be again. I saw high and low, brilliant and insignificant, and how each obtained according to his karma a favourable or painful rebirth.

The Buddha

How the forces of karma transform themselves into a new body was a question which occupied many of the twentieth century metaphysicians. Rudolf Steiner, for instance, believed that if a man had been controlled by his passions, or emotions, then he would, in the next incarnation find some obstacle in his own body which he would have to overcome. This would in no way be a punishment. It would be self-created as part of the soul's evolution. In other words, it would be a mixture of karma and soul purpose. In compensating for the past, he would balance out his karma and his soul would grow. When Steiner examined the after-death process he explained that:

... very special forces indeed are taken into the human individuality in the time between death and a new birth... in the kamaloca [after life] the events of a person's last life, his good and bad deeds, his moral qualities, and so on, come before his soul, and through contemplating his own life in this way he acquires the inclination to bring about the remedy and compensation for all that is imperfect in him, and which has manifested as wrong action. He is moved to acquire those qualities which will bring him nearer to perfection in various directions. He forms intentions and tendencies during the time up to a new birth, and goes into existence again with these intentions. Further, he himself works upon the new body which he acquires for his new life, and he builds it in conformity with the forces he has brought from previous earthly lives... From this it may be seen that this new body will be weak or strong in accordance with the individual's capacity to build weak or strong forces into it.[1]

Here Steiner is reflecting the views of Plato set out many centuries earlier:

Know that if you become worse you will go to the worse souls, or if better to the better... and in death you will do and suffer what like may fitly suffer at the hands of like (Plato: Laws)

Steiner believed that a 'certain sequence of events' was set in motion in the karmaloca or interlife. Following death, a life review would take place in which the person not only saw but felt each and every part of the last life very intensely, especially the emotions – something which is frequently borne out by both near death experiences and regression. Steiner postulated that this occurred because, in life, the brain and mental processes had filtered the emotions. Now, without that filter, those emotions would be much more powerful during the reliving. So, when the soul re-experienced the anger, fear or aversion, envy and so on which underlay his actions, he would do so vividly and would react by saying: 'I must perfect myself so that I no longer come under the domination of my emotions'. That decision would be attached to his soul and would be imprinted as a force on the body that was created for the next birth. In the new incarnation, the soul would not allow itself to be subjected to those emotions, and so a new way of responding to life would have to be created. In this way the soul could compensate for previous actions. However, having attended many such life reviews, I can attest that there are souls who skip this portion of the post death experience and, therefore, return again with the same patterns deeply imprinted.

Most people who explore the interlife find a broad spectrum of agreement on the stages of choosing the next incarnation – assuming that the soul is aware enough to make a choice, some souls simply bounce back drawn by ungratified desires. There is the review of all that has been achieved so far – see the Planning Department in section 1 – usually in the company of guides and helpers; an identification of certain themes or specific qualities to be incorporated into the new life; and a discussion with other members of the soul group who will incarnate at the same time.

Cause and effect

Once you believe in the connection between motivation and its effect, you will become more alert to the effects which your own actions have upon yourself and others.

Dalai Lama

It is clear from regression experiences that karma is the process by which we meet what we have created previously – and experiences that we have planned whilst not in incarnation. Karma is not only a law of retribution but also of compensation and recompense, and growth. There is positive karma as well as negative, and not everything is karmic. A continuous process, it is dynamic and continuous and creates equilibrium.

Karma is often expressed as 'for every action there is a reaction' but its true meaning goes much deeper than this. In the conventional, Eastern, view of karma, an act takes place or a thought occurs and something is set in motion, and reward or punishment is reaped either in the present or a future life. In this view, karma is the fate that shapes the next life and that underlies suffering. Whatever a man, or woman, experiences is seen as the product of previous behaviour and, as the Tibetan Buddhist teacher Chogyam Trungpa Rinpoche puts it: 'what is reborn is mostly your bad habits'.

My own view is that karma is a process rather than a reaction. It is purposeful, concerned with growth and evolution, rather than punishment. It is all-embracing and has many manifestations. Karma operates at different levels, from the personal to the universal. It shows where balance is needed and may involve reparation, or retribution for past actions, and reward and restitution. It does not simply stem from actions and events. It encompasses attitudes, thoughts and desires – and ingrained habits. Purposeful, karma can occur at any time, not just in a future life. Part of the evolutionary journey of the soul, karma is neutral and impartial, neither good nor bad. Nevertheless, 'the weaknesses of the flesh are the scars of the soul' and regression shows that many souls do incarnate to overcome or to make reparation for previous misdemeanours.

> **A Karmic Definition**: *Karma is cause and effect operating in everyday life. What is set in motion has consequences. Karma is purposeful, concerned with growth and evolution, rather than punishment. A balancing force, it is all-embracing and has many manifestations. Karma operates at different levels, from the personal to the universal. It shows where balance is needed and may involve reparation, or retribution for past actions, and reward and restitution. Karma does not simply stem from actions and events. It encompasses intention, words, attitudes, thoughts and desires – and ingrained habits.*

Nevertheless, not everything is karmic. From regressions to the interlife, it is obvious that many people carefully plan what can appear on the surface to be a devastating example of karmic retribution – such as blindness, paralysis and so on – but is actually a learning experience chosen by the incarnating soul to develop qualities such as compassion, empathy or insight either in themselves or in people with whom they have agreed to incarnate. We're going to examine this later in the book but first let's look at how karmic memory works.

Karmic memory is rarely conscious or if it is it quickly gets squashed in childhood possibly to resurface many years later. But, for many people, even without specific memories reincarnation explains the otherwise inexplicable. A few years ago a Polish concert violinist, for instance, appeared on the BBC Radio Programme *Desert Islands Discs*. Describing how she, aged 3, had picked up a violin and confidently played it, she said that reincarnation was the only possible explanation for her prodigious talent and she believed she had lived two hundred or so years earlier in a male body. I found it heartening that unlike so many people she recognised that 'good karma' in the shape of talents and abilities could just as easily travel with a soul as the things that people regard as their 'bad karma'.

It is clear from regressions that even the smallest of actions or the briefest of thoughts can produce karma and sometimes the manifestation is literal. My favourite story in this respect is the woman who, as she was dying and recalling unrequited love, said: 'Next time he's going to marry me'. She burst out laughing and said: 'He did, he was the vicar who performed the ceremony'. I've learned through many regressions that you have to be careful what you wish for or life will take you at your word. The soul is extremely literal in how it manifests karma.

Every moment is pregnant with its consequences. People tend to view karma as punitive but it is actually neutral and non-judgemental. What may be termed 'karmic misfortune' is simply the result of past actions coming round again to be balanced out or, as we will see, of soul choice. Karma is a useful tool for focusing attention on the consequences of actions – past and present. It is through karma that the soul learns and progresses. Consequences may not necessarily be 'bad'. Good karma matures in the same way that more negative forms do. As the Buddha put it:

> Do not overlook tiny good actions, thinking they are of no benefit; even tiny drops of water in the end will fill a huge vessel.

Karma may be a test the soul sets for itself to see how well it has learned a lesson. So, for instance, someone, let's call him Ian, might have had several highly successful, possibly egocentric, outgoing lives. The challenge then could be to avoid selfishness and self-indulgence, learning to think of others. While things went well, Ian would be the life and soul of the party, optimistic and fun to be with. But, the soul asks, can this be kept up under very different circumstances? The test is arranged so that – at first – things go extremely well. Ian has the opportunity to develop a positive outlook once again. And then, seemingly, things suddenly go wrong. Bankruptcy is declared, redundancy looms, a chronic illness develops, or a relationship ends. The challenge is to maintain that happy, positive, optimistic outlook despite the setbacks. To be able to be among people who have 'more than me' and yet not get bitter or resentful. A temptation may be to manipulate previous contacts or to put pressure on someone who 'owes me' so that things can 'get back to normal'. If illness sets in, attitudes may change. On the other hand, the soul might have decided it was time to put aside the outward-orientated approach to life and to develop introspection and inner-awareness. So, the loss of status, job, or whatever, could be designed to turn Ian inward to find different strengths.

Sometimes the greatest discoveries stem from small beginnings and possibly from past life memories. Johannes Kepler (1571-1630) was a Renaissance astrologer, astronomer, mathematician and physicist. He recognized – and brought the awareness back to mass consciousness – that the sun was the centre of our planetary system. His research led to an understanding of the dynamics of planetary motion and much else besides. In a preface to *Harmonics of the World* Kepler said:

> *Yes, it is I who have robbed the golden vessels of the Egyptians to make an offering to my God far removed from Egyptian bounds. If you will forgive me, I will rejoice, but if you blame me I must bear it; here I throw the dice and I write this book. What matter if it is read today or later – even if centuries must elapse before it is read! God himself had to wait six thousand years for the one who recognized his work.*

Kepler would appear to have had a glimpse of a life in an Egyptian temple, possibly as an astronomer priest and probably as one who served a 'different god'. Certainly Kepler's extensive study of Pythagoras and Plato would have brought the concept of reincarnation to his attention. The indictment of Kepler's mother for witchcraft might perhaps show why he hinted at his past life memories rather than speaking openly of them. This was a period when the Inquisition were hard at work rooting out 'heretics' and Kepler's work sufficiently challenged the Roman Church and its established notions to make it dangerous for him. Had his mother, whom he himself defended at her trial, been found guilty his official position as Mathematician of the Holy Roman Empire would have been put in jeopardy. Had he openly confessed to memories of other lives Kepler would undoubtedly have received the unwelcome attentions of the church. As it was, he was able to fulfil his dharma and bring about a revolutionary change in how the universe was viewed.

There are many levels and categories of karma that apply at a personal, group, racial or collective level. It is not necessary to believe in reincarnation to accept karma as karma can arise, and have its consequences, in a present life. Anyone who follows the precepts: 'Do as you would be done by' or 'Do unto others what you would have them do unto you' is actually following the karmic path, whether they know it or not.

Karma implies a continuous process, that is to say, what is experienced now is the result of personal or collective prior action but karma is not static and unchanging. It is continually being set in motion. Karma is active *in the present moment*, not just in the past. What is set in motion today will have consequences: 'good' or 'bad' depending on how they are perceived. These consequences may become apparent in five minutes, a week, in a year or two, or in another lifetime. Positive, constructive karma can be set in motion and reparation can be made to overcome negative karma. Although karma is neutral, its effects may be experienced as difficult and, therefore, perceived as 'bad karma' coming home to roost. On the other hand, the same situation could be perceived differently. It all depends on the attitude of the soul involved. Karma may be looked on as fate but is really an evolving future.

Karma does not decay or become inoperative, but it may go into suspension until the conditions are right for it to 'ripen' and it can be transmuted when the karma of grace comes into operation. The connection between an action and a reaction may be immediately apparent but this is not always so. Karma can be a delayed reaction. A soul may have karma to deal with from a lifetime seemingly many hundreds of years from the present incarnation. Conditions may not have been right for the soul to deal with the karma until the present life. It may have had to develop certain strengths and insights first. Cultural, economic or environmental factors may not have been right. The people the soul needed to incarnate with to deal with the karma may not have been ready.

As time is not linear and chronological, it only seems that way from the perspective of earth, the karma may have *appeared* to take a long time to come around but in the context of eternal time, it has passed in the blink of an eye. On the other hand, karma appears to be speeding up. Many people now find that the consequences of yesterday's actions are returning almost immediately, they do not need to wait for another life.

Karma is a complex process. Some schools of thought teach that everything has to be experienced. So the soul has to know sorrow and joy, pain and happiness, longing and fulfilment. It must be both murdered and murderer, warmonger and appeaser, rake and celibate. In another school of thought, rather than getting itself murdered, the soul of a murderer could become the parent of the soul it had murdered and thus learn to cherish that soul. Once the process is looked on as one of balance, the concept of fault and judgement drops away. All is experienced because the experience is needed. Regression experience suggests that all possibilities are open, there is no one way that the soul will experience and deal with karma.

Balance is also created through fundamentally opposing attitudes to life arising in different incarnations. Someone who is now very introverted and sensitive could be balancing out many lifetimes of extroverted egoism. Another soul who had led many lives as an aggressive male might choose to inhabit a female body or could be a softer, more intuitive male who might choose to relate intimately to other males rather than women. Such a soul could experience what it was like to be on the receiving end of a macho-man's aggressive fear reaction when confronted with someone who was different to himself.

However, not everything is karmic. There comes a time when the soul moves beyond karma and into soul learning. Increasingly, there are people who have incarnated not to deal with their karma but to grow their own souls or to be of service to humanity. And, as we will see, many people may find that their lifepath is a mixture of the two, karma to be balanced out and a soulplan to put into action, service to be given. Karma and dharma work as one.

Before we look at this in greater details, let's examine a complex interweaving of karma from my own experience that may clarify this concept and how other people are drawn into our story and act as triggers or blocks as it unfolds. Over forty years ago I found myself marooned in the African bush. There was a civil war on, so I was restricted to the mining camp where my husband worked. There were no jobs available other than volunteering to run the library once a week. I was bored and depressed as I was suffering from severe morning sickness (a precursor of the pre-eclampsia that would later result in a near death experience at my daughter's birth, which itself reiterated a past life experience and made me realise there was more to life than at first appeared).

'Why don't you try writing,' the sympathetic camp nurse said. 'You'd be good at that'. More than forty-something books later I can laugh at my reply: 'What on earth would I write about?' I asked. 'Someone has already had a book published about her experiences here. I wouldn't know where to begin with a novel. I don't have anything to say'. I was living on top of a vast bed of crystal – a foundation for much of my later work – and through some extremely karmic times although I didn't recognise that until much later.

Sierra Leone was where returned slaves from the Americas were sent regardless of their ethnic origin – and from which many slaves had originally been plundered to feed the collective greed machine. Until recently it had been 'ruled' by Britain who had pulled out leaving the country pretty much bankrupt but, we were assured, politically stable. All that changed as I flew out of the main airport to go up country and we passed over a line of tanks. The army were taking over – and civil war raged for the next forty years. I have written elsewhere about the curse that was put on that mine and what had to be done to clear it.[2]

Ten years after leaving Africa, I had my astrological chart read. I wasn't sure what career to follow and needed some advice: 'You should teach and write', said the astrologer. At that time I was completing a teacher-training degree but knew that schools weren't for me. The record kept by my personal tutor stated 'has very peculiar ideas, should not be allowed near children'. Although I had to fight hard to have that report removed, I really did not think a career as a religious education teacher was in accord with my soul's purpose. 'There are many ways of teaching', the astrologer said enigmatically. The reading I did around that degree regarding world religions certainly helped me much later in life so again I was laying down a foundation.

I had had a few articles published and was keeping a record of my reincarnation experiences. My mentor Christine Hartley, who I had known in many other lives, was a literary agent and she encouraged me, introducing me to her own publisher. 'There isn't much call for that stuff', he said. As usual I was before my time, leading where others were still reluctant to follow. But I knew they'd catch up later, as has proved to be the case.

Then I was introduced to another publisher with whom I felt a – reciprocated – strong connection from Renaissance times. The publisher, who had no difficulty in seeing himself as an historical character, commented that he had brought the same nose back into the present life. There was a remarkable similarity between portraits of the past life character and the present life man, something that occasionally happens. 'You write well', he said, 'we'll have to see about publishing you'. But somehow it never happened.

A few more years went by and then Howard Sasportas and I gave a seminar on karmic astrology. We taped it with the intention of it becoming a book but, although the tape started well, it deteriorated into strange buzzings and mumblings. 'You'll have to write it on your own', said Howard. 'I've just been appointed editor for an astrological series. I'll get a contract out to you'. *The Karmic Journey* was the result. I handed it in and sat back thinking it was done. A copy editor rang me to enquire about some of the references and I went up to London. I could see that the manuscript was covered in pencil marks. I took a closer look. She had completely rewritten my work because 'it sounds better this way'. She was a French non-astrologer who knew nothing about the subject and yet she had changed all my so carefully chosen words. 'Karma' had been changed to 'dharma', which means a completely different thing and so on, and even the names of planets had been switched round. It was a disaster. When I rang the senior editor: 'everyone gets edited', he told me dismissively. I cannot express how incandescently angry I was. That was the moment when I learned that anyone could commit murder if they are sufficiently provoked, he was fortunate to be out of physical reach. He later apologised when he'd seen the extent of the changes but I felt that I could not speak my truth. My words were going through someone else's mouth. It made me wonder.

When I wrote my next book I had a clause put in 'no editing without the author's agreement'. It didn't help. In the second edition a third of the book was dropped without reference to me: the esoteric part about the wisdom of older women. 'There's no call for that', I was told. My words had been thrown away. My next book never really saw the light of day – the publisher went bankrupt the day after the launch. Another project was commissioned but stayed on the shelf for a year while a well known author did something similar with the same publisher. I eventually got the rights back. By this time I had plenty to say and too little time to write. Another book came out without any publicity. It did well but not as well as it could have had more people known about it. My words had finally got out there, but few people were hearing them.

So, I began to wonder again. Just what was it about me and publishing? I did a past life regression to find out. I went into the Renaissance life I knew so well. It had taken me a long time to admit that I could be this figure from history but here he was again. I asked to see exactly what it was from that life that was holding me back now. I was taken to a ceremony in which I had joined an esoteric group – several of whom I recognised in addition to the publisher I had already identified. I had to swear a solemn oath not to reveal the teaching I was about to receive.

It suddenly made sense. In my present day writing, I was revealing many of the things that had been secret then and several members of that group were, albeit unconsciously, trying to keep me silent in our present life. In that other life, the Inquisition was very active and more than one of the group ended up in its hands. In the church's eyes, we had heretical knowledge. But it was also knowledge never intended for public consumption. So there were two reasons for karmic consequences: the first the oath that I had sworn, the other that mentioning such things outside the group, and especially making them public, could easily have brought about a visit from the Inquisition and all that would entail. That imperative had transferred to the present life.

In that other life I clearly trod a fine line between my published work – bringing neo-Platonism to the public eye, my employment as a cleric in the Catholic church and my membership of the occult group. I negotiated this much more successfully than many of my contemporaries as I ended up a cardinal and several of them were declared to be heretics with all that that entailed. But my esoteric activities brought a few heart-stopping moments when discovery seemed imminent and, of course, in public I was promulgating a doctrine I believed in my heart to be false. Hypocrisy. Something I intensely dislike in my present life yet meet time and again. I have to check that I am not committing it myself in thought, word or deed whenever I meet it in other people. Quite a lot of karma had clearly accrued!

In regression, I had to rework that vow of secrecy so that it bound me for that life only – and just to be sure I revoked all similar vows I had ever taken at any point in any of my lives. I then checked in the interlife that I was meant to be writing about these things in my present life. The answer was an emphatic yes. It was time for them to be disseminated to a wider audience. What I didn't do, I now see, was to get the agreement of the group. At the time, I didn't think of it. Sometimes the objective input of a therapist is vital if you are to cover all the bases and I was working on my own.

Things got better, however. It was as though a log-jam had unblocked. Several books were published. Then I realised that one of my publishers, a contact from that past life who had forever been trying to penetrate the esoteric group without success, had misled me into signing away a large part of my royalties. My then agent was embroiled in the situation too but refused to back me up if I took it to court. She said she was afraid her other authors who were published by him would suffer – although he had perpetrated the same fraud on them.

As writing was by now a main part of my work and a major source of income, this was serious. It was time to make a stand. Before I did, however, I pondered aloud why this was happening. Was it karmic retribution? Did it mean that I should not be writing at all? Was it, heaven forbid, new karma being put in motion? 'Perhaps you'd better ask what you did to offend the scribes in ancient Egypt', an intuitive Scorpio said.

Naturally I asked, and was shown. It did not appear to be personal karma but just to make sure I did a tie cutting with the publisher (then one of the scribes), ground up the slab on which the curse had been written and scattered it on the sacred waters of the Nile – fortuitously I was on holiday in Egypt at the time. A part of my soul was retrieved that had been stuck back there. The rest is hazy, especially from this distance as the regression was quite a few years ago. I was releasing the past and did not need to retain it. Once I'd completed that, I was led into a temple and reinitiated into the highest level of knowledge I had attained in Egypt, higher than the scribes whose edicts could no longer touch me. Funnily enough, in fourteen visits to Egypt in my present life I hadn't been able to bribe my way into the uppermost part of the temple where that initiation took place (the only place in Egypt where baksheesh and a smile hadn't got me in). The next time I went to the temple, I could walk in freely. The way had been opened.

I changed my agent (with whom I had a past life connection) and severed as far as I could my connection with that publisher. When I last wrote about this experience ten years ago, I said that no doubt there would be more to discover before forgiveness could finally heal it – recognising that more of the past needed to be released and other insights gained. On checking it out further I discovered that that publisher felt that I owed him something because, in another life, we had once been part of a group working for the same cause but I had died before the purpose was completed. In this present life he appeared to feel that I owed him something. So I asked for forgiveness and once again cut the ties. Then I felt forgiveness encompassing him and everyone else involved in all my publishing karma. My next book, *The Crystal Bible*, was a great success. The wheel seemed to have come full circle. And I thought that was that.

But no, as I said, the working out of karmic consequences is complex. Last night I realised that I was still carrying a soul overlay that I hadn't cleared. Despite having done all that work to release myself from other people's expectations, I hadn't cleared myself of my own imperatives. Part of me was still trying to keep the secrets. I went back through the whole thing again, this time asking that the collective, group and personal levels of the karma be released and that grace would come in so that my soul purpose for the present life – the sharing of knowledge and experiences that will help us all to shift away from karmic consequences into our soul purpose – could manifest. Through this work *The Soulmate Myth: a dream come true or your worst nightmare?* has been freed to fly into the world, as will *The Book of Why*. So unsnagging those karmic consequences took forty years – and I am not complacent enough to think that there might not be more challenges and insights to come.

And, needless to say, three months after writing the above someone tried to hijack my identity by publishing a 'new' version of the most popular of my books and a website with the name of that book is also purporting to be me. So, I am having to look at who I really am, what I value and will fight for in life, and what I can let go and allow the karma of grace to deal with it for me. As the wise Margaret Cahill advised, 'don't give it too much energy, do what you have to do and then let it go'. All the crystal book wholesalers I – and the 'new' publisher – contacted were appalled at what they saw as the deliberate misleading of the public and have refused to stock the 'new' book. So the misappropriation of my title seems to be rebounding already and I bless that author and her publisher for their assistance in selling my books. I don't need to do anything further and I wish the author well. My soulplan obviously doesn't allow much time between insight and a new challenge to my understanding but, equally, the karma of grace is taking care of things for me.

What Carries Karma?

As with the soul, what carries karma depends on the lens through which karma is being viewed. In Buddhist thought, the karma is scattered at death and therefore does not pass to one individual but, potentially to many, although Tibetan Buddhists take a more individualistic view. From the perspective of a Hindu or a Western believer in reincarnation, it is the *atman* or eternal soul. This 'eternal identity' puts on different personalities or personas rather like an actor takes on roles which are played for a period of time and then put aside. The actor, however, remains essentially the same throughout although he may be so carried away by his role that he forgets, for a time, that he is only acting.

In the same way, the soul can become so submerged in the present life that it thinks that the body is all there is – and in most traditions incarnating souls are in any case bathed in merciful forgetfulness so that they do not remember all that happened in other lives. Nevertheless, the karma carried by the soul manifests even though the cause is not remembered. The soul, or eternal identity, carries a knowledge of all that has happened and this is transferred to the body through the karmic blueprint according to which the physical body develops or through the holographic soul (a concept we will explore below).

Another way of looking at the concept of the soul and its karma is to view each life as a bead which is strung together with others. The thread that holds them together is the soul, with the karma passing from the soul into the next life. However, this view emphasises a linear progression and it is clear from regression experiences that linear time, once out of incarnation, has no meaning and that incarnations do not necessarily happen sequentially.

The idea I personally find most useful is that of the holographic soul that carries all the memories and experiences not only of itself but also of other members of its soul group – and maybe even of the whole universe and potentially universes beyond this one. If this is the case, all karmic experience can be 'sampled' by the soul and incorporated into a specific learning experience planned in the interlife and carried into incarnation through a map – the birthchart, 'road signs' – the genes, and the karmic blueprint from which the new body is formed. Or, if the soul hasn't reached that stage of consciously planning the next incarnation, the information in the karmic hologram will pull the soul back into its old patterns.

Transfer of karma to a new body

The physical body is an important repository for the karma to be dealt with in a life. It may be one of the trials or challenges of that life. It is clear from regression experiences to the interlife that most souls about to reincarnate choose the body, and its physical condition, carefully. The body is frequently the 'last stop' for karma as the origin of a physical karmic condition is frequently psychosomatic – that is, created by an attitude in a former life – or is caused by an unhealed former life injury. The root cause is most often a thought, emotion, closed-mindedness or spiritual dis-ease manifesting physically. It is as though the karma 'solidifies' in the physical dimension and, as we have seen, the potentiality for this is created in the womb.

The karmic blueprint

We have already looked in Part 1 at how the physical body is surrounded by the subtle energy bodies that comprise the etheric body and seen what Steiner had to say about karmic transfer to the new body. We saw how, at death, the etheric body withdraws with the soul from the physical and moves to another plane, taking with it the imprint from its experiences whether these are at a physical, emotional, mental level or spiritual level. Ingrained thoughts are recorded, fleeting or persistent emotions are registered, unfinished business logged in and all areas of dis-ease mapped. As the etheric body progresses beyond death, the subtle bodies drop away but the essence of the karmic imprints is carried by the soul as a 'karmic blueprint' that contains a hologram of all that has gone before and which connects to the soul plan for the present life.

When the soul is ready to incarnate again, the holographic karmic blueprint is what manifests the physical body and the new aura – although it may be helped by genetic or uterine conditions that will create dis-ease or disability *or the propensity for such to emerge later in life if the appropriate triggers are applied.* From the moment the soul takes over the new body (and, from regression to the interlife, it can vary considerably as to timing) the karmic blueprint will begin to build a

The aura with past-life blockages

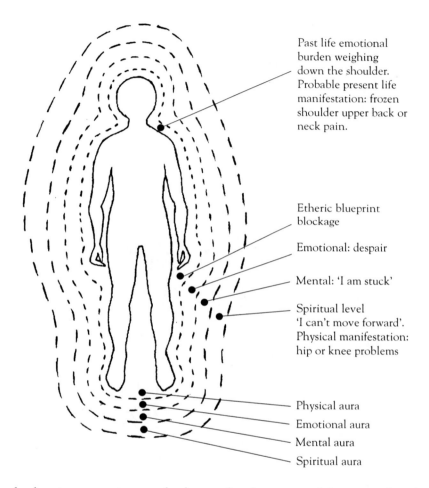

Past life emotional burden weighing down the shoulder. Probable present life manifestation: frozen shoulder upper back or neck pain.

Etheric blueprint blockage

Emotional: despair

Mental: 'I am stuck'

Spiritual level 'I can't move forward'. Physical manifestation: hip or knee problems

Physical aura

Emotional aura

Mental aura

Spiritual aura

body that is appropriate to the karma for the present lifetime and soul purpose. If there is karma that will not be dealt with, this is held in suspension. The new body reflects any fundamental dis-ease in its aura as well as past life imbalances or ingrained attitudes. A physical condition that allows the soul to work with karma may manifest from birth or develop at an appropriate time.

From my own regression work and from the researches of colleagues, I know that certain thoughts or emotions have a particularly strong effect at specific levels and connect to parts of the body. Many of these can be

FRONT[3]

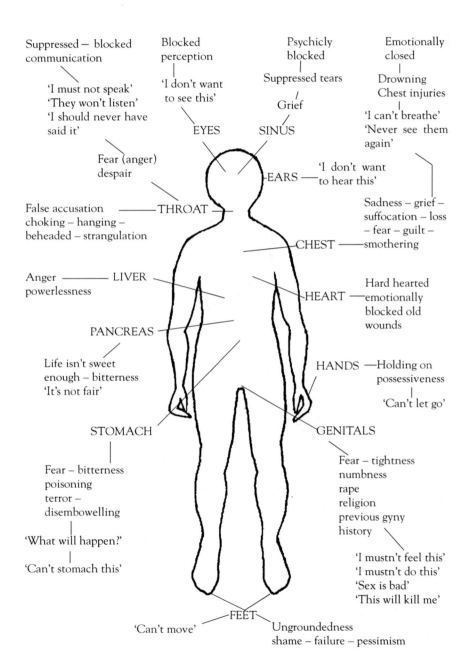

Suppressed — blocked
communication

'I must not speak'
'They won't listen'
'I should never have
said it'

Fear (anger)
despair

False accusation
choking – hanging –
beheaded – strangulation

Anger ——————— LIVER
powerlessness

PANCREAS

Life isn't sweet
enough – bitterness
'It's not fair'

STOMACH

Fear – bitterness
poisoning
terror –
disembowelling

'What will happen?'

'Can't stomach this'

Blocked
perception

'I don't want
to see this'

EYES

Psychicly
blocked

Suppressed tears

Grief

SINUS

Emotionally
closed

Drowning
Chest injuries

'I can't breathe'
'Never see them
again'

'I don't want
EARS ——to hear this'

THROAT

Sadness – grief –
suffocation – loss
– fear – guilt –
CHEST ——smothering

Hard hearted
HEART ——emotionally
blocked old
wounds

HANDS —Holding on
possessiveness

'Can't let go'

GENITALS

Fear – tightness
numbness
rape
religion
previous gyny
history

'I mustn't feel this'
'I mustn't do this'
'Sex is bad'
'This will kill me'

FEET

'Can't move'

Ungroundedness
shame – failure – pessimism

BACK[4]

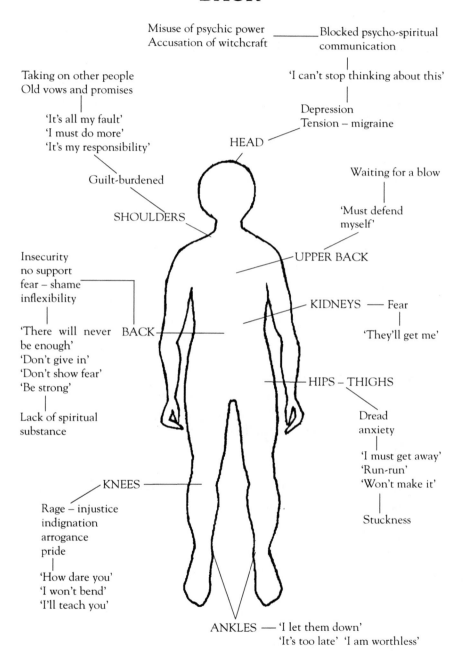

Misuse of psychic power
Accusation of witchcraft _____ Blocked psycho-spiritual
communication

'I can't stop thinking about this'

Taking on other people
Old vows and promises

Depression
Tension – migraine

'It's all my fault'
'I must do more'
'It's my responsibility'

HEAD

Guilt-burdened

SHOULDERS

Waiting for a blow

'Must defend
myself'

UPPER BACK

Insecurity
no support
fear – shame
inflexibility

KIDNEYS — Fear

'There will never   BACK
be enough'
'Don't give in'
'Don't show fear'
'Be strong'

'They'll get me'

HIPS – THIGHS

Lack of spiritual
substance

Dread
anxiety

'I must get away'
'Run-run'
'Won't make it'

KNEES

Rage – injustice
indignation
arrogance
pride

Stuckness

'How dare you'
'I won't bend'
'I'll teach you'

ANKLES — 'I let them down'
'It's too late' 'I am worthless'

seen on the illustrations shown, which may enable you to trace patterns in your own body.

So, by way of example, if a woman, let's call her Pamela, had a past life history of thinking that life wasn't sweet enough, bitterly feeling that it was unfair that she should be deprived of whatever it was she ardently desired, then Pamela would be carrying attitudinal karma and her spiritual dis-ease would be that she grabbed at love or comfort without giving it herself (the primary cause of selfishness and disaffection). Her new aura would reflect the fact that her karmic blueprint was disturbed over the pancreas – the organ associated with bitterness and a feeling of lacking sweetness in life. Pamela could be born with a propensity to diabetes or low blood sugar levels, or a propensity towards pancreatic malfunction in later life and may have, consciously or unconsciously, chosen a family with a faulty genetic pattern around processing sugar. However, if Pamela found emotional satisfaction and joy in her present life, then that imbalance would be healed and the propensity for significant pancreatic malfunctioning might never manifest.

Another example may make this even clearer. Edgar Cayce said that those who suffered from asthma had often 'pressed the life' out of someone else and so were now feeling like they were having the life pressed out of them (which could be regarded as both retributive or symbolic karma depending on other factors). However, in my experience it is just as likely that the person had themselves had the life pressed out of them and could be repeating a pattern. But that person may also have been burned as a heretic or witch and in many cases the asthma would be organically based reflecting the previous death, rather than symbolic karma. Asthma can also stem back to inhaling smoke on the burning pyres in India or being trapped in a burning building. It all depends on how the karmic seed manifests.

Karmic seeds
Let's look at this idea of karma transferring to the body in more detail, and especially at how the result of the same karmic seed and blockages being carried at different levels such as the emotional, mental or physical through the karmic hologram manifests. If someone carries a karmic blockage at the emotional level, for instance, of feeling stuck with something, it will weigh down the shoulder of the emotional subtle

body. It may manifest physically as a frozen shoulder or upper back or neck pain. But if the 'stuckness' arises through a repetitive thought, rather than a feeling, it will register in the mental subtle body and may register as depression and obsessive thoughts, or emotionally as despair, or physically as hip, lower back or knee problems. If the blockage is at the spiritual level, it can manifest through all the levels of the aura.

If we take another example, an elderly lady I regressed many years ago illustrates how not only the physical impact of a past life death can affect the present life but also the consequences of emotional and mental torment that may also have been present. Inga had suffered from severe asthma all her life. She was also using walking sticks because of a chronic hip problem.

In the regression Inga regressed back through time until she found herself in the Middle Ages acting as an intelligencer, a kind of go-between who received the reports from spies and informers and passed these onto the witch-finders. It was something in which she had unwittingly become embroiled and could not break free. Describing herself as an insignificant-looking, lonely man, Inga said she felt suffocated by what she was doing but could see no way out. If the intelligencer had tried to leave or to protect people, he would be put to trial by his employers as they would assume he had been bewitched. He wanted to commit suicide but believed this was a mortal sin and was too afraid of the consequences.

When the burden became too much to bear, he took a horse and rode off without caring what would happen. He was followed and a stab by a sword caused him to fall. The horse then rolled on him, crushing his chest. He died literally unable to breathe and gasped his life away in a most distressing manner that exactly matched an asthma attack. As Inga relived it, the physical symptoms were very real. She gasped and fought for breath, making the most horrendous noises. But, because she was both reliving that life and was aware of the connections to her present life, Inga reassured me from time to time that it was ok to continue. I accompanied her through death and into the interlife. There, the trauma fell away and her breathing quieted. We were able to heal her chest and remove the memory of the trauma from her etheric body.

A genuinely spiritual person, Inga was full of compassion for the man she had been, saying he had clearly had no choice. What did surprise her was how afraid he had been to commit suicide as in her present life she would have had no qualms. It is difficult to recall in the 21st century just how great the fear of mortal sin was only a few centuries ago as, in the thinking of the time, it would result in everlasting damnation. The fear had been stronger than the overwhelming feelings of wrongness and the guilt over what was being done. With that kind of inner conflict combined with the violent death, it was no surprise that Inga's current life played out the drama in such a physical way. The sense of suffocation and guilt that she had felt prior to her death, combined with the actual suffocation through the crushing of her chest, had imprinted itself on her etheric body and her karmic blueprint, resulting in a physical body that continued to gasp her life away. Her feeling of 'stuckness' from that life had also manifested itself in the chronic hip problem she experienced.

The regression helped to explain why, despite her own illness, in her present life Inga had become a pioneering psychic and healer. She had wanted to make reparation. The compassion she was able to show to her past life self and the forgiveness she offered healed the root cause of the asthma, which ceased.

Fate or Freewill?

To what extent we fashion our own destinies is beyond our comprehension but I have found each stage in life offers its own challenge and, surprise, surprise, this does not lessen with time. It merely takes a different form. As the body weakens and disintegrates, the mind, if one is lucky, strengthens in order to take up new challenges. Organises itself to run a personal obstacle race where every added exertion is an accomplishment, and one becomes more and more aware that 'the time is now and the place is here and there are no second chances for a single second.

Pamela Morris paraphrasing Jeanette Winterson

As we've seen, karma generally implies a belief in *continuous* causality, that is: what you are experiencing now is the result of your personal or collective prior action and what you experience in the future will be the result of your present actions. This leads many people who believe in karma to look on it as their fate. Fate implies that the soul is reaping penalties for past actions. Viewed fatalistically, it is what has been earned and it is not open to change.

People who believe in this type of 'kismet' karma hold the view that the future is predestined: what will be, will be. They see no point in trying to change things and extreme passivity sets in. The consequences of this belief are psychologically paralyzing and spiritually demoralizing. There is little point in striving to 'better yourself', to evolve, or to overcome negative karmic circumstances and so nothing is done to alleviate grinding poverty or dis-ease. Kismet is, in most systems, both capricious and punitive. It is predestined. It is what happens, there is no choice. Fate offers no explanation as to *why* people suffer, other than 'this is what they deserve', or perhaps the medieval Christian belief that suffering has merit in its own right.

Even when kismet is discounted, in the fatalistic approach to karma, the rule is an eye for an eye, a tooth for a tooth. If a man murders, he will become a victim; if he injures, he will be injured. However, as we will see, there are many ways of making reparation or restitution. The murderer may achieve a degree of spiritual enlightenment and choose a life of service as restitution. Once the incarnating soul has found another to whom a similar debt is owed by another soul, to perform an appropriate task could be sufficient reparation. Nor does it seem to be spiritually necessary to fulfil every last duty or debt. The karma of grace can operate. There is a point when enough has been done, understanding has been reached, and the soul is freed from the karmic round.

But not everyone views karma fatalistically, and not everyone will experience karma and rebirth in this way. Whilst there are strong links between karma and fate, destiny is an evolving future. The soul has a pattern that has been laid down – the fate or destiny as it were. But it also has free will and the power to change the future. It is the ability to grow, to transform and transmute and to find a positive outcome for karma. The incarnating soul can choose to encounter the result of its own handiwork or to make reparation for the past – no matter how hard a present life that may lead to. This can be a positive choice, both for the soul itself and for other people. The soul may take on collective karma, help someone else learn a lesson, and so on.

It is difficult to evaluate the long-term spiritual effects of traumatic or painful karmic experiences upon the eternal Self; the working of karma is in any case, subtle and far from straightforward. So, while fate and kismet means 'it is written and what is written is unchangeable', it is nevertheless possible to believe in karma and reincarnation and still maintain that the soul is in a purposeful incarnation and that you are fulfilling your destiny rather than your fate. The concept of freewill is one of growth and change on all levels. It is in direct antithesis to all those people who say: 'I can't help it, it's my karma'. This pathway says: 'You are responsible. Clean up your mess'. But it also says: 'You only have to do enough'.

Freewill allows use of the skills, abilities and potentials brought to the current life, and provides opportunities for healing for the wounds of the past. However, it would seem that there are two pathways – and maybe more. The first is that of freewill and personal responsibility: following the soul's choice. The second is surrender to divine will (or to the soul's higher plan) – which could reverse the extreme wilfulness of a former life, for instance. Hindus and Buddhists believe that by submitting to their fate, and aligning themselves with divine purpose, they can move off the wheel of rebirth. For some people who are experiencing a particularly intense and fraught life, the soul intention before incarnating may have been set to have so much pressure piling on trauma that the only thing to do was to give up on trying to will something to change and, instead, surrender to the process.

Surrendering to divine will may be a genuine commitment to divine purpose. It all depends on how clear the alignment is – and how clearly the guidance from the divine or higher self is heard. Many people who believe they are following divine will are actually trapped in the patterns of the past. They attract the same old scenarios over and over again. Regardless of how cunningly disguised, abuse, for example, is abuse no matter whether it is perpetrated by a parent, a lover, or a guru under the guise of aligning to higher will and opening spirituality. An enormous amount of self-awareness is called for on the path to enlightenment.

Belief in karma does not exclude choice that comes in the guise of 'chance'. The incarnating soul can choose to encounter the result of its own handiwork or to make reparation for the past – no matter how hard a present life that may create. It may also be a positive choice, taking on collective karma, helping someone else learn a lesson, and so on, even when this comes about in a seemingly random fashion or by 'accident'. It is much more likely that purposeful synchronicity is at work in even the most accidental seeming scenario.

Karma has been said by some to be a 'get out clause' by which a person can do whatever he wants in the present life, with the possibility that it can always be paid for in a later life. Few believers in karma would wish to take this path as they would recognise that consequences inevitably follow. The 'get out' view does not take account of the purpose of karma – which is ultimately to move off the karmic wheel. Nor can karma be used as an excuse. 'I can't help it, it's my karma' keeps the incarnating soul stuck and impedes spiritual growth. Not everything is attributable to karma, however. The student who fails exams through laxity cannot blame past karma for the failure, for instance. The person who makes an ethical or moral choice which is not in accord with the common good may possibly be acting out of past conditioning, which could be called karma, but is equally likely to be acting out of motives of self-interest, which will accrue karma but will not be caused by it. There is an element of personal responsibility within karmic manifestation which demands that the incarnating soul should own what he or she does and experiences, rather than simply blaming karma from the past for everything.

There are times when rebirth does seem to be unplanned, with fate apparently holding sway. From information gained during regression sessions and particularly when exploring the interlife, it is clear that some souls 'bounce back' into incarnation because of a strong desire to be in a physical body, or to be with a particular person, or because of something left unfinished. They may have made little progress in the spiritual world and 'hang around' the earth plane waiting to incarnate again. If someone desperately wants a baby, they can unwittingly pull this soul to them without any prior decision having been taken. Similarly, if someone desperately wants to be with someone from their past, they can put out such a strong pull that the other soul will be sucked in. The soul who has stayed too close to the earth plane has little choice in the matter, being ruled by desires. It is pulled back by cravings, unfinished business, ingrained patterns, or by its own old promises or vows that have not been rescinded. The major challenge for the present life may be to break the habits of lifetimes or to release someone – or yourself – from an outdated promise. It is these souls who incarnate without plan or preparation that could be said to be 'fated'. A cause is having its effect. But the possibility to move on is always open.

Someone who may appear to be 'fated' because of trauma, illness or difficult life situations may, however, have actually prepared most carefully for the incarnation and will have a profound reason for making that choice. It may be for personal growth and learning, or to aid other people in their lessons or intentions. So, belief in karma does not exclude chance or freewill. Freewill means: 'There is an opportunity to learn and grow.' Fate says: 'This is the future you have earned'. Freewill says: 'Yes, but you have the ability to change it and create a new future'. The key to karmic balance is in knowing when it is appropriate to submit to your karma and when it is advantageous is break a cycle.

Karmic intervention

I have been asked many times whether it is possible, sensible or ethically appropriate to intervene in someone else's karmic process. Rudolf Steiner discussed the question of freewill and karma in a series of lectures he gave in 1910. He particularly addressed the situation where someone was healed by outside intervention of a condition which had arisen out of karmic necessity – that is, when they were making reparation for a previous act. In Steiner's view, 'in a sick body there dwells a damaged soul which has come under a wrong influence'. In this situation, forms of healing that used love would be appropriate to support the damaged soul in finding resolution of the karmic imbalance that had been created. 'Because love is the fundamental essence of the soul, we may, indeed, influence the direction of karma', Steiner concluded.

There is enormous debate, not only within anthroposophy and healing or therapy, about whether a healer (or anyone else) should intervene uninvited in someone else's karma. Some authorities believe that this directly contravenes a person's autonomy and freewill; whilst others hold the view that if someone is able to help then it is their duty (or dharma) to do so – and, indeed, it may be part of a soul contract made before incarnation during interlife planning. I have found that asking that any healing or other work I put in motion should be for the highest good of all concerned ensures that I don't intervene inappropriately in someone else's karmic process. The word 'appropriate' is vitally important.

A young woman asked for healing to be sent to her mother, an Irish Catholic who had had a heart attack. She knew that her mother regarded healing and the like as 'the devil's work' and yet, as a trainee healer, she felt that it was her karmic duty to help because she was 'aware of things that her mother hadn't yet discovered'. A healing circle was conducted for the mother, care being taken to ask that healing would be received in the way that was most appropriate for the mother. If it was her time to depart, then the healing would help her passing. If she could be healed, then it would aid that process. The next day there was a telephone call from Ireland. 'A miracle has happened!' The mother had recovered well. When the daughter went back to Ireland, she told her mother about the healing circle. 'I always knew that you of all my children were special' her mother told her. 'When I looked at you for the first time, I knew you'. Mother and daughter shared the opinion that there was a soul bond between them, and that the daughter had become a healer so that she could help her mother and bring her to a new level of spiritual understanding.

Where does 'duty' come in?
Some cases of apparently fated behaviour come from a contract made between two souls before they arrived in incarnation, other cases arise where someone is caught up in a collective moment such as revolution or war. There appears to be a different karma arising out of carrying out a duty or prior soul contract than karma from volitional acts. In carrying out his 'duty', a person commits the act because he has to – unless of course he uses this as an excuse for behaviour which goes beyond the call of that duty.

So, for example, a state executioner was doing his work when he put someone to death and, provided he carried out his duties fairly and dispassionately, he would not accrue 'boomerang' karma (there would probably have been karmic or soul learning reasons why he became the executioner in the first place). In the past, such a man would generally be appointed to the job with little choice in the matter – it was an hereditary position or was given at the whim of a ruler (so a soul could have made the choice to incarnate into a family where the likelihood of inheriting such a role was strong). If that man cruelly enjoyed his work, prolonging the agony for people for example, then strong karma would accrue, as it would if he had applied for the position in the first place because he knew he would enjoy the work. The same applies to someone who chose to be a torturer because he revelled in inflicting pain. But then, there is the opposite view that someone has to torture so that another soul may learn what it feels like to be tortured and, in another life, then works to assist the victims of torture.

War can indicate someone caught up in a manifestation of fate and any karma would depend on how a man dealt with his place in the greater scheme of things and the situation in which he found himself. If a soldier took pleasure in killing and if he tormented, tortured or raped whilst he was doing it, then considerable karma would result *even though he was conforming to the mores of his time.* But if he was conscientiously 'serving King and Country' from a deep sense of patriotism or had been called up mandatorily and took no pleasure in it, far less or perhaps no karma would accrue. It all depends on the attitude with which he met his apparent 'fate'.

Lack of Personal Responsibility

The 'I can't help it, it's my karma' approach to life takes no responsibility either for having created situations that now need restitution, or for taking on tasks that may prove irksome. A person with this attitude will often blame those around him, or her, for the situation. They may also use the other person as an excuse for not doing something. So, the woman who says: 'I had to sacrifice my career to look after my husband and children' is not taking responsibility for her choice to marry and have children. The son who never leaves home may excuse himself with: 'Well my parents needed my support' and a daughter may use her ailing mother or father in the same way. This attitude can in itself create karma, especially if the person becomes a psychic vampire living off the energy or resources of others, or bullies or abuses the parent.

If someone has agreed in the interlife to help someone learn a difficult lesson; or to look after someone who, for their own karmic reasons, has undertaken illness or impairment, then it can lead to karmic enmeshment and 'bondage' or to freedom. It all depends on how the challenge is taken up once in incarnation. If the person feels held back and blames the other person, they become tied to that person and they will find themselves together in another life as they will have created personal karma between them. On the other hand, if someone can say: 'This is my choice. This is the way I want it to be', they are free from karmic ties as they have willingly surrendered to their soul's road. Ruth White, who has worked extensively with karma, says: 'We are free of bondage only when we are able to make positive statements about limitations we've accepted'. As she points out, to remain karmically healthy 'we should only make those sacrifices for which we take full responsibility'.

Accident or design?

What raises perhaps the most insistent questions are apparent accidents, random events that suck a soul in or someone who is apparently in the wrong place at the wrong time. Can this all be put down to predestination, or soul choice, happenstance or whatever the opposite of serendipity happens to be? Just as not everything is attributable to karma, neither can every event be a matter of fate or freewill. Collective karma outweighs personal karma, for instance, and people can get pulled into events. Accidents do occur and karma works at levels beyond the purely individual. A soul may belong to a soul group that has an agenda to deal with. It is clear from past life regression and interlife testimony that not everything in a life is pre-planned, nor does everything necessarily go as planned. The environment may have its effect in the shape of chemical, functional or economic forces that intervene in life. The engine on an airliner is fouled by birds, for instance, causing the plane to crash and everyone to lose their life. 'Fate' or 'karmic causation' would suggest that everyone on that plane had carried out some action in the past that meant that they had 'earned' such a death. Chance, on the other hand, would suggest that it was mere happenstance that took each person onto that plane just as it was pure chance that took the plane through a flock of birds at that particular time. Similarly, if a chemical or nuclear spillage affects hundreds of people, it could be termed accident rather than karma – although there may be some people caught up within that event who find their karma returning to them. Biological, social and racial factors may take their toll.

Few people would argue that everyone who died in the Holocaust was, for example, irresistibly attracted to that experience because of their individual karma. The Holocaust was part of a social movement and an on-going racial experience of persecution. If karma was operating, then it was more likely to be at a racial or collective level although some people would be working out their own karma or their soulplan through the experience. There are occurrences which, from outside, appear to be random and yet the 'accident' is exactly what the soul (or the race) needs or planned for the present stage of growth. As already mentioned, I have regressed people to the Holocaust who incarnated for the purpose of assisting the souls who would be caught up in it and others who were there for their own learning.

Apparent accidents can happen to an individual soul too. When I was working with a client using a body therapy, Neville began to kick and lash out. All he could say was 'No, no, I don't want to, it's not time yet'. It became clear that Neville had somehow become pulled into incarnation, trapped against his wishes. Then his birth had been induced. He wasn't ready to be born. Eventually he was pulled out by forceps only to be put in an incubator. Neville reported that while he was still in the interlife he had been thinking about incarnating but somehow it wasn't time.

Then, quite suddenly, Neville flipped back into his last death. Again it wasn't time, he had been beaten, kicked and killed. He felt cheated of life, but could not lash out at his attackers. Nor could he make them listen. He flipped out of his body 'into the light'. He was happy there, refusing to look further at that past life but part of him had remained stuck back in that death feeling helpless. That part was saying 'it's no use protesting, they won't hear me. I cannot do anything about this'. Neville had originally consulted me about a lump on his neck – right where the boot that had been kicking him had struck.

He needed to lash out with his feet, to kick away what held him so he kicked and pummelled a large cushion. Eventually Neville found the tranquillity to reflect on his coming back into incarnation. We worked on his karmic blueprint, retrieving the part of him that was stuck at that beating, rubbing out the imprint of the boot on his neck and making the decision to return. I then took him through conception and birth, allowing him to take his own time, and then moved forward through his life healing as we went. The lump on his neck got hotter and hotter. It was spitting 'like frying a hamburger' Neville said, and shrinking all the time. Within weeks all physical trace had disappeared. It is probable that had Neville not been grabbed and pulled into incarnation, he could have done that healing in the interlife, but maybe not. Maybe his indecision would have held him for too long. Maybe he needed to be in incarnation again to work through that previous life. Maybe it wasn't an accident after all, but the result of soul design.

So, to all those who shrug and say 'stuff happens' when asked why terrible things happen I would say, yes maybe it does. And, just maybe, it has been pre-planned. But, at the end of the day, it is not so much what happens to us that is of importance, it is how we deal with it. Whether we let it fester and ruin the rest of our life or whether we find a way to come to terms with it and move on.

Karmic Themes and Soul Lessons

It can be seen that certain karmic themes weave throughout human interaction over aeons of time. Suffering is one such universal karmic theme but there are others such as justice, power, betrayal, forgiveness and love that are equally ubiquitous. Themes work throughout individual lives, and intertwine through the history of a race or a land.

A soul may not necessarily be involved with a particular theme in each and every life but, when reviewed, a *leitmotiv* runs through the soul's entire experience like a river which sometimes goes underground only to surface again when the terrain is right. It is as though the soul has become immersed in that theme, and must view and experience it from all sides before resolving it. Sometimes the soul seems stuck – either in the negative or positive aspect. At other times, it swings between two extremes within it: persecutor and persecuted, for instance. An intense encounter with the theme may be followed by a few lives rest, but the soul will then pick up the theme again and again until it is completed or the lesson learned. Such a moving away from a theme may be a soul choice (see Part 3). Most souls will be working with several themes, some or all of which will be apparent in any one life.

Many karmic themes run counter to each other and frequently work down through lives as pairs of opposites. Power, abuse and control issues, for instance, are the antithesis of empowerment and autonomy; betrayal is accompanied by the opportunity for forgiveness as the betrayer becomes the betrayed. Poverty consciousness, which is based on a deep lack of self-worth, has to be turned to abundance so some lives will be of deprivation, others of wealth. The wealth is not recompense for the poverty. It is a challenge to see how the soul handles both extremes.

Other themes complement each other. Someone working on love tends to incorporate intimacy, companionship, unconditional love and acceptance into the soulplan for several lives, but may also find that cruelty, betrayal and loss are inextricably bound up within the love theme.

Major Karmic Themes

- Suffering, dis-ease and compassion
- Forgiveness, persecution and betrayal
- Victim-martyr-saviour-persecutor
- Love, both unconditional and self-love
- Justice or learning not to judge
- Guilt
- Loss of or attaining individuality
- Attachment and detachment
- Intimacy
- Self-worth
- Control versus freedom
- Power-over and empowerment
- Finding wholeness
- Fear that 'there will never be enough'
- Exile and belonging
- Abandonment and loss
- Independence and dependence
- Deprivation and abundance
- Security
- Nurturing
- Acceptance
- 'Niceness' versus authenticity and congruence
- Restriction and release
- Debts and promises
- Spirituality

Themes naturally fall into groups. Forgiveness, persecution and betrayal go alongside scapegoating, exile and banishment, as do abandonment and loss. Many people do not get the opportunity to escape the results of betrayal or persecution. A soul planning to leave a country to avoid persecution could run the risk of betrayal. Many people unconsciously expect betrayal because of their previous karmic experiences, and may attract it again and again as part of a karmic lesson. When a new country is reached, there is a feeling of exile, of 'not belonging'. The soul may have a deep seated expectation of rejection and experiences of alienation and does not fit into the society. So long as the soul is unable to forgive those responsible for the 'banishment', the theme will recur, with variations, over and over again.

The need for forgiveness often arises out of betrayal or treachery. Being betrayed is one of the most painful of all wounds, and the guilt of having been the betrayer haunts the soul through many lifetimes even when there seemed to be no other choice. If forgiveness is not possible, then the resultant bitterness and guilt erode the soul. It is as though the sense of self is poisoned. The antidote to betrayal, whatever role the soul took, is forgiveness.

Guilt is an insistent and insidious karmic theme. The soul feels culpable, responsible. Some souls seem to suffer from 'existential guilt'. Its source is buried so deep that the guilt is all pervasive, always there. Deep inside, the soul craves punishment for whatever this 'badness' was. When dreadful things happen, this is the soul who assumes it has deserved them because of the past. There are people who are always apologising. They feel guilt over the slightest thing. Such people suffer from other people's guilt, taking it on themselves. They feel they are responsible for everyone else as well as themselves. Other souls may have one or two – or more – acts for which they find it hard to forgive themselves. For many souls in past lives the theme was *mea culpa*: 'I am guilty, I am responsible'. Such feelings of culpability often arise out of religious lives or religious conditioning. The guilt is inappropriate but the soul has not let go.

Some people, however, in the past, may have committed atrocities and offences. They may, or may not, have been punished by society for these transgressions. But they go on punishing themselves. They too need to let go and practise forgiveness. Looking on oneself and others with compassion brings about forgiveness and heals the soul.

Forgiveness is a powerful karmic lesson but one that is not easily learned and so may take many lifetimes to work out – and may appear in the guise of retributive karma or redemptive. Superficial forgiveness is easy, but ineffective. Forgiveness emerges out of a deep struggle to accept things as they are, to see the imperfections and embrace them rather than denying and repressing or, the other extreme, revelling in *mea culpa*.

It is an opportunity to practice unconditional love and compassion. Forgiveness transforms deep, toxic feelings of rage and pain, and their karmic repercussions. The soul may need to forgive itself or others. It may need an opportunity to bring a festering secret into the light and look on its bearer with compassion. It may need to learn how to let go of apportioning blame, or of a deeply ingrained sense of abandonment. If this is the case, opportunities will arise in various guises. Giving up the feeling of being owed anything – a powerful manifestor of karmic reaction – and letting go of the sense that anyone else is responsible for personal pain changes karmic themes, as does cessation of judgement and letting go of the sense that you are responsible for everyone else rather than yourself. Taking personal responsibility for yourself and your actions is all that is possible. You cannot do it for someone else, nor can you judge someone else's actions, nor even your own from the perspective of earth. After all, if there is no longer the judgement that the other person – or yourself – is culpable, then blame is released.

One of the most pervasive themes is the victim-martyr-saviour syndrome. It frequently begins by someone trying to save the world – or an individual – but the scenario quickly turns into the victim or the martyr. Whilst there are subtle variations of this theme played out in families, marriages, jobs and vocations, the underlying question remains the same: 'What did I do to deserve this?' Once the soul realises that it is creating the situation by playing the martyr, then changes can be made, but until that realisation is reached, many lives will be played out in the victim role.

However, there may be more serious karmic causes behind the eternal victim. Humankind has, unfortunately, a history of persecuting or scapegoating anyone with different views. There are some souls who take on this role intentionally, trying to change how humanity thinks, or by practising redemptive karma. There are others who get caught up in a pattern of victimhood or martyrdom from which they find it impossible to escape. And there are those who persecute. Breaking free from this cycle involves learning lessons of tolerance, acceptance, open-mindedness and valuing each person as they are.

Understanding and practising unconditional, universal love is a major soul lesson, as is compassion. In the process a soul may have to experience the difference between loneliness and aloneness, balancing companionship with intimacy and emotional detachment. There may be lifetimes where dislike and hatred are faced and others where cruelty and kindness come to the fore. The soul who is on the pathway of universal love will have lifetimes to practise both letting go and compassionate witnessing, and will then work on merging back into the divine.

A soul cannot know justice without having experienced injustice and so will have experienced lifetimes when it learns about injustice in all its aspects before returning to work on bringing justice to all. One of the most important aspects of justice is that of karmic 'rightness'. Learning not to blame, not to punish and not to criticize but instead allowing the soul to learn in its own way is fundamental to this pathway. As is a close exploration of exactly what 'fairness' entails. Does it mean allowing every soul exactly the same opportunity – treating them as all the same – or does it mean treating each soul according to its own unique self? This theme will take the soul into some difficult byways as it explores the answers.

Recognising your own unique self is part of the theme of individuality, as is realising that you are a part of the whole and finding a way to return to unity consciousness. Issues around self-worth and self-confidence often arise as this theme works it way through lives, which may also include experience of being owned body and soul by someone else – the master/slave experience – and its opposite.

Control and empowerment are huge karmic contrasts. Whilst exploring these themes the soul looks at conforming to the rules or the norm and at challenging these. It explores issues around assertion and use of the will, and of aggression and restriction. It will have experiences of independence, dependence and interdependence. It will find itself in power-over situations and has to seek empowerment and release from all that has held it back in the past.

Fundamental lessons around deprivation often arise from 'poverty consciousness' which in turn comes out of believing that there will never be enough. It can have its roots in neglect or in lives intended to help the soul look at security issues. There will no doubt have been lives of over-indulgence and those of extreme deprivation at all levels. One of the most vital lessons for the soul is to find eternal, inner security rather than the spurious security of material possessions. The soul must also develop a notion of abundance which is not based purely on financial wealth but which embraces joy and spiritual generosity. The soul who is on this pathway may also explore nurturing and parenting issues.

Much karma can arise out of the 'people pleaser' archetype. Someone who tries to please all the people all the time – and usually ends up pleasing no one. This person believes that 'niceness' is preferable to being authentic, and has to develop congruence between inner and outer qualities. A congruence that can only come from fully knowing and accepting oneself and not being afraid to show this to the world. Along the way the need to recognise the difference between spurious 'humbleness' and true humility can arise as can an exploration into the real meaning of sincerity.

Suffering

The rationale behind suffering has occupied men's minds for thousands of years. It is a question that most religions seek to answer. Why, if God is good and loving as most religions teach, do people suffer so much, seemingly without cause?

Karma does, in many respects, explain suffering. If what is set up in one life has consequences in the next, then suffering may be retribution, reparation or a way of learning what it feels like to experience certain situations. Tibetan Buddhists say that suffering is a broom that sweeps away 'negative karma'. It can, however, also reflect a state of inner disease. If a soul has become out of harmony with soul purpose, has lost sight of its divine roots, and feels alienated and cut off, then suffering will arise. One definition of suffering is 'isolation from God', although some religions see suffering as a way of gaining God's favour. If you suffer enough, it must ultimately be rewarded, or so the argument goes. In this view, suffering has merit in its own right. Nevertheless, it is clear from regression work and from the insights gained by psychics, that some souls become stuck in suffering. It may be addictive. It is what a Christian friend of mine describes as being 'stuck at the foot of the cross rather than truly understanding the meaning of the resurrection'. The soul wallows in its suffering, getting immense satisfaction from the depth of that suffering. It can take considerable work to raise such a soul from the ingrained habit – the antidote is often sought in 'ministering to the suffering' where a kind of vicarious suffering goes on, so little karmic progress is made.

Astrologer Alan Candlish defines suffering as 'the pain we experience as a result of [our] own guilt, fear or ignorance' and asserts that 'used positively suffering helps to strengthen and purify the individual'. He separates the overall principle of suffering into 'suffering', 'non-suffering' and 'unsuffering'. Non-suffering involves coming to terms with individual suffering, and putting the insights gained to work to help heal oneself and others. It also requires giving up ego and self (with a small 's' as opposed to Self which is the divine principle). Unsuffering involves 'surrendering ourselves entirely to creation (God)' – see Mario Reading's story in the Conclusion. In this way the soul aligns to its higher nature. It offers the opportunity of 'becoming that which we truly are, acknowledging and utilizing the gifts that are our own and bringing the healing light of love into the world'. Nevertheless, as we have already seen, a soul may in apparent surrender actually be giving up personal responsibility so this is indeed complex.

Awakening Compassion
The positive side of the experience, and the karmic purpose behind suffering, is to awaken compassion in the soul (see also Wilfred Owen's story in Part 3). For this reason, from regression work, it is clear that many souls choose to suffer not as some kind of retribution but as a way of opening to compassion – compassion for oneself and for others. People who take on redemptive karma often suffer in order to 'remove something from the world' as several cancer patients have expressed it. A friend of mine used the Tibetan practice of *Tonglen*, taking the suffering of others into himself and using his death to transmute it on their behalf so that it could be cleared. However, it is equally clear that certain people become stuck in their suffering, relishing the pain and martyrdom because it has become so familiar to them.

Unconditional Love
Suffering can also help to awaken unconditional love. Unconditional love means loving and accepting someone as they are, with all their failings and foibles; seeing what they could be, and yet honouring what and who they are in the present moment. Unconditional love does not force change but nor does it oblige the person practising unconditional love to be misused in any way. It sets boundaries whilst allowing the

other person to be what and who they are.

It can be extremely difficult to stand by placidly whilst someone suffers and yet that may be exactly what is needed. If the soul took on the suffering for a specific purpose, what may be required is the unconditional love and support to go through that process *whatever it entails*. In other words, compassionate witnessing. Similarly, if the suffering is an act of retribution or reparation then it offers an opportunity to practice unconditional love – which accepts a person as they are warts and all and honours that person's innate right to be that way.

There are some people, however, who cope with what other people would see as suffering without considering it so. Keven, a blind man, travelled many miles to attend one of my workshops. He was asked, somewhat coyly, by a woman what he thought he had done to deserve his blindness. Keven replied that he thought he had made a deliberate choice to take on blindness as a learning experience. It had opened him to so many things and taught him independence. The woman, however, had clearly seen his blindness as a form of boomerang karma. But Keven certainly did not 'suffer' from it nor did he see it as a form of retribution. An old Indian wise saying asks:

Who is blind?

And answers:

The man that cannot see another world.
Who is dumb?
The man that cannot say a kind word at the right time.
Who is poor?
The man plagued with too strong desires.
Who is rich?
The man whose heart is contented.

Exploring Karma

As a man casts off his worn-out clothes and takes on other new ones, so does the embodied soul cast off its worn-out bodies and enters other new ones.

Bhagavad Gita[5]

In the present day, many people explore their karma through regression to past lives or through spontaneous 'seeings'. In re-experiencing their former lives, they can gain insight into the forces operating in the present. They can see the actions, thoughts or intentions that set a chain of events in motion. The regression experiences of people all over the world, which are supported by the 'life readings' carried out by the American seer Edgar Cayce and other psychics such as myself, show that karmic manifestation may either occur as a pattern of ingrained actions, attitudes and beliefs which repeat through a cycle of lives – or it can involve 'swinging between two opposite extremes' until a balance is reached.

In the 'swinging between two extremes' manifestation, the soul experiences one end of the spectrum in one life and then rebounds to the other extreme in the next life. So, for example, a man who is overly sensual, lustful and aggressive in chasing women in one life, may then swing to the opposite extreme of celibacy or timidity in relationships in another life. Such swings will continue until a balance is found.

'Unfinished business' draws people back into incarnation time and time again but karma can change and, regression experience shows, that there can be karmic 'accidents' – and what appears to be an accident may not actually be so. In the first instance, as we have seen a strong desire on the part of another could pull a soul into a birth that wasn't pre-planned. The soul being 'sucked into incarnation' before it is ready. From regression experiences, such 'accidents' are rare but nevertheless they do occur.

Life readings
During his life Edgar Cayce gave over 15,000 psychic readings and over 2,500 of those referred to past lives, many of which were devoted to the karmic cause of illness. A devout Christian, he nevertheless came to believe in reincarnation from the information he produced when in trance. He saw himself as Pythagoras and several early spiritual teachers. Cayce worked in a trance state which he had learned when a Persian physician. Wounded in a battle, he had been left to die. Without food or water for three days, he was in agony. By a supreme effort, he detached his consciousness from his body. An ability that stood him in good stead in his current life as he could put himself into trance at will. Cayce first went into trance to find the cause of a throat condition that literally left

him speechless. If Cayce did not do the work he was intended to do – his readings – then his throat closed up and he could not speak.

Cayce stated that he had accrued karma as a strong willed and sensual Egyptian priest who broke his vow of celibacy in order to create 'a perfect child'. He was reborn twice as John Bainbridge, once in the 17th and then again in the 18th century. Both men had a lustful disposition and were restless and unhappy. Cayce said that he had had to undergo those lives as he needed to know extremes before he could help others. At the end of the second John Bainbridge life, he gave his own life to save that of another. Cayce felt that his current lifetime was a 'test for his soul'. His work gave him an opportunity to overcome the pride, materialism and sensuality of his past lives and to serve humankind selflessly.

Cayce gave many examples in his life readings of seeming accidents that actually brought karma and soul intention to the surface. In one, a boy was paralysed in an automobile accident at the age of 16. When Edgar Cayce later read his past lives, the boy had been a military officer of great courage and determination during the American Revolution. The qualities he had developed then were of great assistance to him in overcoming the consequences of his 'accident'. However, Cayce also identified an earlier life as the root cause of the 'accident'. Here the man had been a self-indulgent Roman soldier who 'glorified' in the suffering inflicted on the early Christians – in which he actively took part as he was one of those who fought the Christians in the arena. According to Cayce, the man had seen much suffering but made light of it and the deep religious conviction that lay behind it. Now it was time for him to suffer not as retribution but so that he could understand how it felt and also how the 'purposefulness' of those he had mocked had given them the strength to endure.

My own past life readings seek to identify not only the karma and soul purpose imbued in astrological patterns but also to read the Akashic Record of the soul's lives and interactions to obtain an overview of the reasons behind dis-ease, apparent soulmate contacts, vocations and otherwise inexplicable experiences.

Regression
It's not my intention here to go deeply into the various methods and means of regression although most of the examples I give throughout

this book arise out of guided regression to other lives. I just wanted to say here that although I find regression – and far memory – tremendously helpful in uncovering karmic causes, the roots of soul contracts and the like, I am also aware that some people use these to feed the ego rather than illuminate the soul's journey. It really doesn't matter who you were, as I've already said, it's the *what and the why* that counts. So, if you seek out regression in order to understand, do make sure that the practitioner you choose knows about healing and reframing and is capable of distinguishing between your soul's story and a fantasy in fancy dress however cunningly disguised that may be.

Karma in Action

There are many types of karma, and these operate at the personal, group, racial, collective and cosmic level, each of which tends to supersede the other. Not all types of karma will be active at any one time. The soul usually works on two or three karmic themes during a lifetime but may concentrate on only one if it involves a major life lesson such as a chronic illness or self sacrifice. Three things have a powerful effect on karma:

Desire (often called craving or wilfulness). The human mind has a tendency towards intense attachment arising out of desire or grabbing at something that is intensely craved. According to Buddhist philosophy, attachment is what underlies rebirth. Desire is a compulsion, involuntarily followed. What is wanted, needed or craved for brings about a situation that will provide it – not always a beneficial experience. The soul may be learning to let go of that desire and the pattern it continually creates. The other major attachments are to emotions and ideas – which are still a form of desire. The strength of desire can transcend death and pull a soul back into incarnation to deal with unfinished business or to recreate once again a situation where the desired object can, so it seems, be achieved. Desire keeps the karmic wheel turning.

Purpose is apparent soul intention – something decided in the interlife - but it may be outdated, a hangover from another lifetime that is blindly followed in the present, in other words a soul overlay. Purpose is what the soul incarnates to do and it can operate at different levels. Purpose has to do with the soul's evolution, the incorporation of qualities and

experiences it has identified as being required for further soul growth
and the integration of what is learned from those scenarios. It is often
vocational or spiritual. Purpose can overcome destructive desires,
as when an addict goes into recovery, and it can also compensate for
difficult karma and change a soul's path.

Grace strengthens purpose and helps it to manifest. Grace is an offer
from the highest part of your self to release karma. Opinions differ as
to whether that 'highest part' is of yourself or something other. Edgar
Cayce, for instance, believed it came from God and not from yourself,
whilst I believe that it comes from your own higher self and agree with
Hindus that the highest part of the soul *is* divine.

Grace also operates when enough has been done or when forgiveness
is practised. There are some lessons or situations that simply cannot be
continued with, perhaps because another person is concerned who is
unwilling to learn or to move forward. In such a situation, grace says
that, when the soul has done all it can, it can let it go and no further
karma will accrue. Grace also comes into play when a soul learns to
forgive and let go the past – or seeks forgiveness for itself.

Karmic levels:
- **Personal Karma**

Karma at a personal level is what is carried from life to life by an
individual soul. It has been created in the past and the soul incarnates
to deal with it in the present or to fulfil its purpose. There are many
examples throughout this book of the manifestation of personal karma.

- **Group or Racial Karma**

This level of karma belongs to a group of people. The group can vary
in size from a family, or group of friends, to a tribe, a race or a country.
Most people who become involved in group karma will have incarnated
into that group before but this is not always so. Group karma overcomes
individual. So, a soul who has no aggressive karma may nevertheless
become caught up in a war or other mass movement simply because it
has incarnated into that group at that time.

Annie Besant, one of the founders of Theosophy, expressed the
opinion that a colonising nation such as England was guilty of much
cruelty in the way it took over lands belonging to others. In her view,

thousands of people would have perished prematurely during the conquest and subsequent colonisation of such lands and all these souls would have a karmic claim against England. England would carry a racial karma and would owe a karmic debt to the colonised countries; the inhabitants of England would have a group karmic responsibility and some would have personal karma within the overall group. This claim would operate on a racial or collective level, and a personal claim against those who perpetrated the atrocities would also be present. In her view – she was writing in the 19th century – this resulted in thousands of people being drawn to the English slums 'providing a population of congenital criminals, of non-moral and feeble-minded people'. Her answer to the collective or racial responsibility imposed on England by its colonial acts was that the country should educate and train the people who had reincarnated into the slums 'thus quickening their evolution and lifting them out of their natural savagery'. Other people might see those souls as being drawn into wars and other conflicts with 'victim' fighting 'aggressor'. The equivalent today would be the immigrants and refugees who both contribute to and drain the resources of 'modern' society.

Racial karma may also lie in specific qualities attaching to a race. Dr Hiroshi Motoyama, a scientist and Shinto priest, says that Japan, for instance, has a karma of 'obstinate loyalty and patriotism' but he sees racial karma as present in many countries. Dr Motoyama recounts how when he went to a small town in California he was aware of considerable confusion and unrest amongst the inhabitants. The town was situated in the immensely old Redwood country and the major source of work was felling these ancient trees. The original inhabitants, Native American Indians, had revered these trees, but they had been brutally murdered by the first white settlers and carried what Dr Motoyama describes as 'ferocious animosity' towards white people, particularly the Russians who had first settled there. Dr Motoyama took the view that these original inhabitants were now being reincarnated, causing enormous confusion. They were white on the outside, and Indian on the inside. It was his conclusion that they were collectively carrying the guilt of having murdered their former selves.

If Dr Motoyama is correct in his reading of the situation, then there is another element to this. They are now engaged in destroying the environment that they had so respected in the past. This must create an enormous conflict in their spiritual selves which will no doubt have karmic repercussions.

• Collective Karma

The karma of the human race is collective. It arises from all that has gone before. Although positive collective karma is also generated, negative collective karma is what creates problems for future generations. This arises out of wars, territorial disputes, genocide, religious intolerance and enforced conversion, exile and persecution. No one is responsible for collective karma in the sense of having personally created it, although souls may have been part of its source in conflict, purges, ideologies and other mass movements. Certain people incarnate with the intention of taking on part of this collective karma and clearing it for the wider whole – after all, we cannot change to the Age of Aquarius dragging all the guilt and suffering of the Age of Pisces behind us. The vibration must be cleared before a new way of being can be found.

In the present day, with television and the internet reaching into the most remote of places, collective karma is touching everyone. It can no longer remain a remote event for which no one takes responsibility. So, when news broadcasts show a war or famine together with its effect on children and adults, 'ordinary people' band together to send aid – and to work for peace or famine relief. This could be seen as part of an awakening consciousness of shared humanity, what some spiritual movements would call recognizing the divine spark within each person and the astrological and New Age communities see as moving into the Age of Aquarius. It is a step in the evolution of humankind, the flowering of cosmic karma and unity consciousness.

• Cosmic Karma

There is a need for the whole cosmos to grow and to evolve and regain unity consciousness. It is the spiritual purpose which can override all other karmas. Those Christians who believe in karma say that Jesus' incarnation was an example of cosmic karma in action, for example. They believe that he incarnated to take away the sins of the world, an act of redemptive karma on behalf of the whole. Many gurus believe that they are incarnations of cosmic karma, here to help the world grow in spiritual understanding but the cosmos may make use of individuals in the working out of its purpose.

Types of karma

Within the three major levels of karma – personal, collective or cosmic – there are many types of karma that can operate at each or any of those levels. With all karma, there are credits and deficits. Positive karma is credit paid into the karmic piggy bank and will stand the soul in good stead, while negative karmas are a constant depletion that lead to overdrafts that need considerable work to replenish.

- **Abundance karma**

There are many people in incarnation who have learnt the secret of abundance – which could be called positive attitudinal karma. They have developed the power of positive thought and creative visualisation. They trust that the universe will meet their needs and hold a strong intention that this will be so. In some cases this has been taught as a specific lesson – the temples of Egypt had such a concept as did Jesus when he said: 'Consider the lilies of the field, how they grow; they toil not, they neither spin: And yet I say unto you, that even Solomon in all his glory was not arrayed like one of these' (Matthew 6 v.28).

In other cases, the soul has learnt through the course of many lives to create the right conditions for abundance to thrive. However it has been learned, abundance is one of the most positive of all karmic gifts.

Do you have abundance karma? If so take a moment to thank your higher self and all the selves that you were in previous lives for this great gift. If not, see my book *Crystal Prosperity* which may assist you to develop it.

- **Attitudinal karma**

A past intransigent attitude, ingrained behaviour, intractable or habitual emotional stance results in spiritual and physical 'dis-ease' but a positive attitude, such as a loving nature, optimism or innate trust, brought forward from another life will create positive effects in the present life. So, for example, if a person is consistently generous to those around him, an ability which arises out of an inner sense of abundance, then over his lifetimes he will attract to himself generosity. People will treat him more magnanimously because he has been generous. On the other hand, if someone has always been suspicious of other people, mistrusting them and acting in a miserly fashion, then what he will have created is distrust. He will attract this distrust to himself and may find himself accused by other people of being dishonest or find himself living in unalleviated poverty. Edgar Cayce emphasised many times that apparent misfortune is actually a tool for showing up our own shortcomings, offering an opportunity to redress what he called 'defects of character'. In this he is coming close to the ideas explored in Part 3 of this book that the soul may choose a lifetime with conditions in which to 'grow the soul' rather than actively meeting karma.

Health, wealth and wisdom arise out of positive attitudinal karma. If someone has been openhearted, generous and giving in the past they will have engendered a healthy heart and will attract to themselves abundance and joy. Even when life is difficult, someone with a positive attitude will flourish. They know how to turn things to their advantage, how to be content with what they have, and how to make the most of each day or whatever is appropriate to the circumstances they find themselves in. Julie Chimes, whose story is in Part 3, says that one of her soul learnings is to live with very little and yet be content.

Negative attitudinal karma builds over several lives. It arises out of an intransigent attitude, ingrained behaviour or an intractable or habitual emotional stance. It often manifests at the physical level: a physical condition being a manifestation of soul dis-ease. So, for example, Edgar Cayce stated that there was a strong link between pride in a previous life and crippling disfigurement in the present life. I would suggest that it also links to Parkinson's disease. Attitudes such as believing there would 'never be enough', or that 'there always has to be more', could be a precursor to addiction. Arterial or heart problems can develop from 'hard-heartedness' or a former broken heart, or from being too open hearted or naive. Edgar Cayce asserted that no one could hate his neighbour and not develop a liver or stomach disorder, and that jealousy would produce digestive disorders or heart conditions. Mental states such as doubt can also affect the next life. Cayce said that doubt in one life almost inevitably led to a fear in the next; and from there to dislike, hatred and anger... 'within the inner, psychic world of man there are a throng of weaknesses and imperfections – selfishness, stupidity, envy, malevolence, and greed – that are the source of pain both to himself and to those with whom he lives'.

Rudolf Steiner believed that ingrained attitudes developed across lifetimes and arise out of an imbalance in the soul. So, for instance, someone who had a tendency towards telling lies would do so because he wasn't in touch with his inner guidance. A life previous to that would have been 'superficial' and shallow. The person would not know what it was to love or to be devoted to anything, resulting in 'unsteadiness' in character. In the life lived after the one in which lies were told, the person would have, in Steiner's opinion, 'incorrectly formed organs' because something would be out of balance in the soul and that would result in a 'weak organization' in the body. This would not be a punishment for lying, it would arise from the soul having, in the interlife stage, had a revulsion against itself for not telling the truth. According to Steiner, deeds in one life will be transformed at death into a powerful emotion. This emotion imprints on the soul so that the overall quality of the way of being in the previous life is reflected in the present disposition and physical structure.

Negative attitudinal karma usually arises out of a characteristic approach to life: a stance or fixed opinion which is slavishly followed. The attitude is most often held regarding relationships, another race or religion. It is usually based on indoctrination, ignorance, hatred or fear. The karma may be a repeating pattern with an ingrained attitude carried from life to life.

Some attitudinal karma, however, arises out of how someone was treated in a past life. A person who was abandoned by a partner, for instance, may have problems with commitment in the present life, becoming a 'commitment phobic' who fears intimacy. The resultant attitude is one of holding back, never giving of oneself in relationship. A similar attitude can arise out of a love affair which ended badly, or unrequited love. If, in a previous incarnation, a woman found out that her husband had been unfaithful, in her present incarnation she could carry an attitude of unreasonable and unfounded jealousy which would make itself known whenever her present-life husband spoke to another woman. Many such attitudes towards 'love' arise out of previous experience.

Attitudinal karma often arises out of religious beliefs. How people were involved in religion can have a profound effect in their attitude to it in the present life. Whilst some people carry-over deep religious conviction, and sometimes religious intolerance or fanaticism, other people may go to the opposite of what they knew 'back then'. Angela,

for instance, who had been in a convent in several incarnations, came
into her present incarnation determined to make up for all the 'good
times' she had missed. Her attitude was 'more, more, more' and she took
to drink and sex in a big way. A Cayce illustration of how a present
life attitude to religion arose out of the past was that of a newspaper
columnist who was extremely sceptical where religion was concerned.
According to Cayce, he had been a Crusader in a former life who became
thoroughly disillusioned when he witnessed the gap between what was
professed as religion and the barbarities practiced by its adherents on the
Crusade. His deep-seated distrust of religion passed into his current life.

Some attitudes are persistent and can have violent consequences.
These relate especially to a hatred for anyone who is 'different'. Edgar
Cayce read for an Alabama farmer who founded a Society for the
Supremacy of the White Race. The farmer hated black people with
a particular intensity described as 'fierce and unrelenting venom'.
According to Cayce, in a past life he had been a soldier who was taken
prisoner by Hannibal and sent to the galley of a slave ship. The overseers,
who were coloured, treated him cruelly. One of them beat him to death.
His fierce hatred passed into his present life, spanning three other
lifetimes and twenty-two centuries. His attitude caused considerable
suffering to others. It remains to be seen what the karmic outcome of
his ingrained attitudes will have on his future lives. It seems likely that
he could ultimately create for himself an unhealthy body or incarnate
into one of the races he has so much despised or as a mixed race child to
integrate the dark and light parts of his own being.

Attitudinal karma can subtly mould a personality towards suffering.
The attitudes a soul holds can, of course, change over the course of
several lives and there is usually a pattern of sociability versus isolation
running through lives as the soul first projects itself out to the world and
then turns inward to examine itself. So, a soul could have a 'laissez faire'
attitude to life: easy come, easy go. Incarnations would be passive but
sociable. This soul would probably take on few serious responsibilities
but would help out a friend in need. Then an incident could occur that
would change this pattern. Say in one incarnation the person had a
serious injury. If the response was still placid, little would change. Some
introspection might be forced upon the soul in long hours of inactivity,
but the soul might fill these with visits from friends. But if the soul

saw itself as victim and asked: 'Why would this happen to me, I don't deserve it' it could lead to becoming embittered and isolated. The next life would then carry a different attitude, one of self-preoccupation or self-centredness. Such a person is unlikely to be sociable and so isolation would result and, most probably, self-pity or arrogance.

An 'ivory tower' attitude can arise where all the soul thinks about is itself and what it needs. On the other hand, it may spend all its time feeling sorry for itself. In the karma created through 'sins of omission' as far as its fellow human beings are concerned, the soul could then no doubt attract a difficult life in an effort to balance out the karma. At some point, the soul would realize that it had to look within for the cause of this discomfort. Having done this, it would then manifest lives where it could expand once more into a social being with positive attitudes. Then the test comes. Can those attitudes be maintained in the face of suffering and adversity? If there is a trace of the 'poor me' attitude left, the answer is probably no. If the lesson has been learned, then the soul holds to its positive attitudes and either overcomes or accepts with good grace the situation in which it finds itself.

However, there are times when attitudinal karma can have unexpected benefits for the soul in the current life. In a private regression session preceding a workshop, Marion went back to being pursued by soldiers. She was with a young friend who she described as 'not as well to do as me, his clothes are rougher, dirty but we do the work together'. Suddenly her breathing changed and her manner became anxious, her voice higher:

Now I'm running, we're running [panting]. Through the trees, they catch at my clothes. It's the soldiers. Got to get away.

Now they've got us. They've tied us to a tree. Look at them, the bastards, they just do what they are told. They don't care about anything. They're taunting me now, saying I'm no better than I should be. But I won't let them know how I feel. I won't show them any emotion. You have to be strong when faced with people like this, they're so ignorant and they abuse their position.... Aaah, bastards. No one will ever do that to me again.

I asked her what had happened.

One of them stepped up and killed me. No warning.

Did she know why she'd been killed?

I was accused of spreading sedition. I was trying to make things better for the people. Trying to break some of the power the aristocracy had. The peasants were starving, living in those hovels I wanted them to have some rights... I was an aristocrat myself and my own class misunderstood. They thought I wanted a revolution. So they set the soliders on me and they killed me. I think they were exceeding their authority but it was too late.

While Marion was in the interlife we removed the knife from her chest and healed the wound. Having explored that life a little more, we established that she did not want to do more work at that point – she would have all weekend on the workshop if necessary – so I brought her out of the regression. But I did a 'de-brief' before closing the session. What had struck me forcibly was how cold Marion's voice was when she said 'I won't let them know how I feel, I won't show any emotion'. This turned out to be a powerful pattern in her current life, as was running away whenever possible, but if not she'd front people up as though with complete confidence. When faced with a mob of football hooligans, Marion and a male colleague 'rounded them up' but she was the one who confronted them and told them to break it up. 'They went away meek as lambs', Marion said. 'My male colleague asked me afterwards if I'd been scared. I said no, but really I was shitting myself but I couldn't let him know that'. She had quite clearly carried that dying thought over to her present life. Marion had joined the police 'to make a difference' but told me that her greatest moment of satisfaction was when she was a custody sergeant turning the key in the lock of the cell. 'They were safely put away'.

Perhaps not surprisingly, Marion also carried a deep antipathy to people who pushed other people around simply because they were in authority, a situation she frequently met in the police force but was powerless to change. Not showing her feelings, although useful in such situations, nevertheless had strong physical repercussions. Marion was invalided out of the police with stress-related chronic anxiety – an anxiety that manifested as a pain in her chest exactly where she had been killed in her former life. False accusation too turned out to be a present life pattern. During the workshop Marion was able to release some of the anxiety but needed considerably more regression and counselling to clear this and other past life memories. Learning to show her feelings was a lifelong issue.

If you think you might have attitudinal karma, ask yourself if any of the above rang bells with you. Do you have a negative or ingrained attitude that you need to let go or could you make more positive use of what you learned? What would be a positive attitude that could replace it?

- **Boomerang karma**

Boomerang karma occurs when something a person previously did to someone else happens to them. As Gina Cerminara puts it 'a harmful action directed towards another person seems to rebound on the perpetrator of the action'. Similar to retributive karma, according to most sources on karma boomerang karma underlies a great deal of suffering as it bounces backward and forwards, often between two souls in various incarnations. In my own practice, I have seen little evidence of this unless a soul had refused to listen to 'wake up calls' over several incarnations. Instant boomerang karma happens when, for example, a person having an angry thought about another person and wishing them harm stubs a toe or knock into a door, seemingly accidentally.

In the longer term, that thought or action may have occurred in another life but the manifestation is in the present. An act in one life is mirrored in a condition in the present. Edgar Cayce gave many instances of this in his work. He read for an American professor, born blind, whom Cayce saw, in a Persian incarnation, as a member of a tribe who blinded its enemies with red-hot irons (this could equally well be called retributive karma). The professor had been the officer who carried out the blinding. It was one of the responsibilities of his position. Had he not carried out the task, he would have been punished. Gina Cerminara, who reported this case, raises the question, 'how can an individual be held morally responsible for a duty imposed on him by the customs of the society in which he lives?' This is a difficult area *if karma is only looked on as punishment*. If, however, it is regarded as impersonal, divine justice balancing out former actions or the result of soul choice, then the perspective changes. The man is born blind. He experiences what it feels like to be blind, to have no sight. But he does not go through exactly what his victims experienced – the agony of the process of being blinded. Had he been a man who enjoyed his work and derived sadistic pleasure from the blinding, he possibly could have been born with sight, had a painful accident and then experienced the agony his victims went through – which would then be retributive karma. But he didn't. He experienced exactly the same affliction that he created in others from the beginning of his current life.

In this case, there was no suggestion that the man's parents had been among his former victims. It is often assumed that boomerang karma is a kind of 'tit for tat' karma in which one person has something done to him, and then turns around and does it to the person who did it to him. Having examined all the Cayce readings, however, Gina Cerminara found no case in which the victim in one life became the perpetrator in another:

> *In no case in the Cayce files was the present-life affliction found to have been instigated by the former victim of the person in question.*

My own findings have been similar. In regression, I have found instances where deliberate and direct reversal of roles occurred, but it was usually somewhat 'accidental' or synchronous rather than deliberately inflicted and was frequently accompanied by a vow on the part of the person who was 'victim' the first time to 'get even' or to 'get my own back'. In other situations, great resentment arose *and was held on to past death* (in other words, attitudinal karma took hold). It seems as though, if the situation is resolved within one life, then the personal interplay does not carry over. Only when the animosity is very strong or when the people concerned were in close relationship do they come back together to replay the scenario with different roles. In such situations, forgiveness was called for – and indeed such an interaction could form part of a karmic theme running through several lives.

You can often tell if you have boomerang karma by events in the present life constantly repeating in a 'tit for tat' way. Or by a nagging sense of it all being far too familiar. If you think you are caught up in boomerang karma, forgive and let go. Move off that particular karmic wheel.

• **Communication karma**
The power of words is indeed strong. Their impression can be indelible and lasting. A lie can blight a life. Disparaging laughter, cruel words

and sarcasm impact as strongly, if not more so, than a physical blow. Long after a physical hurt has been forgotten, words echo in the mind. Words of all kinds have a karmic impact: inadvertent, deliberate, tactful, tactless, insulting, repressive, encouraging, complimenting.

It is both the *how*, the *why* and the *what* of that which was communicated that can lead to communication karma – positive or negative. Words have been used to stir revolutions, to revile and condemn people, and to gain power over others. They have coerced, bedazzled and persuaded. Words can encourage and cajole, support and empower. Some people might sincerely believe that what they teach is truth, when really it is a perversion of the truth. People have passed on gossip and scandal, made or ruined other people's reputations. They have told truths and untruths, been open and honest or secretive and devious. Some communication is extremely personal, other transmissions are universal. All have karmic consequences.

In the New Testament, Jesus says: 'Every idle word that men shall speak, they shall give account therefor in the day of judgement. For by thy words thou shalt be justified, and by thy words thou shalt be condemned'. In other words when the karmic reckoning falls due it is words, just as much as actions, that will be taken into account. When Jesus is condemned by the Pharisees for plucking and eating ears of wheat on the Sabbath, Jesus replies: 'It is not that which goeth into the mouth that defileth a man, but that which cometh out of the mouth'. Jesus was repeating words from an ancient Babylonian code. So, the karmic effect of words has been known for millennia.

The effect of communication karma is usually felt in a new incarnation. It can be the cause of physical ailments such as deafness or speech defects; mental or neural imbalances or blockages leading to dyslexia or perception problems; or situations such as misunderstanding, slander and so on where boomerang or retributive karma rebounds on the soul. What was said – or thought – by the soul comes back to that soul. If the soul has used positive thought and has spoken constructively, then 'merit karma' may well have accrued. However, communication karma can indicate longstanding difficulty in expressing thoughts, feelings and beliefs which is reflected in the present. Such difficulties may also be part of a repeating inability of the soul to express itself. Nathan, who found it difficult to string together even the most simple of sentences, traced back a long line of incarnations with communication impediments of one kind or another. Eventually, he came to the core. Nathan had revealed a secret and inadvertently brought about another's death. He had vowed never to speak again. We needed to go back and reframe that decision in order to free up his ability to speak.

We have already looked in the introduction at my own communication karma and I have seen the same theme running through so many authors' lives that I begin to think there should be a separate section here for publishing karma, but authors are not the only souls to have difficult with communication based on past actions so let's look at some sub-sections of this particular karma.

- **Hypocrisy**

Having said one thing, or done things a certain way and yet believed something different, lying most sincerely, being economical with the truth or twisting it for maximum advantage, or pretending to be something you are not, gives rise to the karma of hypocrisy. Hypocrisy arises from a lack of spiritual conviction and inner truth, or a betrayal of truth. A life then arises when that inner foundation has to be regained.

There are people who will do anything for a quiet life. They go along with what is suggested, they agree when something is said that offends their deepest sensibilities, they avoid conflict at all costs. Such people are, on the deepest level, hypocrites and reap the karma of hypocrisy. The karma may return in situations where they are put on the spot, where they have to speak their truth. They may speak their truth, and yet not be believed. They may speak their truth and be reviled for it. Or they may find themselves faced with someone who is a hypocrite and cannot be relied upon. Situations such as these ultimately create a congruence between the outer show and the inner feelings as the soul can no longer bear the tensions engendered when the two conflict. I'm sure we can all come up with modern day versions of hypocrisy especially now that words reach every corner of our world. If we recognise it, it is a step towards eliminating it in ourselves and in our world. But always remember, it is not only the spoken word that creates this karma, it is also the thoughts and deeds of each one of us that contributes towards collective hypocrisy. As does the hidden agendas that lie behind so many actions. Your soulplan for the present life may include refusing to believe hypocritical words instead of taking for granted that the media and those in the public spotlight always tell the truth. But remember too, cynicism has its own karma. Finding the middle way, speaking, thinking and acting in alignment with your soul is the key to unlocking this karma.

- **Mockery**

Mocking other people's afflictions, thoughts, beliefs or actions gives rise to the karma of mockery. It is based on not valuing the pathway that another person travels. One such example is when someone else is debased in some way by the words used. The person judges the circumstances of someone else and mocks them through words. The person who mocked in a past life often finds him or herself living out in the present life the circumstances that were so despised back in that another life.

Edgar Cayce told a crippled polio victim that his illness was the karma that accrued from having been in the audience in Rome when the Christians were thrown to the lions. The crowed had mocked and jeered and he had been carried along with it. It took almost two thousand years for the karma to return.

Acceptance, tolerance and compassionately witnessing someone's plight rather than mocking, especially where difference is concerned, clears this karma.

- **Condemnation and Criticism**

Those who condemned or criticized others in the past may have to meet within themselves the very things they found fault with in the past. As Edgar Cayce put it 'as you have criticized, know that you yourself must be criticized'. So, for example, someone who was intolerant of others and who condemned 'weakness' could find themselves undergoing an incarnation where they became an alcoholic so that they would know what it was to have to confront an apparent weakness – and to be condemned for it by others. A person who criticized another for ignorance could find that the next incarnation involved being an uneducated person who appeared, to those who had received a superior education, to be ignorant but who, in fact, had innate wisdom.

Edgar Cayce gave a reading for a young man who suffered from a dreadful sense of inadequacy which held him back in his career as a lieutenant in the army. The inadequacy was brought about by intense self-criticism. Nothing he did was good enough. Cayce saw him as a literary critic in a previous life. His reviews were caustic and pitiless, with the result that he engendered considerable self doubt in the writers. Now, in the present life, the pendulum had swung and he himself had to experience self-doubt.

Not everyone who suffers from self-doubt will have made a career out of criticism in their former lives of course. But many will have criticized others, inadvertently or as mere social chit-chat. Criticism, like mockery, arises out of judging others. It seems to be a condition endemic to the human soul. People talk about other people, they criticize their work, their appearance, their friends. They may criticize themselves just as much as others, setting impossible standards to meet. Everyone comments on life and some of it may seem innocuous. However, as Edgar Cayce pointed out on many occasions, there is a heavy karmic price to pay. What is criticized in others – even when it has not been voiced to that person – will be experienced in the future. Motive and intention may mitigate this to some extent. Not everyone will be like the literary critic mentioned above. His karmic crime was to be merciless and so bring about deep self-doubt in others. There was no constructive criticism in his prose he simply tore the work to shreds. But even those who engage in constructive criticism tread a very fine line between helping others and eroding creativity and self-worth.

- **Coercion and Persuasion**

Words have been used for thousands to years to influence how people think. The karma will be different if considerable psychological force is applied or subtle persuasion. Motive and intent can also be a factor in the karma that arises. If someone sincerely believes that what they are saying will help someone else, no matter how misguided that may be, then there is a different kind of karmic effect from someone who cynically persuades someone else round to their point of view for their own advantage – and of course a person who is apparently doing the first may have a hidden agenda that points to the second. The former may have to live out a life where the soul gently finds out how misguided it has been, but the latter is more likely to meet the karmic repercussions head on.

- **Ideology**

Attachment to an idea or religious faith, no matter how worthy, can create ideological karma. Someone may have a sincere belief but because of their strong attachment to that belief, often accompanied by a resultant closed-mindedness, karma is created. As Dr Motoyama has pointed out:

Karma results from mental attachment to an emotion, no matter how ideal. Attachment to a sustained love of knowledge, truth, or wisdom, for instance, produces long-lasting karma.[6]

He goes on to point out that the adherents to a religion are often more attached 'to their own self-righteousness than to the ongoing process of self-realisation'.

Dr Motoyama feels that scholars and scientists can also fall into the same trap and my experiences would support this. They may be so attached to their own particular theory or way of looking at the world that, even in the face of contradictory evidence, they cling to it. This is because considerable emotion is invested in what appears to be an intellectual matter. The emotions concerned have to do with pride, vanity, egotism and ambition. They are so powerful that they block out reason, and create karmic attachment. The more passion invested in a belief, the stronger the karma it creates, which is why the Tibetans consider closed-mindedness to be one of the major factors in disease.

Imposing beliefs on other people also creates ideological karma. The beliefs may be religious, philosophical or purely secular. The means used to impose them may be tyrannical and dictatorial – enforced coercion, or they may be subtle and persuasive – gentle inducement. But the resulting karma is the same. Former teachers and law-makers or enforcers, may have ideological karma to deal with as do those who were engaged with religious dogma.

Mac, regressed to being a Jesuit priest who forcibly converted a tribe in Africa – something experienced in another woman's regression who had been one of the small children he taught. In his present life, Mac went back to the country on voluntary service to teach his bricklaying skills as a way of making reparation. Then, when he developed lung and throat cancer, he believed that it was his way of working off that old communication karma.

However, in his present life, Mac had also counselled many people and helped them towards spiritual insights, so he believed that, once the present life was over, his karma would be balanced out. Indeed, he was convinced that the fact that he had lived in a squat for many years, enabled him to die in a pleasant nursing home with caring staff and friends around to help his death, and this was his 'good karma'.

But the power that a belief from a former life can hold over a mind was graphically illustrated by Mac as he was dying. I sat with Mac as he lay in a coma. Although he had chosen not to have treatment, saying that it was his time to pass on, he seemed to be fighting hard to stay alive. Earlier that day, he had pulled out his drip and run amok. He had clearly been very frightened indeed and his nurses called myself and another of his friends in to help him. By the time we got there, he had been heavily sedated. He could not speak but responded, when I asked him to breathe out his fear, by letting out a long, shuddering breath so I knew he could hear me. I tried to talk him through releasing from his body, reading the *phowa* prayer from *The Tibetan Book of the Dead* as he had requested. He would stop breathing for long periods, and then shiver and begin again.

Realising that he was in spiritual trouble, I entered into his world with him. He was surrounded by a ring of hellfire. The vivid beliefs about hell he had held as that Jesuit priest in the former life had returned to taunt him. Taking his hand, I said: 'Well Mac, you always wanted to try fire-walking, how about we give it a go?' We walked together towards the flames, which parted forming a corridor of fire that burnt off his karma.

It is not only at death that such experiences occur. Irrational beliefs, fears and the like are almost always based on previous life experiences. The words that people use in regression often prove to be a key to a strong belief or thought that has been carried over, unrecognised, from another life. That credo or thought will have played a powerful part in creating the present reality and, as such, forms part of communication karma.

If you've been asking yourself why your communication gets fouled up in various ways or why people don't understand what you mean, you might like to go over the above facets of communication karma again and see if you are holding any of the karmas of mis-communication.

- **In a karmic groove**

Many people experience karma as an endlessly repeating cycle, rather like the karmic treadmill although that tends to go round and round repeating exactly the same pattern whereas 'the groove' goes endlessly forward sometimes changing interaction but not the personnel or the fundamental role. This is because of deeply ingrained reactive patterns that have arisen over many lifetimes. The soul literally becomes 'stuck in a groove', going over and over the same old ground, unable to move on. So, a soul may become stuck in a feeling of unworthiness – and will attract many situations that, apparently, confirm that unworthiness. The soul will look to others for support, seeking worth through their eyes rather than finding it within itself. The pattern will be reiterated life after life until the soul can break out of the bondage of unworthiness and learn to recognise its own innate worth.

The 'groove-type' pattern frequently happens in relationships where two souls, or whole families, incarnate together again and again, despite the fact that they have long ago learned everything they had to learn from each other, and had repaid any karmic debts they had. They return together from habit. At some point, they have to learn to let go of each other and move on. (See also the karmic treadmill).

If you suspect you might be stuck in a karmic groove, take a look at the people around you and the way you interact. Have you been there before? Does it feel like the same old pattern? Do the same situations keep coming up time after time, even if you change partners or jobs or location? Then you may well be in a groove.

- **Karma of dis-ease**

Most commentators and teachers on karma see illness either as being caused by 'evil deeds' in a former life or by dis-ease of the soul. The disease may be an imbalance, a reaction or a deficit that has to be rectified. It can be symbolic of a former attitude, intent or action. It may even arise out of ill-wishing or an intentional curse.

The English psychiatrist who worked with past life causes of disease, Arthur Guirdham, found that specific parts of the body were often subjected to repeating patterns of injury and it is quite usual during regression work to find that a 'bad back' in the current life, for example, is the reflection of a previous back injury of one kind or another.

Martha, for instance, discovered that she had been paralyzed during a life as sailor. A spar had fallen onto the sailor's back, exactly where her present life pain was. But another dimension of karmic injury or illness was shown in the remainder of that past life story. Confined to a chair, s/he became severely frustrated and angry, lashing out verbally at the dutiful daughter who cared for what she described during the regression as 'a broken hulk'. It was this bitterness which created a karmic imprint – and a karmic enmeshment between the two of them. In the present life, the daughter had been drawn back to Martha. But she wasn't so dutiful, rebelling against her mother when she tried to control her. Every time the daughter rebelled, the mother would take to her bed with backache, compelling the daughter to look after her. It was a cycle that was difficult to break. Even after the daughter married and left home, the mother would demand her presence. She found it impossible to let go. In past life therapy some progress was made when Martha was taken into the interlife state to look at what she was creating by perpetuating the karmic cycle. But, in the end, Martha preferred to keep her illusion of control over her daughter rather than change her attitude. This carrying forward of an ingrained attitude is a major factor in chronic karmic dis-ease.

To see all illness and disability in this way, however, is to overlook a fundamental part of karma. Ill-health, debility and a weak constitution can also be taken on as a learning experience. The manifestations of karma are subtle and varied. So, illness may be a dis-ease of the soul or the imprint of previous trauma (see also organic karma) but it may also be a soul choice.

Many karmic commentators have seen disease as a way that the soul evolves or balances out previous karma, linking specific illnesses to karma. One of the illustrations that Steiner gives is that of someone whose sense of self is very weak. Consequently the person is dependent and passive. Due to this lack of sense of self, the person performed certain actions in a former life. After death, he would then look at the actions which stemmed from his weak 'I'. He would then feel that he must develop forces which would strengthen his sense of self or 'I-ness'. He would also feel that he had to develop a body that would show him the consequences of his 'weak personality'. In the next incarnation, according to Steiner, he would 'not fully enter into consciousness' – which is perhaps better expressed as lacking perceptive awareness of the forces governing his actions and experiences. By acting according to sub-conscious forces, he would meet opposition. In these circumstances, he would have to do all he could to strongly exert his 'I-ness'. Steiner suggests that a person like this would be exposed to a cholera epidemic. Whilst it seems difficult on the face of it to see how cholera would force someone to assert their I-ness, such soul intentions are supported by interlife work. In other words, the disease is a soul choice rather than being wholly a karmic consequence. Steiner says that, in the next incarnation, the soul and the different subtle bodies will work much more closely together – which would fulfil the soul purpose of the cholera epidemic. The equivalent of this today would be someone who takes on Aids, tuberculosis or some other modern day plague as a learning experience.

Giving the example of what happens to someone whose sense of 'I-ness' is overly strong, Steiner says that he will seek an opportunity in the next incarnation to have no limit for his sense of self and so 'he will be led to the unfathomable and to absurdity. These opportunities come to him when karma brings him malaria'. In overcoming this, self-healing will be developed and he will be set on the 'upward path of evolution'. Today's equivalent dis-ease, in the West at least, would most probably be M.E. This dis-ease strikes hardest at the driven personality, the person who cannot stop, who must get to the top at all costs whether to prove him or herself potent and effective and thus overcome an underlying sense of doubt about those things, or who surrenders willingly to the helplessness of this debilitating illness so that someone else has to take over – for a time at least.

Research by many regression therapists has shown that there are a number of underlying causes, karmic consequences and soul choices leading to dis-ease, the major ones being:

Major karmic causes of dis-ease[7]

- Soul unrest
- Soul intention
- The need to develop specific qualities
- Past life repression of pain that refuses to be ignored any longer
- Attitudinal karma
- Closed-mindedness
- Bigotry or lack of empathy for others
- Unwillingness to help others
- Organic karma
- Direct carryover of affliction or disability possibly in a symbolic form
- Deeply ingrained pattern of behaviour

ptive karma
:velopment of creative potential
t from several past life personas
- Strongly negative past life self trying to manifest again
- Curses or ill-wishing

Let's look at some of these causes and their effect more specifically because they underlie many of the great 'why' questions around well-being or the lack of it.

- **Addiction**

As we have seen addiction may arise out of attitudinal karma – a feeling that there will never be enough or a greed for more, more, more whether in the form of money, love or substance – but it can also arise from organic karma and other karmic consequences. During my time as a drug and alcohol counsellor I explored many stories of addiction and in virtually all of them the seeds of the dependency were there from birth and flowered early. A middle-aged alcoholic told me with great relish how, aged 8, he had drunk a whole bottle of sherry and, for the first time in his life, felt that he was fully satisfied. 'It was something I had been looking for all my young life'. Perhaps unsurprisingly regression revealed that it was by no means his first acquaintance with a bottle.

In the past the effect of morphine and its derivatives, for instance, wasn't fully understood. Not so long ago the British Raj encouraged and controlled a huge trade in opium to China and other countries. This was a method of controlling the populus that has left a trail of collective karma that is still having powerful effects in the world today through Afghanistan and the heroin trade. But it is also having a personal effect on the many souls who were caught up in it as well as those who were indiscriminately given morphine or opium to dull the pain of battle injuries in the American Civil War, the First World War and even the Second World War and of course the drug extravaganza of the Vietnam war. The addictive effects were not fully understood, nor indeed were they of laudanum sedatives and 'nerve tonics' which were taken by Victorian women in large quantities. This has created organic karma, a craving for the substance that is reflected in the karmic blueprint and which can create receptors in the brain that are particularly attuned to morphine-like substances such as heroin or to alcohol and chocolate.

Although we think of 'the drug problem' as modern, someone once estimated that half the population of Victorian England and a large proportion of the urban population in the States may have been addicted to one substance or another. Addiction, of course, deadens pain on several levels, physical as well as psychological. That may underlie the vast number of souls incarnated today who are addicts in one form or another.

As most addicts can't wait to get back to the substance they rarely take time in the interlife to rethink their addictions and so a powerful soul overlay is created. It may take many lifetimes before they reconsider their situation and choose a family that does not carry the genetic propensity for addiction and thus take a step on the path to recovery that will eventually leave them free of any type of craving at all.

- **Eating disorders**

Many eating disorders have their roots in attitudinal or organic karma and, of course, in poor body image. But most have their deeper roots in previous life experiences. A common cause of over-eating in the present life is having starved to death in the past, especially when the last thought in that life was 'I'll never starve again'. But the roots of bulimia often lie in the then socially acceptable practice of stuffing oneself literally to bursting point in ancient Rome, vomiting and then continuing to eat only to vomit again. In one regression experience, Jonathan, a male bulimic, found that he'd had that experience at second hand although he was present. He was the slave who had to hold the basin for his master and who involuntarily vomited on his master – only to be promptly run through by a dagger and killed for defiling his owner. Although that left him with a powerful phobia about other people vomiting, Jonathan also carried from that time a fear of starvation and so would overstuff himself.

Anorexia too may be linked to past life beliefs about the desirable size for a body to be, especially the female body who starved herself to achieve a handspan waist, but it can also link into previous life feelings that the body is 'bad' – from regression session evidence it is clearly a misapprehension under which many a monk or nun laboured – or to sexuality as sinful, and may link into past life sexual abuse. If patterns and beliefs like these are not changed prior to the next incarnation they will be carried over and the hidden thoughts will create over-eating, bulimia and anorexia or whatever socially acceptable form of eating disorder prevails in that life. It only takes two or three lives like that for it to become a deeply ingrained soul overlay that needs in-depth past life therapy and reframing to eliminate the root cause of the disorder.

- **Ill-wishing**

The consequences of ill-wishing in a previous life can be surprisingly strong. The consequences have two ways of manifesting. If the ill-wishing has 'stuck' to the person concerned and been carried in the soul hologram, then they might manifest an illness or condition which reflects the ill-wishing. Such ill-wishing does not have to be deliberate. Simply thinking 'I hope he gets what's coming to him' is enough to set the karma in motion. The ill-wishing may also rebound on the person who had the thought in the first place. In regression, a woman with an ulcerative skin condition was surprised to find that she had, in a former life, voiced the hope that someone would 'rot in hell' for what he had done to her. A few lives down the line, she herself manifested the 'rot'.

Curses are a more serious problem. They carry 'malice aforethought' and a much more powerful karmic charge. Many protracted illnesses and states of disease can arise out of old curses (as can unfortunate life circumstances). If the curse is made by or with the assistance of someone trained in the magical arts, the intention remains 'alive'. No ancient Egyptian would be without an amulet designed to ward off evil spells. In regression, I once had to go back to smash a clay tablet inscribed with a curse which was quite definitely having an effect on my health in my present life. Artefacts may still be around today that express the curse. In the Roman baths at Bath, for instance, hundreds of lead plates have been found with curses inscribed. Some are specific and personal but others were generic. Museums all over the world hold similar tablets that maintain the energy of the curse today (see *Good Vibrations* for dealing with curses attached to objects).

The karma attached to a curse may be very long-lasting indeed. It may pass through family lines as well as through your particular soul's experience. Both the recipient of the curse and the person who placed the curse may be pulled together life after life as they are tied tightly by invisible bonds. Each may in turn experience physically the result of that curse. Much work may be needed to break the karmic cause.

- **Previous life injuries**

As we saw when looking at the karmic blueprint, previous life injuries or blockages can be imprinted and either be manifested from birth or develop later in life. People are sometimes born with a scar on the site of a past life injury or a propensity to damage that part of the body. Even when they do not have a physical effect in the form of a disability, scar and so on, the energetic memory of the injury and the emotional conditions surrounding it can present as the underlying reason for an apparently psychosomatic dis-ease in the current life.

The following is verbatim from an account sent to me some six months after the regression by Howard, a rather shy young man. It shows how vivid the memory of a genuine past life regression is and how understanding develops throughout a session (this one was conducted under hypnosis and not by me) and how sometimes the realisation of the cause and letting go of the emotional pain is all that is required for healing to take place in the current life. You will no doubt notice how the tense changes to the present as Howard shifts deeper into the past life memory:

> My presenting problem was an uncomfortable sensation in my chest whenever someone praised me. It is quite common for people to feel embarrassed sometimes when they are being complimented. It can be uncomfortable when someone 'loves you more than you love yourself'. But this was different.
>
> The therapist asked me to remember the last time I had experienced the feeling in my chest that I was concerned about. I told him it was about a week ago and described the circumstances, what was said and how I felt. He then asked me to describe certain details and to be aware of the precise moment when I noticed the feeling. I described the feeling in my chest, discomfort in my upper chest, and how it became stronger and uncomfortable.
>
> The therapist explained that there may have been some experience in the past which had created the feeling in the first place and that this may have been an appropriate feeling at that time. But we agreed that it was not appropriate to feel this discomfort merely because someone was praising me. He took me into hypnosis and regressed to the first time that I had experienced the feeling. We hadn't discussed past lives, only that there

may have been some experience in the past that had created the feeling.

Suddenly I am in the countryside. There is a feeling of tension and fear. Shouting and anger. I am being killed, a spear through my chest. I am falling, sliding down a bank into a stream.

We run the scene again. This time more slowly. We are North American Indians. There is a battle. I am being killed by a member of my tribe. Why? I am feeling very confused at this point. Why was I being killed by my own tribe?

The therapist then suggested that I would realise the significance of the events. It all became clear. We (the women and children) were being killed by our own tribe so that the enemy could not capture us. They did not kill me because I had done something wrong but because they loved me and were protecting me from a 'fate worse than death'.

I realised that the feelings in my chest when I was being praised were linked to this experience. The spear through the chest, death – but from love not hatred.

Once this had become apparent, the therapist asked me if I needed the feeling any more. Certainly not!

At our next session I reported that I hadn't had the feeling in my chest since the regression. The therapist took me back again to the same scene. The memories were the same but I was free from the emotion.

He never experienced the pain again.

- ## Sexual Dysfunction

Many of the difficulties people experience in their sex life have their roots in the past – and the most common cause is vows of celibacy that have not been rescinded at the end of a life. Women who have a fear of sex, often with accompanying anorgasmia, find that they have been raped or forced to have unwelcome sexual congress in a past life. It is hardly surprising that the memory lingers and, even when everything seems on the surface to be willing and loving, the old memory kicks in and the body becomes too tight and tense to let go.

Robert, who approached me to find the cause of his premature ejaculation, regressed back to a time when he had a passionate affair with a servant girl employed in his house. The affair consisted of hurried fumblings in the linen cupboard and similar locations. He was always enjoining her: 'Hurry, hurry, before my wife finds out' or 'Quick, before someone comes'. It was hardly surprising that in his current life Robert's body still obeyed that command, especially as he set up a similar situation by attempting sex with his first girlfriend whilst his parents were downstairs. The anxiety that they would be discovered by an irate parent brought the inbuilt pattern to the surface once more.

In this case, Robert was repeating an old pattern. In other cases, the soul might have set up the condition of premature ejaculation, or impotence, as 'retributive karma'. They could have felt guilty about sex in the past and the guilt would manifest in the sexual dysfunction. There are, however, more complex cases. Edgar Cayce was consulted by a beautiful woman who had for eighteen years been married to a man who was impotent. She was sensual and affectionate and craved sexual contact. As she loved her husband, she could not simply leave him. Initially she had many affairs but found them unsatisfactory. Taking up meditation, she became celibate. Then an old flame turned up again, and passion burned brightly once more. However, this man was married and she did not wish to hurt his wife. Apparently he had loved the beautiful woman from childhood, but she hadn't known – he had been determined to be able to support a wife before he told her. By the time he could declare his love, his great love was engaged to someone else. When they met again, the old feelings were there but neither wanted to hurt their partner.

Naturally the beautiful woman was confused by the situation and turned to Edgar Cayce, whom she, most unusually, supplied with details. Gina Cerminara, who reports the case, says that the past antecedents of the problem 'inspire a sense of awe, almost, at the singularly appropriate punishment which two erring souls are meeting'. Apparently the woman had in a previous life also been married to her present life husband. He had gone away to the Crusades but before he went, he put his wife in a chastity belt. The wife deeply resented the lack of trust and 'vowed to get even'. As Cayce puts it in the reading:

> Being forced to remain in a state of chastity caused the entity to form detrimental determinations. That this has become a portion of the entity's present experience, then, is only the meeting of self.

In analysing the 'retributive justice', Gina Cerminara says that the man who used mechanical means to impose chastity on his wife was rewarded by impotence. On the surface, the fact that the woman should again endure sexual frustration is, at first sight, difficult to understand. However, Cerminara says that it was her reaction to his unjust action, and her desire for revenge, that created the karmic situation between them in the current life. In the present she was utterly desirable and yet her husband was unable to respond – this was his karmic retribution. Had she desired to get even, she could have taunted him with her affairs. However, in the meantime she had grown in spiritual understanding and could not bear to hurt either her husband or the other man's wife. In 'meeting herself' in the situation, she found the way to redeem the past karma. She was allowing, in Cayce's terms, 'vengeance to be taken by karmic law not herself'.

A woman may, for instance, have had an abusive experience in one life which caused her to fear men. In her next few lives the fear may become ever more deeply ingrained and, because what is feared most is attracted by the soul, she may have experiences that reiterate and reinforce her original fear, experiences that could include abuse or rape. This fear could result in taking up a position of extreme militant, lesbian feminism in the present life – wanting to do away with men altogether perhaps – or in her becoming the eternal spinster. In former times, she could have become a nun.

On the other hand, karma could manifest physically as an inability to engage in sexual activity, inorgasmia or vaginal spasm being typical conditions associated with such a fear: conditions which are more properly defined as dis-ease rather than disease. She may even swing between male and female incarnations in an effort to avoid her fear, living lives as a man where the fear is karma-in-suspension. Eventually, however, her soul will engineer an opportunity for her to face up to the anxiety. This may be through an extreme manifestation of the circumstances she fears but there are less destructive ways of dealing with this karma. She may fall in love with a gentle man who is able to show her another way of loving; or may find herself meeting a man who portrays qualities different from those she has experienced in other lives. Eventually, her fear will be healed.

- **Psychological dis-ease**

Not all karmic dis-ease manifests physically. The dis-ease may occur on an emotional or mental level. Many cases of schizophrenia and mental breakdown have a background of past life trauma: the soul may have been tortured or endured powerful emotional dramas for instance. These dis-eases can also indicate a fundamental conflict and imbalance arising from two very different past life personalities trying to integrate, or a past life personality trying to take over the present life persona. But this is not the only way such conditions can arise. A past life injury can create an etheric block that presents as a chemical imbalance in the present life brain. Psychic disturbances from the past are also common causes of psychological dis-ease. If someone has failed a psychic or spiritual initiation in a former life, that can manifest as psychological disease in the present. It may take the form of recurrent nightmares or have a more serious manifestation such as epilepsy.

From past life regressions, it is clear that some temple initiations used imagery and the power of the mind, whilst others used actual objects to test a pupil. Many people have regressed into lives where they faced an initiation to check how well developed their psychic and spiritual powers were. They would be required to face a 'journey'. Such a journey often entailed meeting, or crossing, a 'pit of snakes' or meeting monsters. If the journey was through the mind, the soul had to remember that it was all an illusion. If the journey was a physical one, there were spells and incantations to awaken the power of 'snake charming'. Should the soul waver, the initiation failed and several people have experienced lives where the remainder of their time was lived in fear and psychotic disturbance. Some of these people have found an echo in their present life – maybe as phobias but also as mental disturbance. The karma may require going through spiritual initiation again, but in a different way. It may be that the soul has to heal that old scar or to recognise that it was all an illusion.

Depression may also arise from past life causes – suppressed anger and rage being an emotional cause, as is loss and grief. Overwhelming confusion or loss of hope may also manifest in the present life as an underlying depression but spiritual dissatisfaction can underlie this ubiquitous condition. If a soul has lost touch with its spiritual roots or purpose, if it cannot remember why it is incarnated, or is vaguely aware that 'I should be doing something with my life', dis-ease will be manifest.

However, we will examine in Part 3 how one young man used apparent psychological dis-ease as a means of giving service to humanity.

• **Phobias**

Phobias often have a karmic cause and stem from irrational, overwhelming and exaggerated fear. They have a past life root directly related to the present life fear and for this reason can be called karmic. Action in the past is producing a reaction in the present. Drowning can create a terror of water, falling off a high tower induces a fear of heights, a tunnel collapsing brings on claustrophobia, for instance. Such fears are specific. A woman who drowned in a deep, still pool was terrified of deep, calm water, but was quite happy on a fast flowing river or the heaving sea. Other people have found that death by snakebite leaves a lasting fear of these creatures.

Some phobias can be symbolic. A woman who was terrified of spiders found that, in a previous incarnation, she had had her hand chopped off. When it fell to the floor, it looked rather like a spider. When she incarnated again, spiders reminded her of that old trauma and all the fear transferred itself.

Phobias like these are a deeply ingrained reaction to the particular stimulus. Anne became terrified whenever she was wrapped in anything tight. If she tried on a dress that had no back opening and became stuck with it over her arms and head, she would scream and become hysterical. If she became entangled in the bedclothes at night, the same reaction would occur. But if someone put their arms around her and held her tight, although she would struggle, she would not scream. In past life regression, Anne found that she had had a sack tied over her head and upper body before being hit over the head and thrown into a river to drown. Her phobia was specific to the part during which she was conscious: material over her face, head and arms with darkness and the inability to move being the phobic trigger. The drowning took place when she was unaware of what was happening to her and did not have an immediate karmic consequence. Through past life therapy, Anne was able to heal the memory and the phobia faded.

However, past life therapy brought up an interesting aside that explained a specific aversion stemming, it seemed, from an act in her present life. When Anne was young her mother deliberately held her underwater whilst teaching her to swim. This terrified her and she would cling to the side whenever she went swimming with her mother. This went on for years although Anne was by then a competent swimmer away from her mother. In regression, she was bundled up in a sack and thrown into the Bosphorus to keep her quiet. Her mother was one of the people who threw her into the water.

Phobias can be more complicated than this, having an underlying karmic cause such as suppressed aggression, guilt or antagonism. This suppressed feeling becomes inextricably linked to the phobic trigger and may result in claustrophobia, agoraphobia and the like. This is rather like attitudinal karma. It is the result of the emotional stance taken at the time (no matter how suppressed) and what the person is experiencing in the present life stems from that old attitude. They are, in effect, punishing themselves and need to learn to break the cycle of stimulus-response, action-reaction.

Phobias can also arise from emotions experienced on someone else's behalf. Edgar Cayce gave a reading to a woman who was terrified of wild animals. He said she had watched her previous life husband being forced to fight wild beasts in the Roman arena. Her fear for him then transferred to her own fear in the present. There are times when fears are not quite phobias, and they occur because they remind the person of a previous event. In regression, Janet, a client of mine found, quite incidentally, that her fear of watching other people standing in unprotected high places came from having been blown off a high cliff herself. This hadn't prevented Janet from standing in similar places herself in her present life and it was only when she saw someone else doing it that the fear kicked in. In the regression, Janet found that she had been relieved to die back then – it hadn't been an easy life. What bothered her was that someone else's life might be brought to a premature close in a similar way. She carried that fear forward into her new life.

So, if you suspect that you are 'suffering' from karmic dis-ease, you need to examine the way in which the dis-ease is manifesting. Is it in your body – organic karma? Is it through your mind and ingrained beliefs that cause psychological unrest? Or is it something that is showing more subtly? Whatever it is, it can be healed by going back in regression to the cause and removing it from the karmic blueprint. But if you are on a soulpath that is learning through the condition in which you find yourself, then you may need to enter the interlife to explore exactly what you intended to learn as it would be imprudent to give up a condition that was part of your soul learning without ensuring you have taken all you can from the experience.

- **Karma-in-suspension**

As not all karma can be dealt with at once, some of it remains in suspension to be dealt with at some other time – which may or may not occur during the present life depending on how other factors progress and whether certain trigger points are reached. Whilst not all of this karma will be positive, a considerable amount of it may well be. If the soul makes a leap forward, clearing or balancing previous karma, then it could be in a position to make use of previous merit or positive attitudinal karma which had been 'waiting in the wings' as it were. This is especially so when the soul has set up a soul intention to be of service to humanity.

- **Karma-in-the-making**

Each thought, deed, action and belief in the present creates future karma. An important factor in karmic consequences is that the soul is building *at each moment* the foundations for the future. Each act, thought, word and intention will have consequences in the future.

If you think you might be building karma-in the making, turn to the section on getting off the karmic wheel for suggestions as to how to reverse your actions.

- **Merit karma**

Positive, or merit, karma is often overlooked. It is as though people believe there can only be negative karma. They disregard the things they 'got right' in the past, the skills they have developed and the wisdom gained, and ignore the benefits and rewards they can reap from that positive karma in the present life. It is particularly helpful to know how to create positive merit karma for the future. As karma shows that we create our own reality, 'good karma' can be created within the present life to sow seeds for a good rebirth.

Merit karma is a reward for things the soul 'got right' in other lives, the lessons learned, the insights put into practice. So, it is money in the karmic piggy bank. Merit karma may be the reason why someone has a smooth and easy life – or receives help as and when it is needed. It often manifests as a talent in the present life. A musician can carry that ability over into the next lifetime, to become an infant prodigy or a natural musician. Equally, a soul may have learnt how to manifest abundance and to trust in divine providence. It will return as someone who can always find a way to make money, or who is naturally 'lucky'. Merit karma also operates on a more spiritual level, bringing an incarnated soul into situations where it will continue with previous spiritual progression, attracting the right teacher at the apposite moment and so on.

To check out your merit karma look at your talents and skills and the things that come naturally to you. These are credits in your karmic piggy bank and, just like investments, they need nurturing and attention to keep them growing.

- **Organic karma**

Organic karma reflects injuries or conditions from other lives and may be encoded into the DNA of the new physical body. We have already seen how a past life death from being rolled on by a horse resulted in asthma and noted that there were underlying psychological factors in that life. Previous actions can affect the body in the present life through the karmic blueprint (see 'how karma transfers to the body'). Over-indulgence, for instance, could manifest as obesity or liver problems. Too much blood-letting in the past could create a tendency to anaemia in the present life. A previous life back injury could underlie a chronic back problem, tuberculosis in a former life could result in present-life lung disease and so on (see also the karma of dis-ease and attitudinal karma).

Nevertheless, even when karma *seems* to be manifesting negatively and operating as organic karma, taking value judgements out of the equation can radically change the picture. For example, during a past life regression, Marie discovered that an abortefactant had been administered to her in a past life, without her knowledge or consent. The resonance had stayed with her soul and had manifested as multiple sclerosis as one of the ingredients had been a neurotoxin. The multiple sclerosis wasn't a punishment for the act of aborting the foetus (to which she had been an unwitting party) but it was a result of the past-life abortion. Marie's soul's consequent dis-ease manifested in her present life as a physical illness. During the regression session, Marie went into the interlife and it became clear to her that her actions during her present life, how she handled and healed the dis-ease and the attitude she had, would affect her next life. If she cleared the dis-ease, she would be born healthy. If she did not and particularly if she became resentful, then she would probably be born with neurological damage as the condition would become more ingrained.

Opinions differ as to the causes of organic karma – and its consequences. According to Edgar Cayce sexual excess in one life can lead to epilepsy in the next life, for instance, but Rudolf Steiner thought that it would result in pneumonia. While it is possible to see the jerking spasms of orgasm in epilepsy, it is less easy to see why over-indulgence in sex would result in lung congestion. In my experience, epilepsy in the present life may also be created by a misuse of psychic gifts in a previous life or by spiritual initiations which failed. The energy field is disturbed, creating imbalances in the karmic blueprint from which the new body develops. According to the theosophist Annie Besant, epilepsy can also arise from alcoholism in a previous life, the soul being attracted to a family whose genetic code has been damaged by alcoholism so that there is a propensity towards diseases of the nervous system.

Positive organic karma can arise when the soul has worked hard to strengthen an organ such as the heart in a past life. This positive karma can stand the soul in good stead when illness or disability has to be overcome.

Organic karma can also arise from soul choices that have caused other people to suffer, and when the soul reincarnates, it has to learn what it feels like to go through that pain or trauma. According to Edgar Cayce, the glands of the body are often utilised in manifesting karma at a physical level. The glands are sensitive to psychic and psychosomatic input and can reflect karmic dis-ease. So, someone suffering from a hormone or brain-chemical imbalance could be put in a position where they were unable to function socially and might indulge in behaviour which they, in former times, would have condemned.

An example Cayce gives is that of a former nun who had been 'stern, cold and intolerant of human weakness'. As a teenager, an endocrine imbalance caused severe menstrual flow. She was unable to have a normal social life, becoming very shy and reclusive. She did not learn how to make relationships. Later, she became a well-known model – put on a pedestal and viewed by other people but lacking contact with them. When she married, it was to a stern, cold, intolerant man. Starved of affection, she became intolerably lonely when her husband was posted overseas during World War II. She moved to a resort town, drinking heavily and indulging in 'loose living'. At first her drinking was to overcome her social inhibitions, but soon she was permanently drunk.

Drink made her throw aside all her inhibitions. This former nun would take off all her clothes and go out in public stark naked. In meeting other people's condemnation of her actions, she met herself face to face. In her previous life, she had had a meanness of spirit that condemned everyone who did not live up to her own high standards. Now she learned at first hand what it was to hunger uncontrollably for something, and understood the overwhelming need to deaden the pain of loneliness with whatever was to hand.

An interesting question arises around organic karma when we consider that many organs are being transplanted directly into new bodies and, as research is showing, the people receiving those organs can become aware of the donor's thoughts, feelings and karma. Does the recipient then take on some or all of the donor's karma – or the donor-soul's life-plan – in the same way that the Jews believe that if you save someone's life you are then responsible for that person? If the idea that the soul is holographic and that each organ has a portion of soul is correct, then a portion of the hologram could be transferred with the organ and the karma could remain active on the physical plane after the donor's death. Would that then mean that the recipient lived out some or all of the karma or soulplan of the donor? This is an area that deserves further exploration, particularly of the interlife agreements and soul contracts that could be involved.

- **The karma of pacts, promises and soul contracts**
The pacts and promises made in another life, or in the interlife, can strongly affect the present. They may involve another person or be personal. If a soul promised to always be there for someone or to 'always look after you', it can create relationship karma (see below). The vow holds the two souls together beyond death. Similarly declarations that: 'I'll never have another child/relationship/etc' or 'I will always love/hate you' can have a powerful effect through many lives. It can pull couples, or parents and children, into relationship time after time or keep them apart until a way is found to heal the interaction that led to the decision. Even decisions to 'always love you' can be karmically blocking. It may be more appropriate for spiritual growth to let go.

Equally powerful can be the promise to mother a specific soul, to provide them with a physical body in which to incarnate. Such promises are, usually, made in the interlife and are, of course, forgotten when the 'mother' incarnates. The other soul, however, waits for an opportune moment to incarnate. This can lead to complications if the first soul takes a different life path to the one envisaged or if the soul contract was not clearly stated.

During a psychodrama on healing the family tree, a young woman whose mother had died when she was a child – and who hadn't been told her mother was dead before the funeral took place – wanted to re-enact the funeral so that she could attend. She selected me as the person she wanted to take on the role of mother so I was the 'corpse' who found myself telling the young woman that although her mother had agreed to give birth to her, she hadn't agreed to stay around and bring her up. For her own reasons, the mother had needed to move on so had had what seemed to be a brief life simply to give birth to her daughter as promised. She hadn't left out of lack of love for her child, but out of karmic imperative. It was a deeply emotional moment for everyone concerned and quite an experience to be given a full Catholic funeral as the workshop included a Catholic priest who had been unable to attend his mother's funeral and so took this opportunity. Sometimes surrogates get to give service for a brief but intensely healing period, at other times it may be for a lifetime.

Yiou had lived in China for the first forty years of her life and then moved to the West. She had, through a series of apparent 'accidents', become a highly successful business woman. As a teenager, she had been very much in love and had married against her family's wishes. Her husband died soon afterwards, under rather mysterious circumstances. She was four months pregnant and she was left destitute. Her family took her back, on condition that she aborted the baby. Although she would very much have liked to have had that child, in her situation she could see no other choice. She then went to work in the family business. She had several affairs, each of which ended in pregnancy and abortion by her choice. (China is a country that uses abortion as contraception and this is not unusual). Yiou began to travel abroad with her work and started using Western contraception, but it failed time after time.

By the time she came to see me, having moved permanently to England, Yiou had lost count of the abortions she had had. When we talked about it, she said that the only child she had wanted was the first one, and yet each time she aborted another potential child, she felt tremendous grief. 'It is as though I am supposed to have that child, no matter what', she said, 'and yet I know I do not want to bring up a child on my own and I have not found a man I would want to be my child's father. And, in any case, I'm getting too old for pregnancy'.

I took Yiou back to scan her former lives to see if there was a reason for the situation but she could not see anything. I guided her into the interlife to seek the reason there. She quickly found a soul who was waiting to incarnate through her. She had promised this soul that she would be her mother and the soul was still there, waiting. I suggested she should ask the soul why the promise had been made. The soul said that the woman had been her mother once before, but had died in childbirth. The mother had stayed close to her child to 'watch over her' in spirit. When they met up in the interlife immediately after the soul's death, they had had a very emotional reunion and the promise had been made there and then. Before incarnating, many years later in earth time, the promise hadn't been discussed again.

Yiou told the soul how her circumstances had changed and how she did not feel able to be a mother. The soul told her that she should stick to her promise. A long dialogue then ensued. Yiou kept begging the soul to release her, the soul was angry and felt rejected. I had to step in and suggest to the soul that she should talk to her guides. (I felt that as she had been hanging around the earth plane trying to incarnate at every possible opportunity, she had made little progress since her last life and was 'stuck in a groove'). Reluctantly she did so, and came back to say that she would go with them. But, she was adamant that she and Yiou had unfinished business that would have to be dealt with at some future time. She wasn't, at that stage, able to offer any forgiveness.

Had she been able to, Yiou would have renegotiated that promise during the therapy session, but it was not to be. I suggested to her that she should spend five or ten minutes each evening, sending love and forgiveness to the soul and holding compassion for her in her heart. In this way, the situation between them would have been subtly altered by the time she left incarnation. As it was, after a few months the soul appeared to her in a dream and told her that she was ready to let the promise go. Had she not done so, the karmic enmeshment would have continued into the next life.

- **Relationship karma**

Relationship karma arises in families, love affairs, friendships and business relationships. The threads of a relationship can often be traced back through many lives. Few important relationships begin in the present life and even fewer are the result of chance. Attitudes, actions and interactions weave a tapestry of which only a small part can be glimpsed in any one lifetime, or a couple may be stuck on a karmic treadmill or be caught up in the 'you did it to me so I'll do it to you' scenario. Souls have a wide variety of reasons for reincarnating together, not all of them based on love. I have treated this subject at much greater length in *The Soulmate Myth: a dream come true or your worst nightmare?* and so have only summarised the main points below.

Edgar Cayce frequently stated that no major human relationship is the result of chance. From a close study of his many thousands of readings, Gina Cerminara concluded that 'no marriage is a start on a clean slate. It is an episode in a serial story begun long ago'.[8] That does not mean, however, that the parties would necessarily have been together before, it was the issues involved that were the serial story. I see in my own work couples and members of families who are starting out together for the first time but the majority have known each other in one context or another.

Certain aspects of relationship karma may be purely personal, relevant only to the one partner in the relationship and not pertaining to a previous life interaction between a couple or family. That soul meets its in-built expectations and confronts attitudes regarding love through interaction with someone *other* – who acts as a perfect mirror to reflect those expectations. On the other hand, couples may have relationship karma that is personal to the two, or more, people concerned. However, some people get together to work on karmic issues that have nothing to do with the other person in a personal sense, they simply share the same issues and are having a practice run as it were before confronting the karma with the person with whom it was generated.

Reasons for incarnating together:

- Spiritual bonds
- Previous relationship carried over
- Soulmate connection

- Unfinished business
- Karmic treadmill
- Habit, inertia
- Dependence and symbiosis
- Mutual support and evolution
- Lessons to be learned
- Redemptive and recompense karma
- Retributive karma
- Attitudes to be transformed
- Debt or duty
- Attachment to mutual unhappiness or happiness
- Soul contracts, pacts, vows or promises
- Love or hatred
- The desire for revenge

Sometimes a bond of true love unites a couple down through the ages, but this is not always so. Hatred can be the cause of powerful attachments. Some people will not let go of someone they possessively 'love', and have to come back with that person until they can love unconditionally and enough to let go. The lesson can be painful, especially when the other person does not recognise the 'love' and rejects the supposed soul mate. Some couples find themselves living the consequence of ancient infidelities. Retribution is a part of relationship karma, as are recompense, reparation and karmic enmeshment but this is rarely a punishment from outside the relationship, more a case of one person being bound by hatred, martyrdom or a sense of 'being owed' and therefore being unable to let go.

In his readings, Edgar Cayce always emphasized that karma wasn't a matter of debt between couples – although I and many other past life therapists have found many cases where the people concerned did feel that they had a karmic debt, subtle or otherwise, which they wanted to repay. According to Cayce, the issue was one of personal soul development:

It is merely Self being met, in relationships so that they themselves are working out… a karmic debt of Self that may be worked out between the associations that exist in the present. [Reading 1436].

So, according to Cayce, if someone complained that their partner was unloving, it wasn't that the partner should change but that the person asking for a reading should take that opportunity to redress what Cayce called 'imperfect attitudes'. They themselves would be well advised to seek to become more loving as this would overcome a previous inability to love. Equally, if they found it impossible to love someone, then they should work on being more accepting and tolerant so that they could develop unconditional love. This approach sounds much more like lessons set into the soulplan for the present life – based on interlife choices – rather than actual karma. I have come across souls who deliberately planned a lifetime with a partner who would cheat on them or remain uncommitted in order that the soul could overcome deeply ingrained jealousy in other lives. Emotions such as jealousy belong to the personality and the ego rather than to the soul and are often seen, in the interlife, as something to be overcome.

If you're asking why your partner is cheating on you or involving you in his or her addiction or a chaotic life, you may have to ask yourself whether you need to move on and let go. Or are you learning forgiveness and unconditional love from the experience? Are you there to be a compassionate witness to your own pain and the partner's weaknesses? But you also have to bear in mind that unconditional love does not mean being abused, misused, walked all over and so on. It means loving someone as they are, warts and all, without being compelled to change them – and without become mired in their pain or their crap. It's about being able to stand placidly by while someone makes a terrible mess but not being drawn in or feeling that you have to rescue them in any way. It is about being strong enough in your own self to say 'no' or 'enough' – and mean it.

Common relationship themes:
- Giving positive service
- Practising unconditional love
- Confronting freedom/commitment dilemmas
- Replaying parent/child sagas
- Replaying victim/martyr/rescuer/persecutor/scapegoat scenarios
- Disentangling enmeshment/dependence and collusion
- Re-enacting enabler-enabled/betrayer-betrayed scenarios

- Re-enacting seducer/seduced scenarios
- Replaying dominance and submission scenarios

For Cerminara, based on the evidence Cayce gave, all relationships are 'sequels to the past' – although her view takes no account of 'karma in the making' nor of soul contracts in which one soul may have been guiding the other through many incarnations without actually being in incarnation. Virtually all the people Cayce read for appear to have been connected within soul groups and some had been in close relationship with each other before. Many incarnated together to continue karmic tasks, to close unfinished business or deal with karma. For quite a number of the people Cayce read for, marriage was a 'repeat performance'. He said that they had had the same partners before. However, there were a number of people whom Cayce warned not to repeat the karmic relationship, and he told others that there were karmic influences that made it unwise to enter into marriage. He affirmed the presence of free will and new choices rather than repeating an old pattern – something supported by interlife exploration.

Not all relationships improve as the karma matures. People can be stuck on a karmic treadmill. In some the interaction changes subtly and yet the underlying dynamics are the same. So, for instance, a relationship which was violent and abusive in its early manifestations may appear on the surface in the later stages to be more kind. And yet, below the surface cruelty may still be present only this time it will manifest on a more psychological level. Sarcasm, endless put-downs, indifference, self-centredness, infidelity, and the like are all mutations of the previous abuse. The couple may be drawn together by hate and a desire for revenge, or they may truly believe that this is 'love'. Until the karma is neutralized, until the underlying attitude changes and the soul contract is renegotiated, they will be drawn back together time and again. The mutations may be many and varied, but the challenge will remain the same.

This does not mean to say that all marriages are between people who have had exactly the same relationship in other lives. In my experience, it may be possible that the parties were married before, but it is equally likely – confirmed over and over again by regression work – that the relationship could have been, amongst many possibilities, as parent and child, siblings, friends and acquaintances, bitter enemies and employer-employee or master and slave. It is perfectly possible to share a life with someone you have never met before, but with whom one has certain karmic issues in common. It is sometimes easier to work on these things at a more objective distance, and the incarnation may be a preparation for working with the person with whom the karma arose in a future incarnation. Even if the relationship is a sequel to the past, it may be that the couple are trying out a different way of doing things, learning new responses, may be even changing roles or gender. They could be exploring interdependence after lifetimes of dependence or extreme independence. Many karmic issues are expressed in relationship.

Like most people who explore karmic consequences and soul choices, I am frequently asked 'why can't I find a partner?' The answer varies of course but what many people are looking for in a partner is someone to make them feel complete, to fill in the gaps as it were. But what if their soulplan was to find the missing pieces within their own self? They are unlikely to find a true mate until they have done so. Being single may have been part of the soulplan for the present incarnation. The soul may be learning the difference between being alone and being lonely. Being alone can bring strength and independence, an ability to be happy in your own company. Being lonely often brings dependence and barriers, repeating old patterns. Souls usually encounter what they expect. So, if at a deep level the soul feels unlovable, unworthy, inadequate or inferior, *for whatever reason*, this is what will be attracted (for a further discussion see *The Soulmate Myth*).

Setting too high standards can be one of the pitfalls in finding a mate. If a previous experience was of 'perfection', then anything else tends to disappoint. If it wasn't, the soul might have decided it has to be this time. Many people go into relationship expecting – or demanding – that everything should be instantly right. If it was, there would be nothing to work on and they'd have found their twinflame. On the other hand, if the soul has always settled for something less, and therefore been disappointed in love, then, once again, that expectation will probably manifest once more or they might enter yet another soulmate relationship in order to learn self-love.

Previous decisions and vows can profoundly affect the ability to attract a mate. If a soul has taken a vow of celibacy in another life, unless this was rescinded there remains a certain 'untouchable air' about that person. They may make subtle movements of distaste and rejection that are perceived subliminally be a potential partner, who backs off. Disappointment or hurt in love, the decision that 'I'll never risk that again' can have much the same effect. It is as though the aura freezes. Consciously the person wants to receive love, subconsciously a little voice is saying 'remember that decision you made, well it was good sense, you'll only get hurt again'. Once the soul recognises that voice and, where possible, finds out where it is coming from, then a new attitude is possible. (Tools such as EFT and Psych-K® can be extremely useful in turning these subconscious decisions around, see Liz Rowe-French's story on page 35).

Reading the above may have triggered some insights already but your present life relationships will soon tell you if you have relationship karma and *The Soulmate Myth* will help you to identify what it could be.

• **Retributive karma**

Retributive karma is what most people think of when they speak of karma. Similar to boomerang karma, it does have the feel about it of retaliation for former actions. In severe cases it may also incorporate an element of punishment and retribution. For example, if someone chopped off another person's leg in a former life, they could have a withered limb in the present life, or become crippled in some way. Disembowelling someone could lead to gut problems in the present life and so on. In other words, what is done to others comes back graphically with a recognisable connection between cause and effect.

The working out of this karma rarely occurs between the two people who were involved in the original action in the previous life – except where it is a case of revenge or a similar scenario. Retributive karma is often a 'wake up call' engineered by the higher reaches of the soul. It can lead to 'soul awakening'. In cases where the soul has failed to learn a lesson after many experiences, karmic justice may be served by a person, perhaps from the soul group, acting as the instrument of 'divine retribution'. The aim is to turn the soul towards a different way of being, to free it from a habit pattern that has become ingrained. The soul may also have a soul intention to learn to give up the right to hurt or see punished someone who has hurt it. Justice doesn't always need to be seen to be done, especially in the concrete form of retribution.

Retributive karma can occur on several levels. It can be physical, as in the case of the cutting off of a limb leading to a withered or amputated limb. Or, if a person has consistently overeaten, gut problems may result. It may also be mental or emotional. Someone who created profound mental disturbance in someone else, may find that psychiatric illness results in the present life; another person may have been cold and unloving in the past, and find him or herself isolated and alone in the present. However, the field of influence can be wider than it. The effects may be felt in the environment, social or external.

Gina Cerminara reports that, in the Cayce files, there are numerous examples where someone wantonly destroyed forests or mined for minerals. The karma would rebound through similar resources. One of my clients, who had relived a past life where he destroyed vast tracts of land in the 'Badlands' of America in a greedy bid to grow 'more and more', had turned to organic gardening in his present life. His enterprise failed, however, due to a drought. After the regression, he felt 'the slate has been wiped clean'.

Roderick was an example of family karma which interwove with retributive karma. His great grandfather made his money in the South African goldfields. He prudently invested the money in houses which were rented out. These houses passed down the family. By the time Roderick inherited them, they were badly in need of repair and had become something of a slum. He failed to make the repairs but enjoyed the extra prosperity that the rents brought him. Eventually the council ordered the houses demolished. Roderick received very little compensation. What he did receive, he invested in silver at a time when prices were rocketing. When they fell suddenly, he lost his money. Ironically, he worked as a solicitor and his main work was in preparing tenancy agreements which were heavily weighted in favour of the landlord. After his karmic wake up call, Roderick turned to representing a group of people whose houses were to be demolished to make way for a motorway. He fought for better compensation for them. Although he wasn't aware that he was clearing his karma at the time, it was an excellent way of 'balancing the books'.

• **Recompense karma**
Put succinctly, recompense karma comes back positively. Reward is given for sacrifices made to help others and the things that the soul 'got

right' in the past when learning a difficult lesson. Recompense is made for suffering or deprivation that the soul underwent, provided that the soul experienced this with a positive attitude and did not succumb to an attack of the 'poor me's' or blamed someone else for its misfortunes.

So if someone took time out to look after a partner who was ill or disabled and they saw this as an opportunity for serving that partner willingly and with love, then in another life they would be rewarded. If an ambition was put on hold to care for someone who was ill, then the person who was looked after might come back as a parent or good friend who helps out in the present incarnation. If someone experienced extreme poverty with equanimity, they would in another life enjoy abundance. If they bemoaned what they were missing out on, then there would be no recompense karma.

In recompense karma, the reward or restitution might come from the person who was helped in the other life, or from another source. Sometimes the recompense is for a small act of kindness. In regression, Archie regressed back to a life where he had given a cup of water to someone who was suffering extreme thirst. He did not know them in that life, but his compassion was great and he helped whenever he could. In his present life Archie had experienced great misfortune. Then one day someone offered him a chance to change his life. He took it eagerly and made a great success of things. But he always remembered his earlier misfortune and offered to others the same opportunity he had been given. To his surprise, during the regression, the person to whom he had given the cup of water was the man who had turned his present life around. Archie felt that his 'small act of kindness' had been out of all proportion to what that man did for him. But, as he saw when he looked deeper in the regression, that act had made an enormous difference. The thirsty man had died, he had been too far gone not to, but he had died following an act of loving kindness that made him resolve to help others in his next life.

In another scenario, Margaret was surprised to find that she regressed back to a very abusive life. She had had a terrible time as a slave. Owned body and soul, and much abused by her 'master', she endured it all stoically and with good humour. She never felt sorry for herself, she simply surrendered to the flow of life. As Margaret had asked for the regression to find the basis of a current happy relationship and the former 'master' was her present lover, we went back to the interlife before that incarnation. Margaret found that she and the 'master' were part of the same soul group. The 'master' had felt a need to learn how it felt to abuse people, especially women, so that he could understand what motivated the abuser. Margaret had volunteered to be the woman he abused so that he would not accrue karma for the future by that act. After her death in that other life, she forgave him and released him, offering him grace. As a result, when Margaret was planning her present life, the man offered to be her life partner. She needed to experience a nurturing relationship and he felt a great soul love for her. Her recompense karma was repaid by a deeply loving relationship which wasn't rocked by difficult times. They were mutually supportive, bringing out the best in each other and finding ways to grow together.

If you want to know whether you've experienced or given recompense karma, look back over your life and see where someone gave you a helping hand or where life flowed easily for you. A small act of kindness may have repaid a service you gave in another life, or you yourself may have been repaying a service by giving such a gift in the present life.

• **Redemptive karma**

The urge to help humankind is an expression of redemptive karma. It is often associated with an act of self-sacrifice or possibly martyrdom. Souls die so that their beliefs can come to wider attention, or that others might live. Others make great personal sacrifices or take a stand to fight for a cause not for their own individual gain or glory but so that the lot of humanity, or their portion of it, will be improved. They may go on, despite setbacks or indifference, in the hope that what they have done will kindle a spark in someone else and that that person will be able to make the difference.

Some souls incarnate to help others or to do something specific for the world. High Tibetan Lamas, for instance, have usually had the opportunity to move off the wheel of rebirth several lives ago. But they come back to help others reach the same state. Differently-abled children may have chosen to come back to help their parents learn a lesson such as compassion and caring. The ultimate example of redemptive karma for Christians is when Jesus is crucified to 'take away the sins of the world'. However, other souls continue to take on tasks that will help to clear collective karma. It is not always immediately obvious when redemptive karma is being practised and a soul's situation can be easily misunderstood.

Redemptive karma may be a reaction to the past. Some souls having been caught up in wars, plagues, famines, etc., develop a deep desire to do something to prevent such things occurring again. When they incarnate, they do so with the intention of finding a way to alleviate the situation. In the recent historic past in the West, this could involve a vocation to enter a monastery or convent so that the power of prayer could be used to change things. In more modern times, this vocation may involve working within the field of medicine, public health, aid or charitable organisations.

Redemptive karma does not necessarily have any connection to a past life. A soul may see, in the interlife, a situation that needs aid. It may feel: 'This is where I can make a difference'. That soul then incarnates with the specific intention of helping humanity by giving assistance in that situation.

I was privileged to have a friend who died from aids (he felt that the capitalisation of the word gave too much power to the disease). At the time, it did not occur to me that he was practising redemptive karma. We did, after all, have markedly different views on reincarnation and karma. He wasn't even sure there was such a thing. But looking back, recalling our conversations and reading what he had written during the course of his life as well as talking to people whose lives he had transformed through his healing work and by small acts of kindness, I would say that Justin was a powerful example of redemptive karma in action. He wanted to do things for other people and he certainly made a difference.

Justin worked in the field of personal development and healing for many years. Early on, he set up a charity which concentrated on healing work with hiv and aids patients. His group would go into hospitals to offer healing, and ran workshops to teach people with hiv how to stay healthy. He explored complementary medicine and used this to great effect. When he himself was diagnosed as having full blown aids Justin used his techniques of positive thought combined with complementary therapies to support conventional treatment. He took part in drug trials so that 'other people could benefit' but there was no suggestion of martyrdom about this act, it was all part of his positive approach to life. He lived way past the normal life expectancy at the time of people with aids, due in no small measure to the support and help of his partner. He overcame major illnesses such as cancer not once but several times. In the process he introduced his NHS consultant to 'complementary treatments', which were introduced into the hospital. He lectured to medical students and was an inspiration to many people. No-one who attended the healing workshops he ran with his partner could believe that he was ill. He was a man who 'walked his talk'.

Eventually Justin contracted a virus that would destroy the oldest part of his brain where the instincts lurk and autonomous processes of the body are controlled, including speech and hearing. An interesting part of the karmic process, as old patterns, having been destroyed, could not then be carried forward after death. He was offered, but declined, treatment that was highly toxic. He rang me to say it was time to move on to the next great adventure. I spent two and a half weeks with him as he was dying. It was an enormous privilege and contributed in no small way to my own spiritual growth. During that time Justin showed no fear. His thoughts were for his family and friends, and for his own spiritual progress. The calm acceptance of his death allowed him to savour each moment with quiet contentment, literally living in the moment. He said and did exactly what each person needed to help them come to terms with death – and later proved to them all his continuing existence after his physical death. It was an exceptional act of redemptive karma.

Many people have seen Aids as a punishment vested by a wrathful God upon people who commit 'unnatural acts' – a judgement which takes little account of the millions of people in Africa and the Far East who have contracted the disease through conventional sexual contact or those who received contaminated transfusions. I have a different perspective. To me, Aids is an opportunity to develop love. The relationship between my friend and his partner, family and friends, and between other people I have known with Aids, was something special. The level of caring and the loving is extraordinary. This is especially so as hiv and Aids can be such an isolating condition. Which was why, when I read Rudolf Steiner on the karmic causes of smallpox, a much larger picture suddenly opened up.

It was Steiner's belief that epidemics are opportunities to make reparation for previous karma. He also felt (at the start of the 20th century) that man's efforts to 'clean up' and wipe out diseases actually prevented people from creating the right conditions for karmic clearing. He pointed out that:

> *If karmic reparation is escaped in one direction, it will have to be sought in another. When we abolish certain influences, we merely create the necessity of seeking other opportunities and influences.*[9]

It was his assertion that smallpox is one of the means of karmic clearing. It is an 'organ of unlovingness'. That is, people who have in other lives created unlovingness will use smallpox to clear it. But, if the disease, smallpox, is removed, then a new means will have to be found to karmically work out an antidote to unlovingness.

At the start of the 21st century, we are in a situation where smallpox has all but been wiped out in the natural environment (it exists in laboratories and may yet be used in biological warfare or set free again through an 'accidental' escape). But we have an Aids epidemic sweeping the third world and the possibility of it becoming global. In England and the States, the fastest growing section of the population with hiv are women who are infected by their partner. Yet little is heard in the West either about how rampant the disease is in Africa, or how it is spreading through the heterosexual community in the West. One theory on how the Aids virus arose is that it came from contaminated smallpox vaccine. In other words, one illness or symptom of karmic dis-ease mutated into another.

When we look at the passionate hatred and isolation that some Aids sufferers have experienced and the unique care and concern offered to others, we can see that this condition could be an 'organ of unlovingness' or an opportunity to express and experience love. In this respect, it may be that those who are infected are actually undertaking a mass act of redemptive karma.

If you want to know whether you are here for redemptive karmic reasons, then your higher self is the best source to consult and your ego the worst. So many people who are giving service inadvertently slip into egostical mode and begin to think they are here to save the world when really they are here to make some small, anonymous act of service. Allegedly offering redemptive karma to the world is an excellent way of shoring up a sense of inadequacy. Be very sure of your motives before deciding you are here to practice this karma!

• **The karmic treadmill**

It is clear from regression work that some souls are too passive to change their role or to break out of a cycle of suffering. They go on suffering because they feel there is some vicarious merit to be gained from it; or they do not take opportunities to change their life, either through fear or a sense of inadequacy. Edwin, for instance, developed the ear condition tinitus when his wife died. This became his, unconscious, excuse for not socialising with people. He became isolated and said that he wanted things to change. However, when hands-on healing brought him to a situation where he could hear again, it became clear that Edwin could not cope with, what seemed to him, the enormous burden of starting up a conversation. Prior to his wife's death she had been the outgoing part of the couple. He had been content to sit and listen. He stopped coming for healing.

Some time later, Edwin decided to try again. We looked at his past lives to see what lay behind his difficulty in communicating. We found life after life where he had been isolated and withdrawn – from choice, he 'liked it better that way'. He had set up a treadmill of non-communication and loneliness which was comforting in its familiarity. In his present life, he and his partner had come together to help him get over this pattern. In socialising with his wife, Edwin had learnt to enjoy other people's company, although he rarely had much to say as he was afraid people would think he had little to contribute. His wife's death had been a 'wake up call', a point where he could either relapse into the old pattern or move forward. Once he understood how he had been on a karmic treadmill, he began to venture out. Picking up the threads of his old social life, Edwin was surprised to find people had missed him. This gave him confidence to go forward.

Other souls experience the karmic treadmill because it is what they have come to expect. They have had several lives where a certain situation or condition prevailed, and they come to believe 'this is how it will always be'. Until they change that expectation, that is how it is.

Destructive patterns that have not been outgrown go round and round. Many kinds of suffering are related to the karmic treadmill. Alcoholism is one example, relationships can provide many. If a soul believes 'there will never be enough love', or 'I don't deserve to be loved' it will manifest relationships where there is no love. The expectation is reinforced, and round the soul goes again. Not only that, children will most probably inherit the attitude so that it multiplies and carries on down through the family line.

The treadmill can also happen when a man (or woman) indulges in irresponsible, promiscuous behaviour, often finding it impossible to commit to a partner. There may be many affairs, outside marriage, or the soul simply moves from person to person using them to gratify sexual desire but giving nothing in return. Then, in the next life, the soul may strive for celibacy or may tie itself to an unsuitable partner for life, perhaps as a result of a momentary whim or 'lapse'. A child may result who suffers because he or she is aware that there is no love between the parents and who feels his or herself to be an encumbrance without which the parent could be free. The unfinished business of karma may be to find a new way of responding to situations.

In this example, the soul might have to learn commitment with discrimination, perhaps having to go through a relationship that has to be recognised as unsuitable and let go of before moving onto the next partner. If the same child has reincarnated within the relationship (a frequent occurrence), the task is to find a way to be loving and responsible to that child without necessarily staying with the other parent.

The unfinished business of a relationship pattern is often concerned with your soul taking responsibility for itself, giving up responsibility for someone else, or learning to be independent or mutually supportive rather than co-dependant and needy. Co-dependence is a common pattern in which the soul feels it will die without the other person. Similar patterns include saviour-rescuer and victim-martyr or persecutor and persecuted scenarios in which one soul can take the dominant role or the partners can alternate roles. Walking away from the situation can be an enormous challenge but maybe the only solution to the recurring motif.

If you find yourself going round and round in the same old circles, it is time to consider whether you are on the karmic treadmill and, if so, what you need to do to step off and take a new perspective on life.

- **'Sins of Omission and Commission'**

A consistent refusal to take action or to learn a lesson or persistent inappropriate action leads to karma. The Book of Common Prayer of the

Church of England defines the sins of omission and commission as 'those things that have been done that ought not to have been done, and the things that have not been done that should have been done'. Omission means non-action, commission action. These 'sins' or 'separations from God' create karma and it is not just acts that have consequences. Not taking action can have as much karma attached to it as taking action – if the action or non-action is ill-advised it can create suffering.

If a soul always behaved in a certain way, or consistently refused to take action, or to learn a lesson, the karma comes around and around until the message is understood. Lives can be experienced as 'sinning' or 'sinned against' as the soul struggles to find a way out of the repeating pattern. Greed, avarice, lust and the like are experienced over and over again, but so is the inability to move beyond something known and comfortable. The soul's failure to take a risk can accrue karma just as strongly as the soul who takes an unwise risk and fails.

So, for instance, a man may grow up in conditions of affluence but fail to share his wealth with those who live in less fortunate circumstances. This is a 'sin of omission'. What he did not do could lead to his experiencing privation in another life so that he would learn what it was like to live under such conditions. If he had achieved his wealth by the exploitation of others, rather than inheriting it or making the money 'honestly', he could have committed a 'sin of commission' and could find himself in a life where he in turn was exploited. On the other hand, he may find himself yet again in a life of ease and plenty if his soul wanted him to learn the lesson of altruism and gratitude.

If life seems to be continually bringing you the same lesson, ask yourself if it could possibly relate to a sin of omission or commission whether in this lifetime or any other.

- **Symbolic karma**

Symbolic karma may underlie many forms of dis-ease. Feelings of guilt, for example, can be 'acted out' in the body and the resultant organic imbalance will reflect the previous life situation. In symbolic karma, the present life condition symbolises what was done or how a person felt in the past. It can be a form of allegory. According to Cayce, a witch-ducker in a former life incarnated again as a bed-wetter, and a man who had 'shed much blood' in the past suffered from anaemia in his present life. In the same way, someone who misused communication in the past could incarnate with a speech or hearing defect. Cayce told a client who had a hearing problem: 'Never again close your ears to cries for aid'.

A physical condition in the present life can symbolically represent the cause of death in a previous life. Mrs Warren-Browne, whose story was told by the Dutch regression therapist Hans Holzer, apparently died of puerperal fever in a past life. Psychic from birth, Mrs Warren-Browne was told by the spirit of the Lord Admiral Thomas Seymour that she had been his wife, Catherine Parr (a former wife of Henry VIII). In her present life Mrs Warren-Browne had a blood condition that led to the death of five of her eight children. Immediately prior to giving birth she would be prone to deep depression and uncontrollable tears. During one birth she saw herself lying in a great bed and dying following childbirth. The blood condition and the depression in the present life apparently mirrored the situation surrounding her previous life.[10]

In the Hindu *Institutes of Vishnu* the hells to which sinners pass after death are graphically described, as is the journey through insect, bird or animal incarnations and finally back to human. As animals and the like, there may be a symbolism between the crime and the result – a stealer of meat becomes a vulture, for instance:

Criminals in the highest degree enter the bodies of all plants successively.
Mortal sinners enter the bodies of worms or insects.
Minor offenders enter the bodies of birds...
One who has stolen grain, becomes a rat.
One who has stolen water, becomes a water fowl.
One who has stolen honey becomes a gad-fly.
One who has stolen clarified butter, becomes an ichneumon.
One who has stolen meat, becomes a vulture.
One who has stolen oil, becomes a cockroach.
One who has stolen perfumes, becomes a musk-rat...

But even when they reach human incarnation again, they have marks which identify their 'sin':

A drinker of spirits, black teeth.
A malignant informer, stinking breath.

A stealer of food, dyspepsia.
A stealer of words, dumbness.
A poisoner, a stammering tongue.
One who eats dainties alone, shall have rheumatics.
A breaker of convention, a bald head...
Thus according to their particular acts are men born, marked by evil
signs, sick, blind, hump-backed, halting, one-eyed.

According to this view, it takes many lives of penance to overcome such karmic consequences and while it may not be actually factually experienced in quite such a graphic way, it does hold an underlying symbolic resonance that can be ascertained through regression.

Similarly in the ancient Gnostic text *Pistis Sophia* Jesus specifically mentions reincarnation and tells the disciples that sins from the present life will influence the next. Some of these sins can be seen as symbolically recreated but others are more to do with attitudinal karma. A man who curses others will, in his next life, for instance, be 'troubled in his heart'; but a thief will be cast into a 'lame, halt and blind body', and a slanderer will be delivered into a body 'which will spend its time being afflicted'. According to the *Pistis Sophia*, it's not just 'sinful' acts that warrant such treatment. An arrogant, overbearing personality would be born into a deformed or demeaned body. A murderer or blasphemer's soul, on the other hand, will be destroyed and dissolved and, presumably, will be no more.

Symbolic karma can work in another way. 'Organ language' in which anxieties and emotional conditions are reflected through psychosomatic dis-ease is medically recognised. If someone loses their appetite, they could be emotionally starved, for instance. If the condition is not rectified, anorexia nervosa could result. A person who has difficulty swallowing or who experiences persistent nausea may not be able to stomach something, either in the present environment or from another life. This may relate to an attitude held, or an act committed by someone else, it may be feelings and emotions in the person concerned, or words that cannot be expressed.

I have a good friend, an American who suffered from 'gas'. She continually felt like there was a bubble burning in her oesophagus which she could neither swallow nor expel. In a workshop meditation, Meredith regressed back to a life where she was handed a poisoned drink. As it went down, it burned her gullet. But what hurt worst was that it was handed to her by her lover. She felt betrayed and that was something she 'could not stomach'. When Meredith reported back, I asked her if she had thought to drink the antidote. 'No', she said, 'I was too mad. To think, I had been taken in by him!' Meredith went back into the regression and took the antidote, but she had a great deal of work to do later to forgive both the lover and herself for having been duped. However, the gas went away and did not return.

In the deterministic view of karma, someone who has put out another person's eye in a past life would be born blind in the next life or be blinded in an 'accident' as retribution and pay back. But whilst one person may experience this 'boomerang' type of karma, it is equally likely that reparation could be made in another, more symbolic way. The person could become, for instance, an eye surgeon who saved many people's sight; or someone who donated their eyes for a corneal graft after their death.

If you want to check whether you are experiencing symbolic karma, let your mind play with word associations and resonances around what you are experiencing in your present life. Your higher self will soon join in the game and slip important insights into your mind if you know how to recognise these.

- **Unfinished business**

Unfinished business is not strictly speaking a karma but it reactivates karmic patterns, creates karmic consequences and stirs up the soul. Meeting someone with whom you have unfinished business or catching a glimpse of a past life contact – whether through dreams, regression or déjà vu – can set the continuation of a karmic process in motion and bring in reactions that are totally contrary to the soul's present purpose. In other words, it can trigger a soul overlay or re-activate a residual thought or emotion that seemingly has nothing to do with present circumstances, although just how the two are connected may be well hidden.

For instance Angelika found that, when driving on motorways, she would 'come to' inches from death as she was rushing towards a concrete pillar or bridge, and yet she was feeling strangely elated. She seemed to have an unconscious death wish. Angelika had met another woman and fell totally, utterly and inexplicably in love: immediately. Soon after they met she had sat down to meditate:

> *I was in this beautiful old house. I was very much in love, very excited. My lover was coming back. He'd been away a long time. We were to be married. That was all I could get at the time but I knew that this lover was the woman I had recently met and that, in that life, she had been a man.*

After the meditation Angelika had thought no more about it, and then found herself being drawn to kill herself. So she came to see me for regression. As the story unfolded the man hadn't come back but she didn't know what had happened to him. Thinking that he had abandoned her, she had eventually killed herself because she 'couldn't live without him'. That feeling that she could not live without him and the fear of being abandoned again, had been reactivated even though the same soul was in front of her in a woman's body. The old imperative had been triggered when the couple met again.

To release the soul overlay, I had to regress the other woman as well. Juliana went straight back to that life in which she had been a soldier called to fight for his country. He had been captured, tried as a spy and summarily executed and hung over the battlements. The problem was, he had had no idea what had been going on as he didn't speak the language. There was no way to let those at home know, it all happened so quickly in the midst of war.

A considerable amount of reframing was needed and so both of them were simultaneously regressed back to that life. The soldier wrote a letter home, smuggling it so that she would know what had become of him. After his death we had him go to say goodbye 'in a dream'. She did not kill herself. In the interlife they were united once more and we made sure that no residue was carried over into the present life. Angelika's suicidal impulses immediately ceased and the pair had a happy relationship.

Unfinished business can also arise if souls were not able to complete their soulplan in one lifetime or where an issue was unresolved but brought to the end by the death or disappearance of one of the parties. If they meet again, the soul overlays will kick in once more, sometimes to the detriment of the current life soul purpose.

You'll know if you are dealing with unfinished business when you are pulled back into a scenario that feels familiar and yet unresolved, or where you feel 'oh no, here we go again, I thought I'd dealt with that'. You need to be clear that both sides know when something is indeed complete.

- **Work and vocational karma**

Although career choices may seem to be random, or based on family expectation, they may relate to karma, especially as nowadays the possibilities to move away from your family roots are endless. The karma of work arises from previous employment or vocations, past behaviour, ethical decisions or choices made. Previous lack of integrity, for instance, could manifest as someone who, in this life, has a business partner who commits fraud. A factory owner whose working practices caused many accidents could reincarnate as someone who had a great concern for safe working practices.

Positive work karma creates skills and vocations in the present life. Edgar Cayce frequently gave career guidance based on a past life. He told someone who had once been in charge of a king's wardrobe, to find a job connected with fabric and costume as this would use his natural talents. There are several sub-sections of work related karma:

- **Technological Karma**

The karma of technology stems from having had to make ethical decisions about the use, or misuse, of technology in the past. It can also apply to having fought against the introduction of new technology – especially when this would have been beneficial to humankind. So, for instance, in regression Wilfred went back to being part of a Luddite group who went around the country smashing up the new mill machines which were taking over people's jobs. He told me that his present life work involved retraining people who had been made redundant. He taught them computer skills as these were the most likely to be required long term. Wilfred had gained his own computer skills after he lost his job as a printer. Whilst being retrained to use the new automated technology, Wilfred 'felt like a machine, there was no skill or soul in the work anymore, I wanted to smash it up' and so he became a teacher of others to help them find their way in this 'alien landscape'.

Technological karma can relate to all periods in history but often involves industrial and technological revolutions and their effects on modern life. It can also occur with someone who misused or was abused by technology and now finds it difficult to adapt to modern technology. Someone who, in a past life, had been severely injured by machinery may have an in-built fear and gravitate towards more artistic or soul-based work, for example.

- **Vocational Karma**

Vocational karma is an opportunity to capitalise on past skills and abilities. In vocational karmic work skills are carried over from another incarnation. A soul who has been a doctor may bring into the present life the urge to heal. If the previous incarnation was more than two or three hundred years ago knowledge of herbal medicine will probably be present as well and could lead to an interest in pharmacology or complementary therapies. A former monk or nun could feel that they still had a vocation, a musician could heed the urge to continue with the music, or a painter to paint. Alchemists return as scientists, psychotherapists or workshop facilitators, healers into various forms of the healing profession.

I did a karmic reading for a doctor who asked me to look at why he had become a doctor despite coming from a family of engineers. 'It was something I had to do', Thomas wrote. I saw him as having been a doctor in Edinburgh in the nineteenth century. A doctor who used corpses so that he could study the mechanism for the movement of blood around the body, dissecting out the heart, arteries and veins in his search for understanding – and who faced considerable repercussions in that life when the source of his research was made public. In another life, he had been a barber-surgeon – practising blood-letting. He was connected to a factory where lead was used to make paint and child labour was employed. He tried to deal with the consequences of environmental pollution which had come about, he surmised, through some kind of poison in the water. This made him exceedingly unpopular with the factory owners. Unbeknown to me, in his present work Thomas specialised in diseases of children's blood. He was particularly interested in environmental factors and their effect – especially that of air-borne lead near to major roads. Clearly he had carried his past life interests forward. Thomas also carried some of the conflict forward. The resistance in England towards his research work on environmental factors was so strong that he had to go to America to find recognition.

Edgar Cayce did a number of vocational readings. He told a man that he had spent many lives working on frescoes for temples, law courts and seats of government. He advised him to take up architecture once he had left art school and to 'combine the modernistic with the Phoenician and Egyptian'. The man did as he was advised and became a leading fresco artist. In another reading, a young woman was advised to give up being a telegraph operator and to take up commercial art as she had been a competent artist in several former lives. Not only did she become a highly successful commercial artist but she also 'transformed her personality in the process'.

Cayce also traced how a series of lives can interact to bring someone to the highest expression of their vocational karma. He told a successful New York arranger and composer that he had had four incarnations which were especially relevant to his present life work. In one, he had been a teacher in New York responsible for introducing music classes to the school curriculum; in the second he had been a German wood carver who made musical instruments; in the third he had been 'jester' to the court of king Nebuchanezzar, and in the fourth he had been in the temples of Egypt working with music. In his present life, his insistence on perfect tone in instruments arose from the German incarnation. His strongly developed sense of fun and wit came from the jester incarnation and his musical abilities from the two other lives.

• **The karma of place**
While this is not strictly a personal karma, just as families, countries and races have their own karma, so too do places and a soul may choose to incarnate because of that karma. Physical locations are powerfully affected by their karmic history. Sites of ancient battles or former sacred spaces in particular still carry an imprint of the events that took place there, although other places may well do the same. People who are sensitive to such things can pick up a psychic resonance regardless of how long ago they occurred. The spirits of those who should have passed on, or guardians of the land, may still remain in place. Karma of place can affect those who live there, whether or not they have set the karma in motion.

Dr Motoyama had a visit from a woman whose son had become schizophrenic and been hospitalised. Before hearing her story, Dr

Motoyama had seen her enter his meditation centre, followed by a 'ghastly-looking warrior'. He saw that the tumuli in which the samurai had been buried had been defaced and scattered. The woman's father had bought the field in which it lay, and dug it up to make a paddy field. This act was quickly followed by a rise in the number of psychologically disturbed people in the family and in the village nearby.

According to the woman's brother, the previous owners of the field had been known as 'the family of ruin' because anyone who bought anything from them ended up in trouble. Dr Motoyama prayed that the soul of the warrior would find rest. A week later, the woman's son was released from hospital, well enough to come home. Dr Motoyama was convinced that, at last, the spirit of the warrior had been relieved of his suffering.[11]

Taking over a site formerly consecrated to a different purpose can have karmic repercussions – and may entice to them someone who can do the necessary karmic healing – but other sites may carry 'good karma', the people who settle there enjoying great prosperity or spiritual inspiration.

If you've lived somewhere that feels 'cursed', 'fated', 'haunted', or 'blessed', then you'll understand how the karma of place has operated in your life. It may be that you have incarnated there to heal the underlying karma through earth healing, spirit release or other means. It may also be that the karma of the place resonates with your own karma and is helping you to move forward in life – although in a difficult and traumatic fashion if the place seems cursed or in a benevolent way if the place is blessed.

Karmic Answers

There are certain questions that arise time and again and in this section you may find the answers to your burning questions or to those which have occurred to you from time to time.

Vocational frustrations

People often ask why they've not been able to follow their chosen career. Even in the modern world of opportunity, it is not always possible to follow a vocation. Lack of finance or education may interfere, as can physical characteristics or temperamental unsuitability. It may not be appropriate for the soul to continue with previous work, although there may be a strong urge to do so. It may be time to move onto other things, to develop talents in a different area. But there may be underlying causes which are much less obvious. There are cases in the Cayce files where vocational choices were unable to be fulfilled and the subjects turned to Cayce for guidance as to why. In his view, such 'vocational frustrations' arose out of 'spiritual defects' which needed to be corrected and which would not have been overcome had the person followed their vocation.

In one such example Cayce read for an extraverted, highly talkative woman who had an aggressive, pushy nature. Her short, squat body combined with difficult family circumstances made it impossible to fulfil her ambition to be an actress so she entered the world of business. Cayce identified her as an entertainer during the American Revolution who had sacrificed personal principles to achieve social status and a luxurious lifestyle. Her ability to communicate freely and her out-going personality had passed into the present life, together with a tendency to talk people into doing what she wanted but Cayce said that, in the other life, she had used her gifts 'without spiritual insight' and, therefore, she had been frustrated in putting her undoubted dramatic talent to use. She was specifically warned to ensure that, in the present life, she did not put her 'expressive gifts' to work without supporting them with spiritual understanding. The inference was that, if she did, something worse would befall her. As compensation for her past behaviour, and to bring out the best in herself she was advised to use her talents in storytelling for children or the disadvantaged. In this way, she would use her gifts unselfishly for the good of others and balance out her karma. Cayce frequently advised, 'determine your ideal, your inner life goal, and seek to accomplish it'.

There are occasions when it is not appropriate to continue a past skill at a vocational level, but it can still be expressed as a hobby. Many people say that they find this frustrating and in which case they may be better employed sharing their talent by teaching others. It may also be that the opportunity to do what one loves or is impelled to do arises after other soul lessons have been learned or karmic consequences balanced out. Many women have needlework skills that were developed in former lives but an elderly man was surprised to find that he had an innate talent for tapestry work. In his past lives, he had been a woman who supervised the making of tapestries for a large castle. Many other people enjoy wood carving and similar abilities which have been their way of earning a living in the past.

Sometimes abilities from two lives collide or come together in harmony. Cayce gives the example of a banker whose past lives gave him considerable abilities in the financial field, which he chose to develop in the present life. He was, however, an avid baseball fan and ran a baseball training club in his spare time. Cayce traced this back to his having been the manager of the state games in Roman times.

Hobbies may become so absorbing that they lead to full time employment as life develops. Another man Cayce read for was involved with gems as a hobby initially, whilst serving in the navy and then as full time occupation when he retired. When Cayce looked at his past lives, he had been a trader on several occasions and dealt in precious stones. He had supplied stones for priests' vestments and so understood their religious significance; and he appreciated them as objects of great beauty that would appeal to collectors. Cayce told him that despite this, he had never really recognized their true value. In his present incarnation, he was urged to comprehend how the vibrations gems gave off could cure disease and so on. (This was long before crystal healing came back into fashion). After his reading, the man devoted the remainder of his life to studying the esoteric properties of gemstones.

Disease as a way of balancing out karma

One of the most frequently asked questions is whether an illness is karmic. Diseases can be tools which the soul uses in its growth towards a greater state of perfection, as in soul intention, but they may also have a balancing function. Rudolf Steiner in his 'spiritual science' suggests that certain diseases are taken on by a soul as a way of balancing out former actions or tendencies, and offering opportunities for developing new strengths. Steiner's belief is supported by reports from hundreds of regressions carried out around the world. Time and again a soul will look for the karmic cause of a disease or condition only to find that it is something they have taken on as a learning situation (see Part 3). Nevertheless, both can be true. The dis-ease may be karmic, and the condition may have been taken on for soul growth. Steiner asserts that 'in karma also lies the curability or incurability of a disease'.[12] In this view, an illness is not only the result of past life events, it also has the karmic aim of enabling the soul to grow and to fulfil certain objectives.

So, it is Steiner's contention that the soul in the present life carries an antipathy towards certain past life behaviours – an antipathy imprinted in the interlife during a life review. Steiner believed that 'forces' imprinted in that state would attract the disease *and* provide the means of overcoming it. In self-healing, the soul would 'lay aside what was a defect in character in a previous incarnation'.

What lies behind chronic disease?
Many cases of chronic illness are a complex mixture of many factors. Some arise as we have seen from soul choice and others from karma. Marguerite, for instance, suffered from a disease that incorporated amongst other things family karma, personal karma including a 'karmic treadmill' and ingrained expectations, redemptive karma, and a desire to grow spiritually.

When Marguerite first contacted me she was paralysed from a 'rare, intractable, complex and defeating familial condition, with no known cause, cure or name'. She expressed 'a burning desire to end this misery', not through suicide but by healing. Marguerite was the seventh known generation to carry a rare, genetically transmitted disease. Her matriarchal family interaction was tight. It appeared that the women in the family had together incarnated again and again with this condition manifesting in each generation.

Marguerite had been taught to view herself as a victim of the family curse from a young age and had the karmic memory of living at least two previous lives with the disease. Her present life hadn't been easy. Her husband had died just before her daughter was born – a karmic expectation that she held from past lives. It was also clear that in her past incarnations Marguerite hadn't felt comfortable in a physical body.

She used meditation and flower remedies to heal the emotional trauma of past and present lives, and worked to befriend her body. Two years later, her paralysis was gone and she was able to travel abroad to see a specialist in her condition. Marguerite founded an association for fellow sufferers, to give hope and pursue the possibility of a cure; and worked on healing herself so that her own daughter would have a better future. Many shamans say that by healing oneself, it is possible to heal seven generations back and seven forward. It was Marguerite's sincere desire that this should so be, and that the spiritual insights and qualities she found would be put to work to help other sufferers (see also Part 3).

What if an illness cannot be healed?

Sometimes an illness appears to have been healed but a relapse occurs. Or, the disease proves to be intransigent and ingrained. Looked at from a karmic perspective, if the illness is chronic and cannot be healed, then it may be that the soul needs to have that particular experience for a longer time, the karma cannot be wriggled out of or it is part of the soul's plan (see Part 3). Although some improvement can be brought about by diligent 'work' (karmic balancing) a complete cure may be impossible where an underlying karmic debt, cause or consequence is particularly strong.

Edgar Cayce brought up an interesting point when he asked 'why does the entity want to be healed?' According to the reading he was doing at the time, the person concerned wanted to be healed so that he could satisfy his physical appetites. He was warned that unless there was a sincere change of heart, mind and intent no more help could be given. Spiritual purpose had to be realigned also, and it was up to him whether he accepted, or rejected, the advice.

The man was young, 34, and suffering from multiple sclerosis. In an initial reading he had been told that, whilst his condition was a karmic one, he should not lose hope as help was available if he was willing to accept it. He was exhorted to change his mental outlook, removing all hatred and malice from his consciousness. He was then given a course of treatment to follow. A year later, he contacted Cayce again saying there had been an immediate improvement which was maintained for four months before a serious relapse occurred. With Cayce in trance, it became clear that whilst the man had followed the physical prescription, the spiritual one had been overlooked. He was told 'so long as there is hate, malice, injustice, jealousy, so long as there is anything within at variance with patience, long suffering, brotherly love, kindness, gentleness, there cannot be a healing of the condition of this body'. In other words, he hadn't got to grips with the lessons his dis-ease was offering him.

The same scenario occurs in many karmic illnesses. The person wants to be healed so that life will 'return to normal', which entirely misses the point that the dis-ease is making. What was normal is no longer appropriate. Changes have to be made at the spiritual level – and often at the physical as well. Unless the person is willing to do whatever is necessary, a permanent cure cannot be effected while the underlying karmic condition will remain. If the illness is designed to bring to the surface patience and tolerance and it brings up bitterness and intolerance, those feelings will ensure the condition remains. Similarly if someone then wants to go back to a life of excess and indulgence, and the karmic cause was over-indulgence (physical or emotional), the cause will be replayed and relapse will occur.

Notwithstanding, there is a danger here that the soul – or other people – might be in blame mode. If the soul blames itself, it does not understand the perfect fairness and dispassionate nature of karma. If it turns to self pity rather than compassion for itself, a new karmic chain will begin. If other people blame, then they are in judgement mode and no one in incarnation can possibly understand all the reasons why someone takes on an illness. Karma is not a question of punishment or reward it is a question of finding karmic balance. That this may entail changing attitudes, beliefs and actions could bring about a karmic cure but there may be a deeper, underlying motive. The soul could be practicing redemptive karma or offering a lesson to someone else. And, in any case, cure does not equal 'making it better'. The karmic condition may be cured without the physical ailment improving, if that is the karmic necessity. The soul will only understand the full ramifications when it returns to the spirit world.

And if the illness ends in death?
Western medicine tends to look on death as a failure. A cure has not been effected, but karmically, and from the soul's point of view, the opposite can be true. Death means enough has been done. The karma could have been balanced out by *the experience of the illness*, not by getting rid of it. The cure lies in the qualities developed by and through overcoming dis-ease at a spiritual level. As Steiner points out, if the illness or condition has been taken on in order to learn or to develop certain qualities, and if the soul has found a point where the physical body and other 'forces' do not disturb it, equilibrium has been reached. There is nothing more to be gained from the illness or condition. The person could recover but the remainder of

that life may not then offer any more opportunities for karmic or soul growth. The soul may, in that case, choose death so that it can move onto another life in which the lessons can be developed further. So there could be karmic or soul reasons why an illness can be cured, or not, and why someone dies at an early age. This is not a punishment, it is a reward.

Short life spans
An issue that is often raised is why some people have short life spans. Is this a punishment? Or is it intentional? From regression work both I and other people have carried out to the interlife, it is clear that souls may have widely different reasons for undertaking a short life. Souls may have had an extremely traumatic death in the last life, or may have committed suicide. They may then choose to have a 'peaceful interlude', a short life which enables them to gently acclimatise to the idea of being in incarnation again or even simply a gentle interuterine experience that allows them to feel earth vibrations without taking on independent life. A soul who committed suicide in the past may choose to live out the time remaining from the 'interrupted life'. Another soul might be on a karmic mission and, once that mission is completed, they may decide then to return to the spirit world.

Some children may come to bring their parents a lesson. Michael Newton reports a case where a client had died from a birth defect in a previous life. During the regression, he was asked 'what was the purpose of your life ending when you were only a few days old?' His reply was that the lesson had been for his parents, not for him and that was why he had elected to come back with them for a short time. Apparently, in another life, those parents had abused a child who eventually died. In their next incarnation, despite being extremely loving parents, they had needed to experience the loss of a child they desperately wanted. In other situations, through caring with great love and compassion for a dying child, parents develop within themselves qualities that they wished to build in, or they support a child while he or she goes through an experience they need.

From my experience, it is virtually impossible to identify the reasons why someone has a short lifespan without a karmic and soulplan reading being done by someone who is able to see further than the present life or by regressing a parent to the interlife to reveal the underlying cause and the soul contracts involved. And, it is clear that a number of children who die 'early' then return to the family once again.

Karmic or genetic inheritance?

It is clear from the experiences of people who, in regression, enter the interlife that a soul may chose to incarnate into a specific family which has a karmic inheritance that matches what the soul needs to experience. This karmic inheritance may be genetic or attitudinal, concerned with race or privilege – or the lack of it. The inheritance may also be a talent or ability, or position that is passed down through the family. It is also clear that, in some cases, a soul needs to experience a particular situation as reprisal or restitution for past actions and, therefore, incarnates into a family that has a specific karmic resonance.

In this latter instance, the experience may not be so much a matter of choice as a karmic necessity or compulsion. Such a karmic inheritance can be at a genetic or emotional level – Dr Bruce Lipton describes DNA as a programme that goes into the computer (the cell membranes of the body), which may or may not run, and which will be affected by environmental factors external to the cell including thoughts, attitudes and beliefs. So, for example, if someone needed to experience illnesses such as haemophilia or Huntington's Chorea or to suffer from alcoholism or addiction then they would incarnate into a family that carried the gene responsible for those conditions. This gene provides a 'seed potential'. Given the right karmic conditions, the seed matures.

Not everyone within the family, however, would manifest the condition for which the genetic potential existed because their karmic pattern may not fit the 'profile' required for the seed to germinate. It may be their karma to live in a family where some members have the condition and others do not and, perhaps, to experience the uncertainty that such genetic issues can engender. They may need to make ethical choices such as whether, being a genetic carrier themselves, they should potentially pass this on to their children in turn. Many other karmic issues arise in families with genetically transmitted diseases.

Skills and abilities often appear to travel through families. Musicians may be made with training, but they are often born with an in-built gift carried forward from other lives. However, they may need help to manifest their talent and part of that assistance may be genetic. It may

ically provable, but it has been postulated there is such
ausical ear' which is inherited. It has a particular shape,
certain resonance when received by it. So, if someone
ausician, it would be wise to chose to incarnate in a family
which has the genetic blueprint for the physical construction of such
an ear. Similarly, they may need to inherit long, sensitive fingers rather
than short pudgy ones which will not have the right span to reach the
notes. Careful planning allows karmic intention and ability to flower.

Nevertheless, there may be other reasons that someone chooses a
particular family. It is not always a matter of heredity. The family may
be ideal in other ways. Newton reported a case of a man who, in the
interlife, explored his options for his next life. He decided that he would
incarnate in New York and be a musician. He was trying to decide
between two families. He thought that he would 'choose the dumpy
kid with a lot of talent'. He commented that the body would not have
the stamina that he had had in the life previous to that, but that he
would have money. Saying that he knew that this sounded grasping and
selfish, he explained that if he wanted to express the beauty of music and
give pleasure to himself and others, then he needed proper training and
supportive parents as otherwise, he was wise enough to know, he would
get sidetracked.

Biology and karma often interact. Cayce said on many occasions
that the glands of the body conveyed karma. The propensity for the
malfunctioning of certain organs or glands runs through families and may
create the 'breeding ground' for symbolic or attitudinal karma to flourish.
So a family which carried a history of heart diseases could allow a soul
with a record of hard-heartedness to manifest that attitude physically.

Similarly, a soul may incarnate into a family with a long history of
emotional or physical abuse. The soul would have the possibility of
being abused or abuser, but could also avoid either condition. Abuse
can arise out of a genetic propensity to conditions like alcoholism but
may also stem from destructive emotional experiences carried through
the family line. Violence, hatred and anger go together and endlessly
recreate themselves. An abused child often becomes an abuser. Many
abused children – and adults – confuse love with violence. They see
violence as a way of showing 'love'. After all, it was the only attention
they got or the abuse brought on such an orgy of guilt in the abuser that

they were then given considerable attention. If a soul has had difficulty in separating love and violence in the past, then it may incarnate again into an abusing family. However, if a soul wants to understand how abuse arises, it also may choose to become an abuser or someone who is abused for the duration of one or more lives. Healing that abuse then becomes an option, as do forgiveness and the operation of the karma of grace.

An angry soul might be attracted by an abusive family as the opportunity is there for the playing out of that anger. Nevertheless, a soul who has accumulated much fear may also be drawn towards an abusing family. Its worst fears would be realized if it became the victim of violence – and this may be the way in which a soul chooses to overcome fear. On the other hand, someone who has been an abuser in other lives may need to experience how it feels to be abused. Karmic choices – or compulsions – are complex and difficult to assess.

'Inheritance' could also work more subtly to create karmic conditions for the soul's growth. A young woman 'inherited' a tendency to intensely painful and prolonged menses. This left her isolated as she often had to stay in bed and her mother worked long hours when her own health allowed. But the isolation, and the endocrine disturbance, allowed the young woman to develop her psychic abilities at an early age. Reading was a solace to her and through this she developed her own creative writings abilities. Both talents had commenced in other lives but were honed and put to use during her present life. She became a children's writer who incorporated spiritual and psychological understanding into her work. Her family background, which might to some eyes have appeared difficult, actually allowed her karmic purpose to flourish.

People are often attracted to families whose emotional make-up matches their own past patterns. So, someone who is angry but who rarely shows this could be pulled towards a passive-aggressive family where, outwardly, things are 'nice' but, under the surface anger heaves and boils and is expressed in devious and, apparently, accidental ways. Another soul might have been attracted to that kind of family because of the surface 'niceness' – and had to face the karmic or soul consequences of those hidden emotions. This soul might have been the 'people pleaser' in another life and then had to face the consequences of being 'nice' rather than authentic. 'Niceness' can be a most untrustworthy quality and one that creates considerable karma.

For some people, it is not so much a question of family and race as of place carrying the karmic inheritance and we have already looked briefly at the karma of place. The earth has energies running through it and can carry the imprint of former events. There are minority groups, like the Druze of Southern Lebanon and Australian Aborigines, who believe they continually reincarnate within their own group or race. They carry not only their own individual karma but the collective karma of the group. This karma is continually being 'worked', each member of the group contributing to its continuation or its balancing out according to their actions in each life. They may also be carrying forward the group purpose.

Some people respond to the vibrations of a place. They may have unfinished business there or simply feel more comfortable in 'familiar' surroundings. T.E. Lawrence, for example, was never at home in England. He did not fit into his family or his society. The only time he enjoyed school was when he studied the Crusades and the military strategies involved. But when he went to Arabia it was a very different matter. He felt he had 'come home'. He became a military leader, said by some to be a genius. It is suggested by Gina Cerminara that, in returning to Arabia, he was completing a life lived sometime earlier as an Arab military strategist who died before his work was done. The place triggered his abilities and allowed him to flourish because, at a soul level, it was his home. Certainly when Lawrence was forced to return to England, he became deeply depressed and soon died in an 'accident'.

Karma or soul-planning?

Many people blame themselves because their child is not 'perfect'. A couple whose child is born with a physical or mental impairment may view the birth as a disaster. They may feel that 'God's punishment' is being inflicted on them – or on the child – and find it impossible to handle the resultant tensions. They will not necessarily seek out what is best for the child and often blame each other. Such bitter marriages rarely last and one parent often takes on the job of caring for the child. Even when seeming to accept the situation, they could be ignoring its deeper meaning – and the opportunities it brings for personal and family development. Another couple might do all they could for the child, but want to turn the child into a 'perfect-child' instead of accepting the child as already perfect in his or her own way. Such a couple would, most probably, be guided by 'experts' who told them what to do. This could involve abandoning the child to 'its fate' or trying to force the child to conform to the 'norm'. Some parents of such children fight for their child, especially for their 'rights' or to get them education or treatment so hard and so continuously that they don't know when to stop fighting or when to stand back and let their child take responsibility for their own life. Yet another couple would do all they could to bring the best possible quality of life to that child, allowing the child's full potential to emerge whilst accepting and loving the child as he or she is, treasuring him or her as a unique individual. This couple would perhaps look at more unorthodox methods of helping the child and seek ways in which they themselves would grow through the situation. They would experience the child as a gift rather than a punishment, a beloved child.

As we have already seen soul choice may involve choosing a difficult incarnation. A learning disability or physical impairment can be the incarnating soul's choice. The soul may be offering a gift to the parents so that they can grow and practise compassion or tolerance, or it may be an experience the soul itself has decided to undertake. It is impossible to assess from the perspective of earth whether such a situation is retributive, regressive or growth-inducing – although the birthchart interaction does offer clues. The impairment could be the result of lifetimes of ingrained attitudes or thought patterns, or a physical injury carrying forward from another life; or a seeming accident of birth. The same applies to many other situations.

Getting off the karmic wheel

So, is it possible to get off the karmic wheel without having to reach a high spiritual state of enlightenment first? Well, it's clear that a 'positive', constructive and magnanimous approach to life can balance out previous 'deficits'. So, karma can be changed. But it should be borne in mind that karma is ultimately about balance. Nature abhors a vacuum, and so does karma. It's no use simply eliminating reaction or karmic consequence, a positive response must also be cultivated. In some spiritual systems, emotion is something to be 'overcome' but it is more harmonious to be a person who stands within their emotions, experiencing them but not overwhelmed by them, for instance. Recognising emotional stimuli and mental triggers assist in getting off the karmic treadmill but new pathways need to be initiated. Letting go of attachment needs the balance of dispassionate non-attachment, as otherwise repression sets in.

In-built attitudes and prejudices can be overcome, and beneficial attitudes developed. Inappropriate acts can cease, and actions taken that are long overdue. A new pattern of thinking can be created, and spiritual practices incorporated into life. Avoiding excess in any direction is wise, whether it be towards the spiritual or the material. In this way, 'meritorious' karma will be cultivated and the soul will move closer to its goal of spiritual evolution.

Of course, acts of kindness and compassion and the like cannot be done on the basis of storing up positive karma for the future. That kind of motive will not create positive karma or soul evolution. Such an act has to be unselfish, and the soul is often unaware of having clocked up the 'good karma' in the first place until hindsight is applied.

In *The Last Days of Socrates*, Plato has the great philosopher offer his advice for ensuring a good future for the soul. He says that 'a man must abandon bodily pleasures and adornments as foreign to his purpose and likely to do more harm than good'. If this man 'has devoted himself to the pleasures of acquiring knowledge; and so by decking his soul not with a borrowed beauty but with its own – with self-control, and goodness, and courage, and liberality, and truth – [he] has fitted himself to await his journey to the next world'.[13] A Buddhist would recognise this teaching as one that could bring enlightenment and liberation from the wheel of rebirth. Freedom from desire and the cultivation of positive qualities are universally agreed to lead at the very least to a good rebirth and at best to cessation of reincarnation.

Although karma and reincarnation do not usually feature in Islam, the Bektashi Sufi sect accept rebirth, especially into animals. Their founder Haci Bektas Veli lived during the thirteenth century. Amongst his teachings were several intended to guide the soul to live a good life and to create a positive future:

> *Even if you are hurt, don't hurt others.*
> *Be master of your deeds, words and passions that none may be harmed by them.*
> *The foundation of spiritual awareness is respect for others.*

The beauty of a man's soul is reflected in his speech.
Never demand from others what you find hard to give yourself.
Vilify no person and no people.
Only true learning leads the way from darkness.
Blessed are those whose lights dispel dark thoughts.
Never forget that even your enemy is human too.[14]

Tibetan Buddhists would add to this the practice of compassion for others which William Bloom calls compassionate witnessing. Unselfishness and small acts of kindness accumulate into a huge reserve of merit karma. Giving to others creates future abundance. When Jesus said: 'Do as you would be done by' he was giving practical advice for getting off the karmic wheel.

Part 3

Beyond Karma: Moving into Soul Choice

I am the enemy that you killed, my friend. I knew you in this dark.

Wilfred Owen, Strange Meeting

*A*s I've already said, not everything is karmic. If you've read through this book so far and have not yet felt 'yes, that's it, that's the answer' you may find more insight in the soulplan that results from interlife planning – which is based on your soul's choice not your karma. I have been present at many planning meetings taking place in the interlife or 'Bardo' as the Tibetan Buddhists call it. Sometimes my presence has been made possible by accompanying someone from their last death through the interlife decision to come into incarnation once again. At other times I have read the Akashic Record of that planning meeting when doing 'far memory' astrological readings. Initially it puzzled me that a soul's purpose could be so at odds with previous karmic experiences – and that members of a loving soul group could become the instruments of trauma and dissension in the present life. But as I attended more of these meetings, it became clear that souls could put aside their karma if appropriate and that loving souls would often volunteer to help a member of the soul group go through some extremely difficult experiences for the sake of their soul evolution.

Equally, it was clear that people often chose a life to experience the effect of something they had perpetrated in another life in order not only to balance their karma but to grow their soul. Such a decision may cause considerable discomfort before it is resolved, especially when the underlying reason for the experience is not immediately accessed. A woman who had been strongly racist in a past life, for instance, fell head over heels in love with and married a black guy on the spur of the moment. She faced considerable racism. The 'love' had quickly fizzled out and her husband had left her before the mixed-race child was born. Her relationship with the child – the result of a soul contract with a soul

who also needed for his own reasons to experience this kind of abuse –
was extremely difficult until she realised what lay behind the contract.
Once she adjusted her own attitude, her relationship with her son healed
and she was able to support him in his journey.

For the longest time, however, I seemed to be the only person
exploring the interlife. Of course, I wasn't the only person working this
realm but those who wrote about it back then seemed to do so only in
the context of karma and breaking karmic patterns. In *Life Between Life*,
written in the late 80s, for instance, Dr Joel Whitton and Joe Fisher, who
use hypnotic regression techniques, commented on one of their cases:

> *Ben understood at once that by acting with restraint towards his father*
> *in the crucial incident with the carving knife, he had wrestled a karmic*
> *predicament into submission.*[1]

This seemed to be a good example of karmic process but, comparing
it to Julie Chime's experience below, I wondered, was soul choice also
involved? In other lives Ben had apparently killed people who had
treated him badly and in the present life was brutalized by his father. In
his youth he had snatched up a carving knife intending to kill his drunken
father but stopped in response to an 'inner voice'. When he explored
his interlife planning, Ben had discovered that he was learning how
to remain calm under extreme provocation and that his vicious father
was someone with whom he had previously had 'a series of antagonistic
relationships'. There was however no sense in the interlife of Ben's father
being a loving soul group member who had volunteered for the task. As
the authors said, there was still much to be understood. Julie Chimes,
on the other hand, when attacked by a woman wielding a carving knife
found a much greater part of herself and her life's work (see page 192).

In 1994 Michael Newton published *Journey of the Soul*, his record of
taking souls into the interlife to explore a 'curriculum for the soul' that
was planned there. Newton taught others how to take clients into the
interlife to assess their soul's purpose and his work was taken up with
enthusiasm. By 2007 when Robert Schwartz invited participation in an
ongoing study of pre-birth planning, this idea had taken deep root in the
consciousness of regression therapists everywhere.

When I read Rob Schwartz's book *Courageous Souls* it was a lightbulb
moment. Here was someone writing about what my clients had

encountered time after time: conscious planning and roles undertaken by the soul group. Rob also emphasized personal responsibility and soul choice as a route to spiritual evolution and holistic consciousness. My only question was why Rob had used only mediums and channels to gain the interlife information. His answer was that, at the time, it was the only method he knew. Once the book appeared he made contact with hypnotherapists and others undertaking this work, but I was the first karmic astrologer. I was struck by how many statements Rob made in his book that I use all the time. Insights that have arisen directly out of my interlife work:

- A soul chooses 'lack of' what is most wanted in order to understand and appreciate what having it means.
- Pain is temporary, the resultant wisdom is eternal.
- Souls use forks in the road as a means of growth.
- Illness is dis-ease, the final manifestation of emotional or mental difficulties.
- Blocked energy creates dis-ease.
- The healing journey is one of remembering (or re-membering).
- There is no fault or punishment.
- Soulmates are the core team not just the person you fall in love with.
- We can exercise freewill to create challenges that were not part of prebirth planning.
- Time is an aspect of the physical dimension.
- Time is a web, not a line.
- Little is as it seems.

As we shall see, a superficial reading of the living out of soul choices rarely reveals what is beneath. There are times when I desperately want to contact people and ask if we can explore their interlife choices because the most amazing things come from very unpromising beginnings. For instance, when I switched on the radio the other day, a photographer was describing his childhood experience of extremely difficult family circumstances, in which they lived in dire poverty in two rooms with no inside plumbing or facilities, and he received no education. As he said: 'an ideal place from which to have to escape and make a new life'. He volunteered for the Air Force, ironically spending much of his time in a barbed wire fenced encampment in Egypt, which was just as much a prison as his home had been. But that, and a spell in Nairobi during the Mau-mau troubles, gave him a taste for exotic travel.

On his return home he took a picture of a family member who had been murdered. He sold that photograph to a paper and was on his way to a career as an outstanding war photographer – who in his latter years now photographs landscapes that offers a balm to the soul. But even as a war photographer he was always conscious of the humanity and suffering of those he photographed – always, as he said, bearing in mind 'that sad little boy from North London with no education'. His photographs brought home to those who would otherwise never see it both the horror of war and its moments of great courage and human interaction. He also underwent captivity and isolation. His was a life of compassionate witnessing and recording of the depths and breadth of the human condition. His life could be the result of soul choice in the interlife in that he deliberate chose a family background that would impel him out into a different world. What sounded to me more like karmic memory was his comment that he always took a box of *Redybrek* with him wherever he went because he had a dread of waking up hungry.[2]

I am fortunate to be present when someone explores the soul choices made in the interlife and gains a great insight. I had known Ruth, for instance, for over thirty years. Abrupt and to the point, fiercely self-reliant and stubbornly independent, she prided herself on being, as she said, 'a tough cookie'. A talented musician, she'd had a high flying job but had to retire due to ill health so she moved to the country and explored her 'alternative interest' of astrology and, of course, her beloved music. But a recurrence of the heart condition that had taken her into retirement (literally a broken heart following the break up of a soulmate relationship in which she had been the dominant force) and drastic treatment to reduce the fluid build-up in her body also revealed that she had extensive breast cancer. She looked back at her relationships and the great losses in her life and seemed to come to terms with them, allowing herself to grieve and heal. When she had another heart attack she thought 'yippee, this is it, I'm off'. Ruth was unafraid of death, believing totally in reincarnation. The paramedic who revived her was surprised to find himself roundly cursed for having done so.

So, a very frail Ruth came to a workshop to ask 'why?' 'Why have I survived, what else do I have to learn?' As she went back into the interlife she discovered that, surprisingly, she had, in fact, incarnated to learn not to be so self-reliant. In other lives she had been overly independent, bossily pushing everyone else away and being the one who did things for others – things she thought they needed rather than what they asked for. Now it was time to learn how to receive, to be open to allowing others to help her and show their unconditional love for her through service. This was not the time for her to do it herself, in receiving she would also be giving. 'Oh gawd', groaned one of her friends who was also present, 'if she does that as thoroughly as she's done independence we're in for a tough time'. And so it proved. For six months, as her health rapidly deteriorated Ruth, finally, after a huge struggle, allowed herself to receive. As she did so, she became so much more loving. She learned that love is a reciprocal process. She was no longer afraid to show her love for people, nor afraid to allow them to demonstrate their love for her. Her transition to the spirit world was peaceful, in her sleep, simply slipping away into another world. Exactly as she'd wished it to be. Her soul was satisfied that she had completed her purpose for this life. Death was her reward.

Cancer does seem to be one of the great soul learning experiences of life – for both those who have the dis-ease and those who are intimately involved. It appears to have an inextricable connection with anger, grief and acceptance, and the need to resolve unfinished business. It has been medically recognised that loss of a loved one can trigger cancer and the core loss is often in childhood. Death of a sibling or parent is something many children have to face and, in the not so distant past, was not something that was discussed. I have met many people who were never told that the parent or sibling who was so ill had died and who were sent to school the next day while the body was removed. They were not told until after the funeral had taken place – if they were told at all, so never had the opportunity to say goodbye or to grieve properly. As the parents were grief stricken, their own needs for love and understanding went unmet. Nor did they have an opportunity to express their anger at not having been told about the death nor had the chance to say goodbye. There is also a belief that cancer, and especially breast or oesophageal tumours, have as an underlying cause a tendency to over-compromise and not get things 'off your chest'. As Elizabeth put it: 'my mum stewed and fretted about stuff because she couldn't confront it. My father was pretty fragile emotionally, having had several mental breakdowns, and he relied on Mum to be strong for them both. She was in an impossible situation where she felt she couldn't disagree with him – he could be pretty arrogant – but inside she was raging and frustrated. In effect she was completely incapable of expressing anger'. Elizabeth realised that although her mother was incredibly strong to deal with such powerful and destructive emotions, it was likely that in doing so she had possibly created the situation for the breast cancer to develop which eventually claimed her life. She had also set in place a family pattern of non-confrontation. 'Sometimes you could cut the atmosphere with a knife'. Elizabeth knew this was a pattern that had to be healed in her own life as she grew older and started to attract forceful men who tried to block her communication; however hard it was, she had to find the courage to speak up so as not to follow the same path as her mother.

Amelia, who developed aggressive breast cancer as she came up to her sixtieth birthday, realised that in order to heal she first had to contact and release her anger and then had to speak to her mother as a way of healing herself and her relationship with her mother – who had been unable to face her young son's death and had completely withdrawn from her remaining child, never admitting to the loss.

Breast cancer is often to do with issues of nurturing and soul nourishment and can sometimes occur when the link between mother and daughter is too overpowering, when too much is demanded or given and the breast says 'no more', separation has to occur and if it's not by death then it can be by loss of the breast. Laura, who story is below, had to have a mastectomy a year after her mother's death. It seemed to be the final resolution of the long family saga – her daughter had become estranged after years of neediness and karmic entanglement, just when Laura's mother's own extensive cancer had been diagnosed. That cancer brought healing and resolution between Laura and her mother, and Laura's cancer between Laura and her daughter but, although Laura was able to finally express her anger to her mother, she was unable to do so with her daughter. When we spoke to Laura's higher self about the loss of the breast, we were told that the daughter had, etherically speaking, been clamped to it so strongly and it had absorbed so much of the toxic relationship between the mothers and daughters that it had to go. This was a deep lesson about letting go and the difference between unconditional love – which loves and accepts but does not allow invasion or depletion by the other person – and the kind of co-dependent, needy, greedy, grasping at support that often passes for love but which facilitates one or both of the parties remaining mired in their own karmic patterns. But it was also a lesson in expressing feelings such as anger and in not seeing it as 'unacceptable'. Laura let go and forgave so completely that she needed no other treatment and healed rapidly.

Another woman, Lucy, said that as a child she had lost her beloved brother to cancer, her mother to grief, and her father to alcohol. She, however, was given the gift of knowing her father in the last eighteen months of his life when he had to stop drinking because he had oesophageal cancer. This particular cancer often has at its root unspoken words and feelings that have been swallowed down again and again. Lucy said that before he died the aggressive, bullying man she had known right through her childhood suddenly became an intelligent, funny man again who was able to express his love for her and his grief and anger at the loss of his son. This led her to her life's work, preparing those who would be left behind, especially children, to deal with loss of a parent or sibling. She worked to make the last days, weeks and hours happy ones, full of loving memories and deep sharing which included all that had been left unsaid. Lucy also brought up her own family in a very different way to what she herself had experienced, creating a haven of warmth and love in a stable household where everything could be discussed. She is someone who radiates love and healing to anyone who meets her and her soul light shines bright.

One of the most important things that the idea of soul choice brings to us is that apparent tragedy can then become part of the plan and enrich the lives of others. Years ago I met a woman whose young daughter had just died. The child had been in a coma for a week. Her mother was a natural psychic and kept seeing her child 'alive and well and brimming over with joy'. The child kept reminding her mother that this was all part of the plan and asked her to please let her go. Through her death she would be released to act as a guide for the souls of children who passed unexpectedly to spirit, and her mother would be the medium through which the children could communicate with their grieving parents. They would still be together, but not physically. The mother did as she was asked and became a full-time medium and grief counsellor who helped numerous families.

Many of the answers to questions upon which I have been musing arrive when I switch on the radio. So I was not surprised when, having put out the thought that I needed some more positive examples of how apparent tragedy can lead to soul evolution and practical service to humanity, I heard the story of Ron and Pauline Friend on 'The Call' on BBC Radio 4.[3] Ron and Pauline Friend's son Martin was one of eight people murdered in Uganda by Hutu rebels from neighbouring Rwanda while on a trip to see mountain gorillas. Sixteen people had been taken hostage, eight were released and eight killed. There was no apparent reason for the arbitrary and random division of the group into who would survive and who would not. Martin's parents said that, very quickly after receiving the news, they realised that anger and bitterness was a pointless reaction to the killing. They would never know exactly what happened or who was responsible. But, as they saw it, they had a choice about how to respond. As their son had intended to climb Mount Kilimanjaro on his trip, his father did it himself the following year and raised £130,000 for the charity Children in Crisis. Becoming more involved in the charity's work, the Friends went out to Africa. There they realised that the answer to the problems in that area were to educate the young, as most people had been denied the opportunity to read and write due to the ongoing war situation.

Pauline Friend said that she had met one woman who had lost four sons and that, while she couldn't say she was yet at a point where she forgave, she nevertheless felt she could move on. The couple's way of moving on was to found a school in the area in memory of their son. By his death, Martin changed the life not only of his parents but gave hope to hundreds of children.

This is in direct contrast to another woman I knew whose son was murdered at around the same time. She made his room and her entire life into a shrine to grief and has never moved on. If she could have embraced the idea of soul choice and soul evolution, she could have let the past go and be released into new soul growth.

When someone is murdered and especially where the killer is never 'brought to justice', or when you are in an abusive relationship, you have a choice. You may feel like a victim or you may become strong. Your soul may have wanted to learn to give up the right to hurt or see punished someone who has hurt you, in other words to forgive and let go. In the soul's eyes, justice doesn't always need to be seen to be done. What is needed is to see the gift in the experience and put that to work in your ever evolving, everyday life.

Soul Contracts: a covenant for life?

I was the soldier, you in the cell
You were in prison, I was your guard
I loved you, I shot you, to save you from hell…
I had to stop the horror to follow
My love for you saved you, by ending your life.
My darling, I had to, you had once been my wife.

Jewelle St James, Jude

The extract above is from a poem channelled to Canadian author Jewelle St James during her search for her past incarnations. It follows on from her 'soulmate' experience with John Baron (see *The Soulmate Myth*) in which Jewelle was shown a past life in 17th century England in Petworth. In that life the man she loved died prematurely but promised to return to her. Jewelle was later to find that the details of that life had been revealed by her 'soulmate John Baron' to prepare her for revelations of a much more traumatic incarnation as a young girl who died in Auschwitz. *Jude* is the story of her soul group's incarnations and interactions, the soul contracts that held them together, and the healing they finally found.[4]

A soul contract is an agreement usually but not necessarily made willingly in the interlife. It may that the incarnating soul will undertake a specific task, in which case a contract has often been made that the higher self will keep the soul on track, or that one soul will interact with another in a specific way. However, it may also be an agreement that is carried over from a previous life or even from a previous interlife which has not been reconsidered or renegotiated before the present incarnation and which is no longer applicable. Soul contracts can also arise from pacts, promises and vows especially those such as 'I'll always love you/look after you/be there for you' as in Jewelle's case above. Such contracts can be positive and constructive or destructive and positive soul contracts that are not completed in one life may be unwittingly carried over to another and become destructive. Sometimes a soul contract appears to end in a destructive event, as in Jewelle's death in Auschwitz when she was shot by a young German soldier she had known earlier in that life but also in another life when he was her husband. He stepped in to save her from further horror and so it was actually a positive act by a member of her soul group.

Soul contracts are most often made with members of your soul group but not inevitably so – and you may find that members of your soul group are still trying to insist upon a contract being carried out that is no longer relevant to your purpose or appropriate to the life you have mapped out. Contracts that have passed their sell-by date or which are in direct contradiction to the intention of the present life lie behind many of the karmic conundrums that people endure as they compel certain behaviour no matter how much the soul may wish to override them. This is why soulplans sometimes fail despite all the good intentions they embody.

Do you have a soul contract or soul overlay?
- Do you feel you have a purpose that you are not fulfilling?
- Are you sure you've got a soul purpose but don't know what it is?
- Do you have an overwhelming urge to look after someone?
- Do you demand that someone looks after you?
- Does someone demand that you look after them?
- Do you feel you owe someone something?
- Do you think someone owes you something?
- Do you feel there's unfinished business/karma somewhere in your life?
- Do you feel like there's a hidden agenda?
- Do you feel you're on a mission/have a task to perform etc?
- Are you compulsive about certain things?
- Have you ever said 'it must be karma'?
- Do you repeat the same kind of patterns/relationships?
- Do you feel you have a soulmate?
- Do you yearn for one particular person as a resolution to all your problems?

If you answer yes to more than one or two of the above you most probably have a soul contract operating in your life. The question is, is that contract personal or does it involve someone else – and is it still relevant?

Exercise: ascertaining your soul contracts

In accessing the soulplan for the present life (page 22) you may already have come across several soul contracts but there may be more. This visualisation uses the same framework as attending the planning meeting but if you have not yet done this, please familiarise yourself with the preparation instructions on page 23.

Close your eyes and breathe gently, setting up a slow, unforced rhythm. Bring your attention deep into yourself and let any thoughts that are not relevant to the answers you seek to simply float past and go on their way.

Picture yourself in a sunny meadow, let yourself feel the grass beneath your feet, smell the flowers, feel a gentle breeze on your face. Enjoy this lovely place for a few minutes and then let your feet take your across the meadow to a building you can see in the distance.

As you open the door to this building, you will see a lift in front of you. Step into this lift and allow the doors to close. You will see a button marked 'contracts department'. Press this button and allow the lift to take you swiftly up to the level you need. As the doors open, your higher self will be standing waiting to greet you. Spend a few moments greeting your higher self.

Your higher self will then conduct you to the contracts department to show you the relevant soul contracts you have and explain things to you if necessary. The contracts may be presented in written or pictorial form. Study them and make sure that you fully understand all that they entail. If the contract is still relevant and appropriate for the current life, hand if back to your higher self. [If not, see the instructions below.]

Ask also that you be shown outdated and outgrown soul contracts that have passed their sell-by date and which may trip you up when putting your soulplan into action. Allow these overlays to be torn up or to be reframed into something more positive and appropriate to your current stage of life. [See below]

Before you leave, ensure that you clearly know the soul contracts you are honouring and the part that you and other people are to play.

Ask too whether you have agreed to specific roles and, if these are no longer appropriate, adjust or reframe as appropriate. [See below].

When you are ready to return, your higher self will take you back to the lift. The doors will be open, waiting for you. If appropriate your higher self will step into the lift with you. Press the button for the ground floor. When you step out you will be back in the building that leads out onto the meadow. If your higher self has joined you in the lift, ask that it will be available any time you come back to the meadow.

Walk back to the centre of the meadow. Then breathe a little deeper, move your hands and feet, and open your eyes. Take time to adjust to being back in your physical body. Then get up and stand with your feet firmly on the ground, feeling your connection with the earth. Have a warm drink and then write down your experience.

Make a note of your soul contracts, what you contracted to do and who you contracted with. Remember that these can be renegotiated in future if necessary.

Exercise: renegotiating soul contracts

If your soul contract is no longer relevant, it can either be reframed into something more appropriate, or let go entirely (see below). Renegotiating can take several forms, you may want to slightly adjust an agreement or completely change it. Working with your own higher self and the higher self of the other person ensures that this goes smoothly but if the other person's higher self will not cooperate or if your own higher self is insistent on you fulfilling the contract, ask yourself if that is because you are trying to wriggle out of a valid agreement which, while you may not like it, still has relevance. If that is the case, ask how the contract can be fulfilled with grace, ease and forgiveness. Add the following section into the appropriate place in the exercise to ascertain your soul contracts:

Ask that the other person's higher self will join you and your higher self in the contracts department.

Discuss with the other person's higher self how you feel about the contract, where you feel it is still relevant and where it is not. Remember to be open to hearing the other point of view. Then find a way to reframe the conditions set out in the soul contract that will be agreeable and fair to all parties. Once this agreement is reached, have it take the place of the original agreement.

Write out your renegotiated soul contract and keep it where you can see it to remind yourself that things have changed.

Tearing up past-their-sell-by date contracts

There are times when, with the best will in the world, contracts simply cannot be honoured. This often occurs in relationships. If a contract was based, for instance, on another soul fulfilling certain intentions or putting a soulplan into action, which you offered to support, then you can set a time limit on the contract. If the soul has wilfully refused or been unable to make the transition to a new way of being, or has made no effort to put the soulplan into action, you can end the contract without any karma or consequences accruing. Occasionally both the higher selves concerned may take some convincing of this, in which case unilateral action on your part may be necessary if you are sure that you have done all you can and want the karma of grace to come into operation – although this will not work if you are trying to wriggle out of something that really is in your soul's best interest. Add the following at the appropriate place in ascertaining your soul contracts:

> In your mind's eye, take the contract and tear it into small pieces. Place the pieces into a fireproof dish and set them alight. As the paper smokes and burns, let forgiveness and thanks go to the other person but set them and yourself free from the contract. When the fire burns out, the contract is ended. Ask both higher selves to honour the fact that you have rescinded the contract and to release any agreement made between the two of them regarding the contract. There is an old occult law that says if you ask three times, the request must be honoured and the contracts must be rescinded so, if necessary, repeat the process three times and hand the charred dishes to the higher selves, blowing away the ash as you do so.

To reinforce this, you can also write the contract on a piece of paper and set light to it as a tangible release, remembering to let go with forgiveness as you do so.

Soulplan or ego script?

When you look at your soulplan, do make sure that it really is the soul or higher self's purpose and not the ego that you engage with. Many of us are here to assist this planet and humanity through troubled times of great change and potentiality. Egos may see this as the end of the world, higher selves tend to see it as an opportunity for much needed changes to occur, but the ego can try to take over and give you an heroic mission that is far beyond what you really planned – and it's not always the higher self who communicates even though it may appear to be.

If someone or *something* tells you that you are here to save the earth, you might want to look back to what happened when someone had a similar belief about humanity two thousand years ago. It can so easily become an ego sacrifice – something appropriate to the Age of Pisces but not to that of Aquarius. Aquarius is about individuals working together for the good of the whole but, with the planet Uranus which is the 'ruler' of Aquarius, travelling through Aries, the sign of self, I and ego, until 2019, the emphasis will be on an individual's contribution and the responsibility each takes for their part in creating the whole.

A Stranger in Paradise

People are like stained glass windows. They sparkle and shine when the sun is out, but when the darkness sets in, their true beauty is revealed only if there is a light from within.

Elisabeth Kubler-Ross

As I was musing on what should go into this section an email came in from an old soul friend, Julie Chimes saying that she was about to be on Radio 2 discussing forgiveness. As I was going to be away on that day I thought I'd miss it, but I went down to breakfast just in time to hear a trail – a clear signal from the universe to include her as she is someone who really walks her talk and fulfils her soul purpose.

Julie has an extraordinary story to tell. Some years ago she was attacked by a paranoid schizophrenic. At the point of death several times, somehow she pulled through. In doing so, she opened a remarkable reservoir of forgiveness that she brought to the whole experience – and which has become her life's work. Having been stabbed repeatedly, weak from loss of blood, she suddenly moved out of searing pain and everything became still:

I was on a trapeze, swinging amongst the most brilliant stars I had ever seen, suspended in a vast, black velvet night sky, I rocketed back and forth, through the heavens. The speed exhilarating – the vision intoxicating – my entire being exploding with the excitement of its new-found freedom, beyond the straitjacket rigidity of its earthly overcoat. There was no sound except the rhythmic beating of a heart. Time did not exist. Nothing mattered. I knew some tiny part of me was being stabbed, and it did not seem to be of any consequence.... I was so incredibly alive... I became aware of thoughts, calm, loving, soothing, beautiful thoughts.

She could distinctively see the frenzied attack, from a bigger perspective, and, from there, Julie felt a sense of oneness with her assailant. Knowing with certainty that she would not die, Julie looked directly into her attacker's eyes and said: '*I love you.*' She felt an overwhelming sense of love and compassion for this woman who had inflicted such harm. Julie's perception of the world changed in that moment. She moved out of time: past, present and future were laid out before her. She thought of Christ and immediately found herself kneeling before him at the crucifixion. Feeling utterly desolate, she asked him where he was going and how she would find him when he was gone.

He replied: 'Everywhere you look you will see Me'.
I flew back into the heavens, the screen before me was now filled with a light, which shone with a brightness beyond anything I had ever seen. All the images of life blended into a sea of dazzling points of light... somehow everything was me... I was part of a magnificent whole.

Julie found herself in a wonderful garden where an orange-robed man was supervising two boys practising martial arts. Although he did not use words, she clearly heard his instruction to watch the class. He was showing the boys how to move slowly and turn the attacker's strength against him. Looking at Julie he said: 'It is very simple. It will get you out of any situation'.

Back on earth, with a broken knife slicing at her chest, Julie put the lesson into practise. Instead of struggling, she ducked. Her attacker fell forward, the knife embedded itself in the stairs, and Julie slid away. In danger of collapse, she was surprised to hear someone in her head instructing her to leave the house immediately. Unable to move alone, she was guided by the voice and, once more, told to use the power of her attacker. She allowed herself to be propelled backwards to the front door.

When Julie left her body this time, there was no magical place waiting. She was immediately told to go back to her body. Resisting, she was assured that she would survive and that, despite the desperate condition of her physical body, she would not be crippled. Suddenly she found herself back in her body. Once more she was instructed how to handle her attacker. This time she was told to intercept the knife with her right hand. With an enormous amount of trust, she did so. Eventually she was able to open the front door and stagger down the drive, where she collapsed. Urged on by the voice, she crawled onto the road, pursued by her attacker still wielding the knife. One woman saw her lying there bleeding and passed by on the other side of the road but a young man confronted the deranged woman, removed the knife and called an ambulance. Julie's partner, a doctor, arrived. He took her to hospital in a police car.

In hospital, Julie received more communications from The Voice, or, as she came to call it, Veritas. It guided the process of her recovery and explained it was part of Julie's soul learning programme. This is Julie's understanding of Veritas taken from *A Stranger In Paradise*, the account of her extraordinary experience:[5]

> *You kept reminding me that You were me. I didn't understand. You promised me I would. And now I think I am beginning to. You are the part of me who remembers. The part who is not sleeping. The part of me who is all seeing. The part of me who knows only love. The part of me who could take me beyond my physical and mental limitations. The part of me who would teach me how to sustain the knowledge and encourage me never to stop again on my journey into infinite love. Slowly the state of awareness awakening within me realises it is the destiny of every particle of consciousness to reveal the One within. And with this comes gratitude. The knowledge that I am ordinary, the heart of me the same as everyone else. And with that knowledge a vision of where the path leads.*

The path led Julie to teach spiritual development and reconciliation and her love touches everyone she meets. Not only did she forgive her attacker but also the people that ran away including the woman who passed by on the other side. Years later she said:

Knowing and experiencing the wondrous inspiration and guidance from the place within, I now know that the purpose of human birth is to reveal this part of ourselves. All suffering in humanity occurs when this deeper place is not accessed or known. The quest becomes to learn how to distinguish between the constant clatter of the limited conditioned mind (accompanied by the ego's insatiable need to be right whilst also taking everything personally) and the Inner Voice.

A journalist once asked, 'Your assailant heard voices too and she is classed as schizophrenic – aren't you the same?' It was a good question, a big question. My answer then and now is that the voice of the Self has the qualities of love, compassion, wisdom and strength, and each word is permeated with these expansive qualities, spoken only to uplift, encourage, inspire and unite us. Throughout eternity the saints, sages, mystics and gurus have spoken to us about the mysterious and sacred spiritual awakening and have guided our footsteps on the path heading towards home. Since the moment that dear old carving knife entered my chest my process of awakening began, and until my last breath this life is dedicated to the spiritual journey. We each have our own unique moment of touching the feet of the Divine but some of us need rather dramatic cosmic kicks to shake us free from our delusions!

Through writing, 'one to one' counselling, and leading seminars, workshops and discussion groups, I have become a guide for those who are ready and willing to embark upon the greatest adventure available to human consciousness – namely the search for Truth, to know the inner being.

It was on Julie's soulplan to take this teaching and especially that of forgiveness and reconciliation to a wider audience. She thanks her attacker for being the catalyst that brought her to the place she needed to be.

When I checked back with Julie as to where she is now she said:

A modern saint of India said that, 'Everything happens for the best'. I can now look back over the years with the benefit of 20/20 hindsight and see the truth of this profound statement. A well-known therapist came, uninvited, to 'heal' me when I was recovering from my injuries and told me 'It was my karma' and I must have done something terrible in a past life. She then got a migraine and had to leave. I realised then that our karma is not about being punished for wrongdoings – this is a very limited view of a complex subject. How boring it would be if destiny was only a rigid linear pre-ordained set of events? It is true we come into this life with a certain amount of 'historic' karma accrued from past lifetimes, which creates our life circumstance. Yet although none of us can truly know what the next moment will bring, we do have total freedom in the way that we deal with it, and this attitude plays a major part in creating our future karma. There is always a choice and it is worth asking, 'Am I burning off my ignorance or am I adding to old limitations? In any moment we have a myriad of possible futures awaiting us – and none of them are wrong – simply pathways that will ultimately lead us to what I call 'The Point of Knowing'.

Life is an exquisitely designed game of hide-and-seek. I have always been grateful for all the difficult times in my life, as hard as they were to bear, because they have moulded and shaped the person I am today. Think of the pressure required to create a diamond! The ego tends to flop around in a permanent state of rage and restlessness, never accepting anything that comes its way and yet acceptance is a golden key and the only way to open the door leading to profound peace.

So I have accepted what happened to me, not in a passive, beaten way but more an alive, dynamic excited way. So why did it happen to me? My suffering has enabled me to reach into areas that I would never have been permitted to enter, to speak with an authority I would never have achieved through intellect alone, to meet and share stories with audiences around this world and to make changes that can improve human rights. I now understand the journey of forgiveness and the remarkable healing power it bestows upon us. Above all, I can now love with a capacity that is ever deepening. What more could a woman ask for?

'Wait for me I will come back'

Wait for me, I will come back
Though from Death's own jaws.

(*Author unknown*)

Some of the strongest evidence for other lives comes from those who have been pulled back to their wider family through circumstances and promises that occurred in a previous life, especially where that life has been cut short.[6] I have written elsewhere about Simon Jacobs but as his story is graphic, evidential and insightful, and includes an interlife planning meeting script – one of the few I have on tape so can transcribe exactly – I'm using his experience again here including a part that has not been previously published to illustrate the why's and wherefore's of soul contracts and the way that the soulplan manifests. As a child, Simon suffered from a recurring nightmare:

> *The dream was of being in uniform, definitely camouflage uniform. Wearing a helmet, lots of kit all over, webbing, ammunition pouches, rucksack. The picture is of a large glider, and the back of the glider is open. It is empty inside and I am running round the glider.*

As Simon described it to me when we first met:

> *The dream would go from being a smooth black and white photo, to almost clear, then it would go very distorted as though someone had moved the contrast button, very mishmashed.*
>
> *We were running around woods, a Northern European setting, leaves on the trees, a lot of emotional energy. And then nothing. So that was about it, no distinct pattern to the thing. Always the glider, what I was wearing, a sense of panic, a sense of urgency, a sense of drama.*
>
> *It is very obvious what point of history we were at. It can't have been much prior to 1945 because no one ran around in camouflage at that stage, and it can't have been after then because of the gliders. We haven't used gliders since 1944-45 in a battle situation. So that focused the time.*

This nightmare pursued Simon until he undertook past-life regression with me in his twenties. It is common for people who have undergone a traumatic previous life death to dream of it – especially if they incarnate again relatively quickly and with a specific soul overlay. In his first regression Simon experienced being Captain Myles Henry, an Intelligence Officer for 10 Para at the Battle of Arnhem. As Simon was to later verify, Myles Henry was killed saving a wounded colleague. Simon relived his death in graphic detail – and his life before that date. All the details in his regressions were later found to be correct. Simon's life had run parallel to Myles in several respects: he joined the Army at the same age, starting out as a private but being promoted to an officer, and his career trajectory took the same path. Paralleling Myles' experience

although in a different country, Simon spent time in Northern Ireland
during the fighting there, and, unknowingly, left the army at the age of
which Myles had died.

The following is an extract from the transcript of the first regression
(as it was long and repetitive I've cut it somewhat). Initially there was a
great deal of waiting around unable to see anything, which Simon later
found was due to fog which delayed the mission for two or three days,
and gave rise to considerable boredom and anxiety. Then suddenly he
was in a glider and about to parachute into Arnhem:

> [Simon]: I'm in a wood. I'm wearing green trousers and black boots.
> A lot of kit on. There's a lot of kit. I feel strong, fit. I've got a smock
> on and a helmet, with a strap. Carrying a machine gun – it feels quite
> light, though. Not heavy. It's dark, it's very dark. There's no light
> anywhere. It's dark in the wood. We're waiting for something.

> [Judy]: Are there people with you?

> [Simon]: Yes, lots of people, all dressed the same. All around. We're
> all together. All waiting to go. Here we go – moving off. We're walking
> through the woods in the night. Walking along, there's a long line of us,
> looking out the whole time, keeping our eyes peeled. Listening to the
> sounds, stopping every so often. I can see some glowing lights, getting
> closer to them. Looks like some vehicles – our vehicles, looks like. I
> think jeeps. They've been hit – they've been on fire. We walk past
> and there are bodies, wearing the same as us. We hear the owls. Keep
> walking. It's a bit sandy under our feet. There's grass as well. Scrubby
> trees. The sun isn't up yet, it's just the light beginning to break. It's
> cold. Far off we can hear machine guns firing.
>
> Now I'm talking into a radio. [startled] What's going on? It's
> the enemy – Germans. They're up there, in the woods. They've got
> vehicles. And guns, on wheels. That's what we hear. We're engaging,
> but it's very difficult, because of the woods. [becoming more agitated]
> We can't see them. We don't know quite where they are, or how many
> there are. We're all gathered now, we've stopped, we're gathered
> around, trying to get more information on the radio. It's getting lighter
> all the time. The sun will be up soon, maybe we'll see the Germans
> then. But the woods are very thick. I can hear a lot more firing now.
> We need to get much closer, to find out where they are. So we start to

go forward. We're running through the woods. We can hear the rounds cracking in the trees. Big guns going off too. Rumbling of tanks a long way off. Can't see them, though, we can only hear them, hear the Germans.

Must find our chaps. They are firing into the woods. Trying to see the Germans. But there are obviously a lot of them, an awful lot. Must be some kind of defensive line. Haven't got enough fire power. We just keep firing, firing.

Got to get back now, to help another officer. Running in the woods. Running, running. Tell him what it is, what the problem is. Where we are, stay where we are .... German soldiers (?indistinct)

[very breathless] Find him. Find him in the scrub. Everyone is digging into the sandy soil. Got to get cover. Can hear the German vehicles on the road. The tracks, and then more fire. We send somebody over to find out what's going on. It's all very confused, we don't know what to do now. We're stuck. Our chaps are pinned down, in the woods, can't see the enemy, there's not a lot we can do. We try to go to the other side of the road, but there's more Germans there. Try to outflank, more Germans, there's a long line. There's nothing we can do at all. Everyone's so tired. People are calling for ammunition and stretchers. It's not a happy scene at all. It's very frightening. There's a lot of shrapnel in the trees, flying about. Wood splinters. Got to keep your head down. It's odd, 'cause the sun's out, shining through the trees, the shrubby trees. We spend a lot of time trying to keep our heads down. No one's really sure what to do. This goes on for ages. So much noise. No birds. [Simon was getting visibly tireder now – his speech which had been rapid and repetitious became much slower]. Everywhere there's bangs and cracks. I feel quite sad. My mouth's very dry. I reach for a sweet, a boiled sweet, unwrap it. A red one. I put it in my mouth – that's better. There's no water left.

Going forward again through the trees. We're down, crawling and sliding on the ground. Forward to the right. To D Company. They've dug in, as well, little scrapes. One or two wounded. But not too many casualties.

[agitated again] Messages coming through, telling us 'move back. Withdraw from contact. Break off'.

*Back through the woods – not good to withdraw in daylight. But
we must. We're on our own. In the scrub. Moving.*

*What's going on? What's the matter with him? He's crying.
Wounded. In the leg. Lot of blood. Can't walk at all. Let's grab him.
Carry him to the farm. To the aid post. He's not heavy. [breathing
heavily now]*

*Oh God! (Groans). Such a lot of blood. We're running.
[indistinguishable] Through the woods. Going through the bushes
towards ... farm ... Where ... mmmmmm ... uh uh (louder) (gentle
sigh and murmurings) ... Bright light. Very bright. So bright. Awfully
bright. (gentle sigh). I feel safe, so safe. Very relaxed, very comfortable.
Very safe. [long silence].*

As the regression had lasted a long time I brought Simon back for a
debrief and to check what had gone on. He said that he had been shot
while carrying a fellow officer who had been wounded and that he had
been going in and out of consciousness before he died, after which he
was in a very peaceful bright place but he wasn't clear on this so we
decided to check it out in another session.

Second session

[Judy]: *Can you go back and tell me what happened? You were going
through the woods, and came out of the woods. If you look down on
that scene, what happened?*

[Simon]: *With the man. The three of us are there with him. We're
carrying him. It's difficult to see. Then we went to the light. I went on
my own. There's no one else – just me – to the light.*

[Judy]: *Who are you, what's happened?*

[Simon]: *Going back down. There's a body. My body. It's my body.
Bye bye. My life is over. Such a relief. [big sigh] It really is. And we go
to the light – it's very calm there. I feel better. I was so tired.*

[Judy]: *Is there anything in that life you need to do, to go back and look
at?*

[Simon]: *Search for the child – there was a child – a little child – a child
I've never seen. She's not been born. It's too late now. It's too late to
see her. I must go to the light.*

[Judy]: *Can you meet her soul on the way to the light?*

[Simon]: *No. She seems to be born now. She's not there. It's too soon.*

(Simon later found that her mother had gone into premature labour when she heard that he was missing in action and that the child was indeed a girl).

[Judy]: *Is there anything else you need to look back at?*

[Simon]: *Saw a woman. She's so small. A wonderful woman. She's alone without me, but I must go.*

[Judy]: *Say goodbye to her – let her go.*

[Simon]: *Goodbye...... Goodbye...... Beautiful...... Must go to the light.*

[Judy]: *Go fully into the light. Let yourself get all the healing you need. [Pleasurable sounds]. Go to the level where the healing is.*

[long silence]

[Judy]: *Are you still in the light?*

[Simon]: *Yes – it's lovely here. Mmmm...... So comfortable.*

[Judy]: *Is there anything you need to do, or need to know while you're in the light?*

[Simon]: *What's next?*

[Judy]: *Let yourself move to the point where you're deciding what comes next. Before the next conception, where you're planning your next life.*

[Simon]: *For some reason I feel busy. It's going to be a big one, the next one. Got so much to do. Got to be very, very strong.*
[Judy]: *Is there going to be help and strength for you?*

[Simon]: *God's going to be with me. He'll be with me, because we've got to tell them. And the guides will help with that process. They want to. There will be help. It's God's will. He's so wonderful, he really is. He's here. We must go. Must get back for him. Such a lot to do.*

[Judy]: So let yourself come to the point where you're looking down on the new parents, ready for conception.

[Simon]: Driving in a car. So happy. Such a happy time. So peaceful – beautiful mother. They're the right ones. Must go now. I'm with them now. Ooh [grunts, body writhes, as though trying to move down the birth canal]

[Judy]: Just let yourself move very smoothly, so that the birth is easy.

[Simon]: Not again – oh no, not again. I don't want to face it. Oh God.

[Judy]: Let it be a good birth, so that you can move closer to your purpose. You can rescript the birth. Just speed time up, and come forward to this moment now, back into the room with me.

Myles Henry was an, at that time, unknown distant relative but Simon had to go to the Imperial War Museum to verify the details of his death as he wasn't in touch with that side of the family. He describes having the war diaries of 10 Para presented to him:

I opened up the diaries and found the entry relating to Myles Henry. It gave me huge tingles up and down my spine. He was killed with another guy trying to rescue a fellow who had been wounded, trying to take him back to an Aid Station. Myles Henry was badly wounded and died later that night without regaining consciousness.

Simon is absolutely convinced that this was his former life:

I just know it happened. I know it was me. I can't not believe it, there are two many pieces of the jigsaw that come together for it not to be believable.

It was only much later however that Simon found confirmation of the more personal details of his regression such as the fact that Myles' wife had been pregnant at the time of his death and went into premature labour on receiving a telegram announcing 'missing, believed killed'. The wife of Myles Henry wrote her life story for her family and Simon was able to obtain a copy.[7] He also went to Arnhem and found evidence on the ground for his past-life memories. He was able to pinpoint exactly where his field-grave was, for instance and several other details that were not exactly as the war diaries had stated were proved to be as Simon remembered them. Later Simon met some of his old colleagues – several of whom have accepted him as the reincarnation of Myles Henry. One actually said: "Not only do you look like him but your whole character and manner is identical".

In the book Myles's wife, Pamela wrote about their 'soulmate meeting' and their great love affair. She quotes a poem written at the siege of Stalingrad which meant a great deal to them and which ends:

Wait for me, I will come back
Though from Death's own jaws...
And the reason I've come through
We shall know, we two
Simply this: you waited as
No one else could do.[8]

Sentiments that may explain her very long life, and Simon returning to the same family, albeit to a different branch and in another country to that in which she was living. Hopefully one day the full story of this extraordinary love story and its effects can be told as Simon was able to contact her family. For me, the most poignant moment in her autobiography is when Pamela says:

Never was I officially notified that Myles had died of wounds... I never gave up hope. Throughout the days and nights, throughout the years that followed. And now as life draws to its inevitable close, my destiny fulfilled, that hope grows stronger.

Simon's interlife planning told him that he had to make a difference. An avid cyclist, he has been cycling marathons the length and breadth of England to raise money for his favourite charities, 'Help for Heroes', which supports casualties from the Gulf and Afghanistan wars and his local air ambulance which quickly transports road accident and other casualties to hospital for treatment. Myles Henry's imperative in his last act before he died had been that he had to get the casualty he was carrying back to the aid station for assistance, and Simon returned with a soul overlay that required him to do the same – and a soul intention to make a difference.

Strange meeting

I came out in order to help these boys – directly by leading them as well as an officer can; indirectly, by watching their sufferings that I may speak of them as well as a pleader can.

Wilfred Owen to his mother

We've just seen how one soldier returned from World War Two and this is a story of a different kind of return but with an equally strong soul purpose. I chose lines from the First World War poet and pacifist Wilfred Owen to open Part 3 and include this particular section because Wilfred is someone with whom I have had a profound soul contact and whose life and interlife I have explored intimately. Surprising perhaps given that he 'died' in 1918 in the last days of the war that was supposed to end all wars. Wilfred was a paradox. A slight, shy man who abhorred war and was bullied by his senior officers and yet was given the George Cross for conspicuous gallantry and devotion to duty in exterminating a German pillbox, Wilfred believed that it was his soul task to chronicle 'the truth untold, the pity of war, the pity war distilled'. He wanted to show the inhumanity and futility of war and yet in doing so he became a willing sacrificial victim as a service to humanity. The lines to his mother were penned just before his death. But Wilfred is a wonderful example of how a soul is very much alive even though technically 'dead' and of how interlife planning both precedes and follows on from a physical incarnation.

I first met Wilfred Owen when Robert, a historian, sent me birth details and a photograph of a man named only as Wilfred along with his own birthchart and asked: 'what connection do I have with this man?' My reply was that Robert appeared to be living out something that the man himself had been unable to complete, in some strange way they were now sharing a life and Wilfred was living vicariously. I saw that Wilfred had been killed in the closing stages of the 1914-18 war and that Robert had been his batman during that war. At that time I knew nothing of Wilfred Owen. Robert responded:

I have remembered my death in that life when I was killed crossing a field with a comrade in that war so, it would appear, I was not with Wilfred when he was killed, but I believe I knew him well.[9]

From what I have since seen, Robert and Wilfred had in that life an extremely intimate relationship that had to be kept hidden – they would both have been shot had it become known. The intensity of the brief relationship opened the way for Robert to become Wilfred's amanuenses in this present life.

Robert told me that Wilfred Owen had appeared to him and asked him to complete and publish several of his fragmentary poems. Thus began a very intense period of contact for both Robert and myself. The result was an extremely powerful performance piece compiled by Robert from Wilfred's previously unseen poetry and a volume of 'completed' poems. Soon, Wilfred was also appealing to me to tell his story, which I did for the first time in *The Hades Moon* as Hades was a realm with which Wilfred was intimately acquainted. But now, Wilfred would like a wider truth told, that of the choices his soul made and the service he gave to humanity. In many ways, his poetry, so often reworked and refined but rarely completed, is a compassionate witnessing of man's inhumanity to man. Wilfred 'loved the sorrows of [the] changing face'. As he said in his poem, *The One Remains*:

I sometimes think of those pale, perfect faces,
My wonder has not looked upon, as yet;
And of those others never to be met,
And often pore I on the secret traces
Left in my heart, of countenances seen,
And lost as soon as seen – but which mine eye
Remembers as my old home, or the lie
Of landscapes whereupon my windows lean.

So, let's go back to the beginning and look at Wilfred Owen's soul planning for his short incarnation. He was a delicate, psychic child who had an intensely passionate, overwhelmingly symbiotic relationship with his mother and resultant lack of connection with his 'stiflingly respectable' father and siblings, who deeply resented his bond with their mother. As a teenager Wilfred had to keep his homosexual leanings to himself, his father would never have approved, and he hid it from his beloved mother who was not prepared to share her 'darling boy'. All pre-planned. Wilfred wanted not only to intellectually understand suffering, sacrifice and alienation he wanted to immerse himself in it so that he *knew*. This he certainly achieved through four years in the trenches, but he also witnessed the small kindnesses of his fellow soldiers to each other and the hope that never died. He was indeed the Poet in Pain:

> *Some men sing songs of Pain and scarcely guess*
> *Their import, for they never knew her stress.*
> *And there by other souls that ever lie*
> *Begnawed by seven devils, silent. Aye,*
> *Whose hearts have wept out blood, who not once spake*
> *Of tears. If therefore my remorseless ache*
> *Be needful to proof-test my flesh*
> *The thoughts I think, and in words bleeding-fresh*
> *Teach me for speechless sufferers to plain,*
> *I would not quench it. Rather be my part*
> *To write of health with shaking hands, bone-pale,*
> *Of pleasure, having hell in every vein,*
> *Than chant of care from out a careless heart,*
> *To music of the world's eternal wail.*

Wilfred had a strong karmic bond with his father, who worshipped at the collective altar of war, and it was to please his father that Wilfred first volunteered as a soldier and then returned to the front after treatment for shell-shock. Both parents featured in the interlife planning, his father's rejection was an important part of his soul plan as it pushed him into something that was the opposite of Wilfred's own pacifist beliefs and yet enabled him to carry out his wider purpose. Like so many young men of his generation, Wilfred Owen knew before incarnation that there would most probably be a war and that he would be unlikely to survive. Indeed, it was to be through his war experiences that the poet would be born and through his death that his poetry would become widely known so death was part of his plan. His intention – and soul service to humanity – was to show the awfulness of war in all its horror not its glory:

> *If you could hear, at every jolt, the blood*
> *Come gargling from the froth-corrupted lungs,*
> *Obscene as cancer, bitter as the cud*
> *Of vile, incurable sores on innocent tongues –*
> *My friend you would not tell with such high zest*
> *To children ardent for some desperate glory,*

The old Lie: Dulce et decorum est
Pro patria mori
(It is sweet and fitting to die for one's country)

The need to keep his true self hidden led to an intense, secretive inner life that was the foundation of Wilfred's poetic genius. His father's abhorrence of his son's romantic sexual leanings and the repudiation of who he was at his core would have a profound effect upon Wilfred's life and friendships. From the interlife planning meeting before that incarnation, it is clear that Wilfred deliberately chose this alienated outsider position as it was essential for all that he would become. As his biographer Dominic Hibberd expresses it, 'his poethood began in secret darkness, born out of a tradition which had made the poet both the prophetic voice of the people and a solitary, damned figure, a dreamer cast out from sunlight'.[10] There are fragments of an epic poem begun by Wilfred prior to the war and continually reworked throughout (after his death his ultra-respectable family destroyed what they saw as damning papers so only fragments remain). Starting as a poem that goes into 'hell's low sorrowful secrecy' to meet an old hag who offers to become his lover, it metamorphoses into a saga of erotic initiation and subsequent rejection that takes him into Hades. The poem features a descent into the Plutonian underworld that Robert Christoforides believes to be 'spiritually and emotionally autobiographical' and Dominic Hibberd 'a shadowy but insistent pattern, a secret myth which he seems to be making out of his own experience' – very typical of a Pisces experience of the world which somehow goes beyond the purely personal into the realms of the collective unconscious and higher unity consciousness. A dreamy, sensitive Piscean and yet powerfully Plutonic in his 'incarnation map' – his birthchart[11] – Wilfred was no stranger to hell. He was incarcerated three times in shell holes during that unceasingly hellish war for several days at a time, twice with dismembered, decomposing corpses as his only companions and at least once having an out-of-body, near death experience that culminated, not surprisingly, in severe shell-shock. Out of which some incredible poetry arose, including 'Strange Meeting' in which he becomes reconciled with his dead enemy who is his friend and soul companion. As Jon, one of Robert Schwartz's case histories observed 'after you've been bumping butts with the Angel of Death, you get a little appreciation for where you've been'.[12]

In Wilfred's case, the Angel of Death led him to Craiglockhart and the ministrations of the remarkable Dr Arthur Brock, a pre-planned soul group volunteer who guided him to look upon his experiences on the battlefield as a 'purgation of the soul'. Dr Brock, who is one of the best examples of compassionate witnessing in action that I've come across, believed that rather than being denied and repressed, such things should be confronted so that they could become grist for the creative mill. As Dominic Hibberd put it, Wilfred 'had to reconnect himself with his past and put it to work'. Under Brock's care Wilfred's poetic abilities increased dramatically and his 'hideous memories' became poetic images of great potency. Wilfred described his fellow inmates as:

These men whose minds the Dead have ravished.

But it was amongst these men that Wilfred was able to face up to what Brock called 'the phantoms of the mind'. At the urgings of another pacifist war poet and Craiglockhart inmate Siegfried Sassoon, Wilfred's poems were gathered together for a book, although Wilfred would not live to see it published and the typescript is lost. When Wilfred recovered from his shellshock he was graded fit for active service but not on the front. His father sent him a telegraph 'gratified to know you are normal again'. Just the prompt his soul had been waiting for. Wilfred immediately volunteered to return to his regiment. This small retiring man walked with utter calm through the devastation that was Ypres tending to his men and giving them heart. Their orders were clear. 'There is to be no retirement under any circumstances'. Just before sunrise on 4 November 1918, Wilfred was killed while trying to take a raft across the canal. The engagement was called off just minutes after. The war to end all wars ended precisely seven days later. Wilfred's mother had engraved on his war cemetery headstone lines from his poem *The End*:

Shall life renew these bodies?
Of a truth, all death will he annul?

Two days later Wilfred appeared to his brother Harold who was on a ship off the coast of South Africa.[13] Wilfred Owen's body may have been gone but his soul was profoundly alive and his poetic legacy ensures that neither he nor the horror of war will be forgotten even while it continues to be glorified.

Was it for this the clay grew tall?
O what makes fatuous sunbeams toil
To break earth's sleep at all?[14]

Curious as to how this sensitive soul had felt after he'd been torn from life, I asked Wilfred where he had been in the period before he attached himself to Robert – he'd already told me he couldn't leave the earth until he'd completed his poetry and, although time as such does not exist on other realms, I wondered whether he'd experienced a gap of time and, if so, how he filled it.

His reply that 'I was with Charlie Chaplin learning with him' perplexed me until I discovered that Chaplin himself had been haunted by the memory of being wrenched from his mother's arms, aged 4, as she was taken to the asylum and he to the workhouse. These two small, quiet men were curious reflections of each other and yet in other ways the antithesis: the perfect way for Wilfred to learn through someone else's experience. Like Wilfred, Chaplin endured many weeks of illness as a child and was entertained by his mother but Chaplin's upbringing by his bohemian theatrical family, which inspired his acting career, was the opposite of the stifling 'proper' English childhood that Wilfred experienced. Perhaps this is why Wilfred wrote introverted poems and Chaplin made films that lodged him firmly in the public's eye – although it is tempting to believe that Wilfred may in some small way have influenced Chaplin's choice of subject. Chaplin's mother's life was dogged by mental illness so they had many periods of separation and Chaplin toured the music halls with his alcoholic father until he died when Chaplin was twelve. It was these experiences that gave Chaplin's eyes the look of pathos that underpinned his comedy – and which gave rise to films portraying the plight of the alienated outsider and highlighting social injustice, such as *The Immigrant*, and *The Great Dictator*, which revealed to the world the way that Hitler was treating the Jews, released just before America dropped its neutrality and entered the Second World War. Both men were perfectionists. In the same way that Wilfred obsessively reworked his poetry over and over again, Chaplin shot and reshot his films, working without a script until the final version was as he had envisaged. At the end of his long life Chaplin opined: 'life is a tragedy when seen in close-up, but a comedy in long shot'.

Saying that he had immersed himself in Chaplin's comedy as an antidote to all the suffering he had endured, Wilfred was nevertheless aware of a deeper purpose that lay behind Chaplin's films – and of the anguish that Chaplin himself had endured. Although British, Chaplin remained in the United States during the First World War, refusing to return home to fight. He was accused by many in Britain of being a coward – exactly what Wilfred's father had said when Wilfred was hospitalised with shell shock.

Chaplin's first child was born in 1918. He was severely disabled and died after only three days. Wilfred tells me that this was an ill-judged attempt on his part to incarnate again too quickly and that it was part of the soul split he had endured when blasted into a shell hole. Seeking a safe haven, but without consulting the higher self, the split-off soul part had been drawn to Chaplin and the Little Tramp, a figure that Wilfred perceived as a romantic refuge from trauma. During the pregnancy it became apparent that this plan could not work. The split-off part incarnated as the baby, thus securing a link to Chaplin, but the disabilities reflected the soul fragmentation. As it was prior to Wilfred's death, the soul could only become whole again after both child and adult died. This is one of those extremely complicated situations where time has to be taken out of the equation as otherwise it is impossible to comprehend. And even then, it is very difficult to get your head around. I've had quite a few years of thinking about it now, and this is the first time I've been able to write about it but still don't feel that I fully understand the processes involved. I have, however, seen enough similar cases to know that it does occur, as does the kind of attachment to and learning through another soul that also took place. Wilfred has made me much more aware that, before moving attached souls on as I and other soulworkers tend to do because I assume they are stuck, I should always ensure that I ascertain whether it is appropriate for them to continue their learning in this way or whether they should go fully back to spirit so that they can make a new life choice to continue learning through their own body.[15]

Through shadowing Chaplin's life closely, Wilfred was able to see how an inauspicious beginning could be turned around. Chaplin said of his best known character, the Little Tramp: 'a tramp, a gentleman, a poet, a dreamer, a lonely fellow, always hopeful of romance and adventure'. An apt summing up too of his soul's alter ego, Wilfred Owen.

Laura's Story

A child forsaken, waking suddenly,
Whose gaze afeard on all things round doth rove,
And seeth only that it cannot see
The meeting eyes of love

Quoted in Middlemarch

The words above held a particular resonance for a woman whose soul journey I have accompanied for the past twenty-five years. She is one of my soul sisters. Laura has been a source of profound learning for me and I stand in awe at her capacity for forgiveness and the love that she radiates out to the world, not something I say lightly. The story that follows may sound like one of karmic retribution for some unknown or unacknowledged wrong but it is actually one of profound soul growth and evolution as well as an act of service to a family group and to a group of alienated outsiders: the mentally ill. When I asked Laura for her story she promised:

I will write from my heart starting with the small 4 year old – feeling abandoned – never knowing what it was like to sit on mother or father's knee or cuddled by them…

But in fact she needed to go back even earlier to her first memory:

My first memory as a child is one of violence. It was towards the end of the Second World War. I was three years old. Each time a warning siren sounded, my mother used to put me on the floor under the table, a common practise in those days, as the only protection against any bombs that might land. I remember my father becoming very angry, shouting "Bloody Hitler", kicking my dolls pram and other toys that were dotted around on the floor. That was the first and only childhood memory of my father as after that I had no contact with him until I reached seventeen. I was told much later by my mother that he was a violent man. He would not work, "Gentlemen don't work", he would say.

My mother took a secretarial job at that time, working for my future step-father. The next memory I have is as a four year old. I was living in a children's home. The headmistress took me into the parlour where my mother and a strange man were sitting. "This is your new Daddy" said my mother, "Kiss him" – I took one look at him, screamed and ran out of the room. I believe that was the moment that we took an instant dislike to each other. At that point I was informed that my surname had been changed to that of my step-father.

This was Laura's introduction to abandonment and rejection, issues that are embedded deep in her astrological chart and in her karmic history.

So began my life in the children's home. I made some good friends. We had a lot in common, as, for various reasons our families had deposited us there. My mother and step-father went to live abroad. They had three sons. On rare occasions they would return to England and take me to stay with them. This was a terrible ordeal for me. My mother referred to her sons and my step-father as "my family", as if I was nothing to do with any of them, and I certainly didn't feel anything to do with them. From time to time there was talk of my visiting them abroad, but that never happened. I was expected to be my mother's kitchen servant. If my step-father ever caught me sitting down, reading a book, he would shout at me to "Get back in the kitchen and help your mother". These times were pure misery. Sometimes my mother would look at me disapprovingly and say "you look just like your father" as if this was a sin and my fault. I remember falling over and cutting my knee. "That is God punishing you because you are bad". She would tell people in front of me how bad I was. When items in the house became mislaid, I would immediately be accused of stealing. I was always relieved to go back to my friends in the children's home and would count the days. I was criticised constantly by my mother and could never please her. I used to envy children with loving parents and homes.

When I was about five, I became aware that I had a very loving Grandmother who lived by the sea. She used to visit me, regularly write and send parcels of sweets. Sometimes I would go and stay with her. Together with her son, my uncle, they would spoil me, taking me to the fun fair on the pier, buying me candy floss, toffee apples and visits to restaurants. An especial treat was going to the local department store for tea, listening to the Palm Court Orchestra while I enjoyed my favourite chocolate éclair. Every night my grandmother put a shilling under my pillow while I was sleeping, she said Fairy Joan had visited. She introduced me to magical thinking! When it was time for me to return to the children's home I thought I was rich. We would play a game, where my grandmother would pretend to talk to Fairy Joan, then put on a funny voice, like a ventriloquist, and be Fairy Joan. As I got a little older I began to be aware that my Grandmother was no ordinary grandmother. She was a very fine natural born clairvoyant. This was how she earned her living as it was her only means of support. She introduced me to a different and exciting world. Her like minded psychic friends, always showed me utmost kindness, and, although I never realised at the time, between them were instrumental in gradually expanding my consciousness and provided the supportive family I lacked elsewhere in my life. My Grandmother started to take me aside and confidentially whisper to me "Never tell anyone we are Jewish". I didn't understand the significance at the time, but this was something she repeated in hushed tones whenever she saw me. As I became older I was able to understand that, indeed after the war, it was not a good idea to let anyone know this fact.

Despite all that had happened to the Jews during the war, in England they were still at that time treated like alienated outsiders so this was Laura's first conscious taste of being the outsider, something that would soon accelerate as she was torn between two faiths. She was also the alienated outsider within her own family:

Grandmother explained other details of my family background. My real father (who was not Jewish and came from an aristocratic background) agreed not to contest the divorce with my mother provided my mother and step-father promised to always look after me. This promise they broke when they dispatched me forthwith to the children's home. I was also told of another complication: My paternal grandfather would have nothing to do with me as my mother was Jewish, and my Jewish step-father felt the same, as my birth father was non-Jewish. It seemed I was neither fish nor fowl at that time. In an attempt to fit in with all the other children I lived with, I decided to have myself christened.

I wore a crucifix around my neck with pride. It gave me a sense of belonging, of not being different. The next time I visited my mother she looked in horror at the crucifix, I could see she was angry with me. She grabbed hold of it and pulled it off my neck, breaking the chain "You are not Christian, you are Jewish". I didn't know what to make of this. I couldn't understand why she was so displeased with me. I hadn't done anything wrong as far as I was concerned. In fact I had had encouragement from the Priest who christened me, and the children's home brought me up as a Christian.

One day, I must have been about twelve, while staying with my mother and step-father, I was so utterly miserable and desperate I decided to run away to my Grandmother. Having no money, I stole the train fare from my mothers' purse and set off. Grandmother, always giving me unconditional love, explained to me that as happy as she was to see me I would have to return. I was in deep trouble and had made things worse. So much so that my mother accused my grandmother of encouraging me, which she never did, and of taking my love away from her. Mother was always very jealous of our close relationship. From that day she refused to have anything more to do with my Grandmother. This was a source of great pain to Grandmother for the rest of her life. In fact I can remember her saying to me many times "She is my daughter, I will always love her, my wish is to see her before I die". She never did get her wish. Over thirty years later when my Grandmother died, my mother asked me to take her to the funeral. I can remember my mother standing at Grandmother's grave side, and as she shovelled earth into the grave saying "Forgive me Mummy". I had never witnessed anything other than her hatred until then.

At this time both my mother and step-father would say the most cruel things to me about Grandmother. She was feather-headed – her psychic gifts were a lot of rubbish. This distressed me greatly, I loved her deeply and I knew her gifts were genuine. So Grandmother and me began to have a clandestine relationship. I ran away at least a couple more times, which made matters even worse for us both. Around the age of fifteen, I finally decided to run away to a young adult friend who lived a three hour train journey away. Thinking no one would possibly find me. For two days I felt free and happy, until to my horror two policemen came to the door. The friend, who I foolishly had trusted, had betrayed me! I was not mature enough to grasp that she had no choice as I was a minor. I was immediately taken to a Remand Centre for young offenders, hauled in front of a judge in court and told that my mother reported I was beyond control. I would have to stay in the Remand Centre until my case came up. It would then be decided what would become of me. This was a ghastly experience. It was a locked prison, I had to wear prison uniform and abide by extreme rules. I was mixing with young criminals of every sort, treated like one, and found nothing in common with them, or the staff. I had no way of contacting the outside world and felt completely abandoned and alone. The day arrived for my court hearing. My future would be decided, and so it was with utter dread I was taken from the Remand Centre. Shaking like a leaf, I glanced over and saw my mother glaring at me. Then something remarkable and unexpected happened. The kindly judge, having listened to various derogatory accounts about me turned to me and asked me where I would like to live. I immediately said my Grandmother, and my wish was granted. My mother and step-father were furious at the verdict, they wanted nothing more to do with me and I felt the same about them.

So began at long last a happy loving chapter in my teenage life. I was curious to meet my father. I enlisted the help of my Grandmother. The tea-time meeting took place at a London Hotel. My father seemed charming and genuinely pleased to see me – gave me his address with an open invitation to visit him and his wife. They both made me most welcome. Somehow, word got back to my mother and step-father that I had made contact with my father. Predictably they were enraged by this. They made it clear that they wanted to cut all association with me and that I was no longer to use their surname. I reverted back to my father's name and was delighted not to have that association any longer. I discovered that my father could be very charming but also very violent and cruel. He never displayed this cruel side to me, but I was to witness these actions towards his wife, my step-mother.

At nineteen I began a relationship. I became pregnant. Life was full of hope and promise, but not for long. I found myself confronting a future with a baby and without the man I loved, in other words I was to be an unmarried mother. My Grandmother was always there supporting me. Again, somehow word got back to my mother and step-

*father. My mother contacted me saying, there was no way I could have
the baby, that I should have a termination, otherwise I would bring
shame on the whole family. I refused.*

*I had my baby, staying in hospital for a few days to recover. I loved
every moment looking after my baby. The time came for the two of us
to leave. I went to the nursery to collect my baby to be told that the baby
had already been taken by my mother and the staff had instructions
not to let me know where they had gone. I was underage and had
no rights it seemed. My baby had been kidnapped. I was devastated,
and resolved that I would do whatever it took to get my baby back.
Something remarkable happened again. I was renting a flat from a
kindly couple who, when I returned empty handed, and told them what
had happened, agreed to do everything within their power to help me.
Eventually, after many enquiries this kindly supportive couple drove me
to an address. There we found my baby with a foster mother – we were
just in time as my baby was about to be legally adopted. After a lot of
arguing and threats we left with my baby. My mother had betrayed me
all my life, never given me a kind encouraging word, only criticism. I
felt this act was the ultimate betrayal I could never ever forgive her. I
despised her and the way she treated me.*

*During the next few years I had no contact with my mother, and
had no wish to ever see her again. I did hear that my mother had made
it plain to my half brothers that they were not to have any contact with
me. Word got back to her that I was to be married. She contacted me
and made it plain she did not wish to have any part in the proceedings,
she was particularly aggrieved as my father was going to be present. I
did not feel I could welcome her anyway. Time passed. I had son. The
grapevine was working again and my mother contacted me, enquiring
after my son, asking his name. When I told her we had chosen my
father's name, she cruelly said she wouldn't want anything to do with
him. She was true to her word. So both of my children were denied the
experience of a loving grandmother – but they did have a few precious
years of love from their great-grandmother before she passed on.*

*A few years later I had a serious accident which left me in hospital
unable to walk. My recovery was a long painful uphill struggle.
Eventually, although still in pain, I was discharged. I had good friends
who helped me. My children were teenagers by then. One day, in*

desperation, I contacted my mother, explaining my predicament. My husband and I were divorcing. Her attitude was you have made your bed, lie on it. What made things worse was that she chose to take my husband's side in the divorce. Around this time my father died. My mother asked me if he had left me anything in his will. He hadn't. She accused me of lying. I wrote a letter to her saying that it was a pity she chose not to believe me when I was telling the truth and that I was not responsible for her relationship with my father.

Time passed, my daughter was at university. On leaving school my son went to work on a kibbutz in Israel.

So began a new chapter in my life. Little did I know what was in store! I became a Samaritan and took a job working as a secretary/ receptionist in a care home. Life settled down into a different rhythm.

One day, when my daughter was with me on holiday, I had a revelatory dream. In the dream I was in a jungle that seemed impenetrable. I saw a red light flashing ahead of me and I saw and heard a telephone ringing, I felt desperate to reach it as I knew it was my son trying to contact me, it was so urgent and he had something to say to me. I was trying frantically to reach the telephone, fighting through the undergrowth, but held back by the dense jungle. In the morning when I awoke in a state of panic, I knew my son was in trouble in Israel. I told my daughter that I must go out immediately to see him. Without hesitation she said she would accompany me. We travelled out on the first available flight and found that my son had been discovered unconscious with blood coming out of an ear. (I will never know how this came about). It was quite obvious to me that something dreadful had happened. I could see it was imperative that he return with us to England with utmost haste. This provoked a huge argument with his father who was unable to grasp the seriousness of the situation. I was immensely grateful for my dream. It was so clear and precise. My son was calling me. He was in deep trouble. How right my dream was. I found my son in a truly awful confused state. His father was extremely unsupportive, harsh and unloving. From a young age my son tried hard to please his father, he was never good enough. It was tough growing up rejected by both his father and grandmother.

This was the beginning of a devastating mental illness, which shattered his thoughts, perceptions and feelings, hijacking his mind making his entry into the adult world a descent into chaos and inner darkness. I was utterly bewildered. What had happened to my frail golden haired son? A gentle sensitive young man who was transformed by voices and delusions, on occasions becoming aggressive.

"If hope were not, the heart would break."

These are words that came to me when I was in the depths of despair when Oliver first had his breakdown (although I did not know that he was breaking down at that stage). I couldn't understand what had happened to my golden boy with his whole life ahead (he is now 43) and I was ignorant. How right my dream was because Oliver was at the beginning of his terrible descent into schizophrenia (I call it that, but you know what I mean, it was so much more)... this was how it all began – from then on his condition started to run amok with all our lives.

Thus I embarked on an odyssey to find my son's lost mind. First I sought help and advice from the 'professionals' as I floundered about in isolation and despair. I was enraged by the lack of interest and competence of those people who stood by, doing nothing to prevent his decline. Each one of them said that they couldn't do anything unless my son harmed himself, me or someone else. On numerous occasions his GP suggested I take my son to see him but he refused. My son did not believe there was anything wrong with him, that the problem was other people. Once again I turned to my mother for help, but she wasn't able to hear me. Eventually my son was seen by a psychiatrist and sectioned under the Mental Health Act. He spent the next ten years in hospitals. Each weekend I visited him.

I joined a support group for relatives of the mentally ill. This depressed me even more. It seemed to me we were all helpless victims. Each meeting reinforced these feelings for me. I had to find another way and left the group. It was then I determined to find out all I could about mental illness. I wanted to be in a position to learn and understand as much as possible in order to help my son and the victims.

I embarked on a two year counselling course, which involved working closely with patients like my son. I followed that with a four year psychotherapy course. I became a volunteer on a helpline specifically for mental illness. I even started to give talks to trainee volunteers for the helpline. Very gradually it dawned on me that my life was becoming much more rewarding and fulfilling. For the first time in my life, in spite of my grief, I started to meet people who supported me in a loving way. I was blessed to meet some very fine and wise teachers who assisted me in developing a sense of a presence of spiritual aspiration beyond myself by which my life is guided towards the light.

I learned so much. There is a psychic aspect to schizophrenia that is little understood. Because of damage to his aura and chakra stems either in this life or a previous one my son has a too open auric field and involuntary access to areas of the lower astral plane. The voices are a mixture of thought forms from other lifetimes, his own guilt feelings, his own poor self-image and other entities that come into his sacred space uninvited. It seems as though he is also in touch with helpers endeavouring to bring him some healing and integration. In chronic cases of schizophrenia, such as my son, there is also a biochemic aspect which requires him to take medication.

Not long after I first met Laura she asked me to tune into her son and to see what his purpose in incarnating had been. I spoke to Oliver's higher self and, with his permission, went to view the planning meeting before Oliver was born. Although he had his own issues to deal with, Oliver's main purpose in developing his mental condition was to help troubled souls move on from the asylum in which they had been stuck for many years. He acted as a portal, showing the souls the way as he was able to all too easily leave his body and take them to the light. This was deeply spiritual work and his mother had incarnated to assist him. Some years later I met a young Greek-Cypriot man who had grown up next door to this particular asylum – a former Victorian workhouse – and who, as a child, 'played with the ghosts'. He said that gradually he realised that they needed to move on and that one of the patients appeared to him – in his etheric form – and said that he would take them into the light as 'this was his job'. Leaving the asylum (as it was always known locally), which was closed down so that its inmates could experience 'care in the community', was deeply traumatic for Oliver who, not surprisingly, felt like he was being pulled out by his roots. 'Care in the community' failed miserably. Many of the former patients were left to wander the streets with nowhere to go amid an uncaring and often hostile world. Oliver was fortunate in that he had Laura to fight for him and to get him into the sheltered care environment he needed. Laura also picked up on the redemptive karma and service aspect that lay behind her son's 'disease':

> I also came to see that there is also a collective reason for my son's condition – by being ill in this way he (and most others who bear mental illness) carry some of the collective shadow so that others don't have to carry it. There is a level at which those who are ill enable those who are well to be well and this applies across the whole spectrum of disease. So there is a strong purpose to my son's condition for his own karma/ evolution and as a service/sacrifice to society. There is a greatness in the souls of those who make such sacrifice.
>
> I learned my deepest pain can give me my greatest joy. My son has schizophrenia, and his torment engulfs me frequently. But what joy when he took me out to lunch and paid for it with money he had earned from creating his own art work. What a joy and a privilege to spend Christmas lunch with him in the community where he now lives with all the other residents. To pull Christmas crackers together and see their smiles. What joy to sit in his community garden on a beautiful summer's day and celebrate his birthday with all the residents and staff, who work so hard to make it such a special occasion. Losing my son to schizophrenia feels like a bereavement with no body to grieve over, because the son I knew is no more and yet his body remains. Schizophrenia has brought with it indescribable despair, as over the years I have watched helplessly as the illness runs amok with our lives. It not only destroys its immediate victim but I have seen and spoken to countless families whose lives have been torn apart, including mine, in my work as a therapist. My son continues to be my greatest inspiration and teacher, and all those like him. I honour him, and feel unconditional love and complete gratitude towards him. I realise that I am who I am today because of him. He is like a fragile beautiful flower, an innocent, trusting, loving child without guile. His consultant said to me he thought it was heroic of me to take him away on holiday to the sea for a few days. I am not the hero, my son is, and all those like him.
>
> A few years later, my daughter married. There was great excitement when she became pregnant. I was looking forward to my first grandchild. We were looking forward with such joy to holding, nurturing, and protecting the new little being. This beautiful little boy

did not stay with us long. He appeared perfect, but on the fourth day it became apparent that he had a heart defect. My distraught daughter sat up all night holding her little one until he died in her arms. My mother telephoned me to enquire about the baby. I told her what had happened. The callousness of her reply was unbelievable. "We all have our problems". She made no contact with my daughter. After the little one's sudden and cruel departure the pain, black thoughts, and unanswered questions swirled around and around. My daughter was overwhelmed with grief, she felt robbed, confused and bitter. I tried to give her as much support as I could. We were both grieving in our own ways. I asked Martin Israel, my teacher and friend, why such things happen. "Souls have their own reasons", he replied.

These days I endeavour to find my own way, to be eclectic, to design and practise my own spiritual life and awareness, through reading, through practicing exercises that appeal to me and through continually exploring the interface between psychology and the spiritual path and psychology and alchemy. There are no easy answers, but I feel a sense of trust in the meaningfulness of whatever happens in life and live more calmly from day to day and seek direction in the art of being.

Finally, after a lifetime of despising my absent mother, of feeling such absolute hatred and loathing for her, with assistance from wonderful teachers, and years of working on myself, I have reached a stage of forgiveness towards her. I have learnt that forgiveness is a state of being. Two years before my mother died we were able to have a profound talk. She told me that she thought she was doing the best thing for me when she put me in a home as a child. She was able to tell me that she needed my love that she was proud of me and did love me. I told her I loved her. I could see she reacted as she did with me because she didn't know any different. She acknowledged she hadn't been a very good mother. I visited her often. She was developing dementia and cancer. She was very loving and benign. All her venom towards me had dissipated. We spent some good times together, laughing, singing old songs from her youth, playing fun games. I massaged her hands. As she took her last breath on this earth plane I was privileged to be present and to repeat several times so that she could hear me, "Go to the Light". This felt like the completion of our journey together.

This was not the end though! There was to be a further twist to my story. I received a phone call from one of my half brothers informing me that the family was arranging for my mother's body to be flown from the UK to a Mediterranean country where she had lived. She was to be buried there according to the orthodox Jewish tradition. I flew out to meet my mother's coffin and attend her funeral. On arrival, I was informed that I would not be allowed to attend her funeral as according to this particular tradition it was men only. I requested a meeting with the Rabbi as I wished to try and understand why this was so. Basically his explanation to me was that the women are segregated from the men in case the men looked at the women and had lustful thoughts. The Rabbi suggested that, if I wished, I could stand at a discreet distance, outside the cemetery gates, unseen and watch the proceedings. I declined. It did not seem appropriate. I was also told that I would not be allowed to attend the stone-setting ceremony at my mother's grave, for the same reasons. Many members of the Jewish community came up to me. They spoke of how much they had loved and respected my mother and of her great generosity to the community. They spoke of the many acts of kindness she had done. I did not recognise any of their descriptions.

When Laura returned from that funeral experience which reeked so much of the old rejection and alienation she had experienced at her mother's hand, I asked her what she thought she had learned from all this? Her reply was 'perhaps to be more tolerant, less judgemental and that forgiveness is a state of being'. My experience of Laura is that she is one of the most forgiving and compassionate people I have ever known. Exactly a year after her mother's death we did some work together to help her mother's soul pass on – she was being held back by her Jewish sons, Laura's half brothers, who were holding onto her as much as she was holding onto them. Neither side could let go. Unbeknown to us a religious service was being held at exactly the same time to help the soul to move on. Laura was able to speak to her mother from her heart and finally express her anger at how she had been treated. "I didn't know any different," her mother said sadly, clearly feeling rather sorry for herself, but she had finally heard what her daughter had to say. Having offered unconditional love and forgiveness to her mother yet again, Laura was able to let her go with love and her grandmother arrived to take her daughter to the light and to reconciliation. We then went into the interlife to explore exactly what Laura's soulplan had been for the present life. I began by asking her why she had chosen this particular family group as, although we knew why she had chosen to incarnate to assist her son, we had never explored her soul relationship with the rest of her family:

> [Laura]: To give them an opportunity to change and to grow. They knew no different, they hadn't received love and didn't know how to give it. I wanted to be the means by which they could develop it and I was fully prepared to accept it if they couldn't.

> [Judy]: Was this an act of service?

> [Laura (sounding surprised)]: Yes, it was. I hadn't thought of it that way but that's what it was. My beloved Grandmother was there to support me, to give me a beacon of hope and the love I needed to go through the experience. We had agreed on that so I wouldn't be totally alone.

> [Judy]: Why were you willing to take on what could potentially be such a difficult life?

> [Laura]: Well, first of all to become much less judgemental, to look at the reasons behind things. I wanted to learn how people could be affected by outside influences – as I could myself. And then to become more accepting of the alienated and mentally ill among us. I wanted to offer unconditional love and compassion to those who were undergoing serious mental suffering of all kinds. I had already offered to support Oliver in his spiritual work among the mentally ill but I also needed to know myself how it felt to be abandoned, alienated and unloved, to be immersed in that grim world of the outsider. Only then could I truly understand what they were going through. And finally, there was that old chestnut, forgiveness. I wanted to understand that it was a process, a way of being rather than a single act.

The picture gallery of the soul

*Only within yourself exists that other reality for which you long. I can
give you nothing that has not already its being within yourself. I can
throw open to you no picture gallery but your own soul.*

Herman Hesse

Elizabeth, who we met briefly when looking at the effect of cancer on her
mother, wanted to know why she herself had chosen such a difficult life.
Her mother and father had both died while she was pregnant with Mark,
her second child, and she had had to nurse them as well as cope with
her own young family and her grief. Although intellectually she knew
that these deaths had, finally, released her to move across the country
and establish a life for herself, and to then leave her unsatisfactory
marriage and set up her own business which fulfilled her interests and
soul intention – which eventually led to her meeting her twinflame –
she still felt there was unresolved business especially at the emotional
level as she kept crying and became emotionally wound up whenever
she thought about her parents' death.

Initially, I spontaneously took a look at the Askashic Record on her
behalf. I was not working from her chart, merely from the soul contact I
had made with Elizabeth. However, the reading was not handed over to
Elizabeth. Instead I sent it to Gabriel, her twinflame, who agreed with
me that it would be better for Elizabeth to do her own session exploring
her interlife planning and the past life reasons before reading what I had
seen. In that way we could compare the experience with the reading –
we had already agreed to use both in this book – because I knew that
things were often presented to the soul in several different ways:

*At the interlife planning meeting there are seven family members present
who are part of Elizabeth's wider soul group and, standing behind them,
their higher selves. They are sitting around the table with various advisers
and guides. Elizabeth is in the centre chair with Miriam, her mother and
Alex, her father, on either side. Her two present-life sons and their father
Brian sit around the table and, at the other end, Gabriel, her twinflame
is waiting silently to take his part in the proceedings. Elizabeth sets out
to the group her feelings on what she needs her next lifetime to achieve.
She is aware that for many lives now she has experienced huge grief*

and enormous anger and frustration following a massacre that she had to witness but could not halt. She knows that, had she spoken out, she would also have been killed. But she has no details of that life.

She is also aware that, in later lives, she experienced the premature deaths of her children and her parents and somehow felt that this was a karmic punishment but, again, has no precise details. She feels she is intimately connected with death but is stuck in the grief process rather than being able to move through it. She has come before those who guide her soul's progress to ascertain what kind of life will assist her to move on – and to find her soul's purpose in experiencing these and other losses. She also wants to find a way to be able to express her anger and frustration clearly rather than having to hold it all in as she recognises that this could cause physical dis-ease in the life to come. She also wants to know how to fulfil her highest purpose and what she can do to serve others.

On the opposite side of the table a large screen is set up and Elizabeth's higher self asks her whether she is prepared to view the life that began this long process. As he asks, Elizabeth puts out her hand as though begging for support, saying she is not sure she has the strength to go through it again. Gabriel, her twinflame comes to sit by her and takes her hand, quietly offering his strength and compassion. No words are necessary. Miriam, Elizabeth's present-life mother, moves away, saying she cannot bear to watch as she already knows the details. Her father Alex sits frozen in place, but mutely calls to his wife to return and support him. Her mother returns to put an arm around him, but resolutely faces away from the screen.

On the screen a scene appears: a Roman province to which a state visit is taking place. A Roman emperor and empress sit in a high box above an arena. In close up, the empress's face is stiff and unnaturally still, it is Elizabeth. All around the arena a crowd are gathered, although they have half-heartedly cheered the arrival of the emperor, they are subdued and mutter to each other. Clearly all is not well. It is a period when control of the empire is breaking down. Soldiers move among the crowd plucking the dissenters out and marching them away.

The doors of the arena open with a screech and a ragged group is pushed into the centre: men, women and children peer around uncertainly, many shading their eyes as if exposed to daylight for the first time in many days. With them are those who were plucked out *of the crowd. A voice announces that these are 'Christians' who have been accused of sedition and fermenting revolt and they are about to be punished. Anyone who has been perceived to be a troublemaker has been placed in the group regardless of whether they are actually Christian. The people plucked out of the crowd are, for the most part, well fed and healthy but the remainder of the group are malnourished and many can barely walk and have scurvy, sores and various physical damage. They have no weapons. Elizabeth's present life father and sons are part of this group along with members of her that-life family and friends. Her present-life mother Miriam is one of her attendants and, although Christian herself, has to hide that fact. Like Elizabeth, she has to watch poker-faced or she will be killed. This is where they both learn to hide their emotions.*

A group of gladiators march into the ring brandishing tridents, spears and nets. They begin to attack the group. One man steps forward, holding up his hand and eloquently asking the emperor for leniency, requesting that they be allowed to practise their religion in peace saying that they have no gripe against Rome and no wish to challenge the emperor's authority. It is Gabriel, Elizabeth's twinflame. The emperor merely turns his thumb down at the request, not speaking.

The screen then flashes back to another scene from the same life in which Elizabeth is attending a secret Christian service along with her mother (her former nurse who had become her attendant), her father and other friends and family. Gabriel is the priest holding a grail cup to give communion. Her marriage to the emperor is an enforced, political one and Gabriel is the man she has loved since childhood. Because he took on the Christian faith at an early age and heard a call to the priesthood, she and her family embraced Christianity. When the emperor became aware that his wife was Christian and attending rituals, he had the priest banished to the colonies and told his wife that, if she contacted him again, they would both be killed. There does not appear to be jealousy, just cold anger that his wife could ally herself with people that he believed to be the enemy – he is a secret follower of Mithras and sees Christianity as in direct competition although the Mithraic religion at this time was a religion for soldiers and not for women. The state religion is something different again to which the emperor pays lip service. When the emperor knew that they would be visiting the province, he sent word to 'round up the Christians to provide the entertainment for the crowd'. The administrators took advantage of the order to get rid of many who were trying to break away from the empire.

As the emperor's thumb goes down, the gladiators attack, going for the weaker members of the group first and attacking them with spears in their sides and through their eyes. These gladiators are former criminals who have been given the choice, fight or be killed. Few who fight do so because they enjoy it, it was a choice made to save their life. Brian, Elizabeth's first husband in her present life, is amongst this group as is Duncan, another of her present-life partners. Both men are extremely angry that they are being used in this way but cannot say anything. They know that if they do not fight aggressively with apparent relish, they will be stripped of their weapons and put to fight wild animals with their bare hands.

Elizabeth has to sit without moving throughout the massacre – as does her attendant. If she closes her eyes for a moment, her emperor husband taps her thigh warningly. She has to watch her beloved twinflame be killed along with so many of her family and friends. She watches while Alex, her present-life father attempts to flee and is brought down, her compassion goes out to him for trying to escape and she sends him strength as he is killed which makes a karmic link between them as she silently promises him help and support for his soul.

Finally the whole group have been killed and are dragged out of the arena and later dumped in a common grave. The emperor feels that some of the gladiators were tardy in their fighting and they are stripped of their weapons and wild animals are released into the arena. Although one or two manage to kill the animals – mostly wild dogs – with their bare hands, most gladiators die. Throughout, Elizabeth has to sit poker-faced and then, finally, has to hand the victors a trophy. One of these, Duncan, will in her present life be one of her partners, but he looks on her with hate and anger, silently vowing to get even and to bring her and all she represents down.

Elizabeth's higher self then briefly shows her a chain of lives where the grief becomes deeper and more and more personal as she loses those close to her. Interwoven through these lives are her present life family, friends and partners – and Duncan wreaking his revenge.

"Why," Elizabeth keeps asking, "Why did I choose a life like that?"

"Well," says her higher self, "Initially you did it because you wanted to inure yourself against pain, to learn to shut down your emotions. You felt that you had been too soft in too many lives, too easily hurt. Far too sensitive. But also you knew that these members of your soul group would elect to be killed because of their religion and you wanted to be there to support them so that someone looked on them with love and compassion in their final hours – especially your twinflame. You were giving them soul service. What you didn't realise was just how this would tie you all together throughout many incarnations with so many unspoken emotions".

At this point Duncan, who has been sitting unnoticed in a corner, enters the discussion.

"You could have stopped it," he says accusingly. "You could have stood up and said no, the crowd would have been on your side but you failed us. You let us suffer. But you always come up smelling of roses, you're always the successful one. You owe me".

Elizabeth's higher self steps forward to remonstrate but Duncan walks off, out of the room, throwing over his shoulder as he goes "Wait till we meet again. I'll get even with you".

Elizabeth and her family then plan the roles that will be taken in her present incarnation. Gabriel, her twinflame, will enter her life only after she has faced many of her life challenges, but he will assist her in fully understanding all she has been through and in putting her soul service into action. He will be her 'reward' for all the insights she has gained up to the point he arrives in her life and they will then mutually support each other as they go forward into the future together.

Her two sons, both of whom were deeply wounded in that Roman life and in subsequent lives, would come to her because she had the wisdom and the compassion to find a way to help them heal – and the younger could have the difficult interuterine start in life that he needed for his own soul purposes. Her elder son, who would be born with dyspraxia and other difficulties, needed her to fight to get him the revolutionary treatment that would enable him to lead a normal life. Brian, her present life first husband, was willing to father the two boys and be part of her initial challenge in meeting repressed anger – but *also, when they had resolved their personal difficulties, to be a support for her in her business. (Although it was clear that, in return, he hoped for the support and insight he would need as he met his own emotional challenges). It was not quite a member of her soul group who unselfishly loved her enough to help her learn a very hard lesson, but it was close. What was not planned, and only barely glimpsed, was that Duncan would intervene in her life, bringing with him all his angst and blame. But in dealing with him and learning the soul lessons he could offer her, she would then be ready for Gabriel.*

When it was time to choose the parents for her present incarnation, Elizabeth, rather than turning to Alex and Miriam, was requested by them to be their child. They had their own soul contract. Alex knew that he was a deeply wounded soul and that his life would be difficult. He had already asked Miriam to be his rock. He knew that he would probably have several breakdowns as he explored the stresses and strains of mental instability. Now he asked Elizabeth too to be part of his support system. He knew that she had the soul wisdom and the strength that he needed. Both Alex and Miriam knew that they would probably return to spirit around the same time as Alex couldn't face life without her and she would be worn out with the feelings she would have to repress. Miriam knew that she would need healing time after the relationship, rather than another partner, and felt that this could best be effected by a return to spirit where they could still be together and find healing. So, they offered Elizabeth an opportunity to immerse herself so deeply in grief that she would, in time, simply have to find a way through. Part of this would come from recognising that they were eternal souls who had their own journey and soul lessons, as was she, but part would also come from the way Elizabeth handled things, the insights she gained and the steps she took to heal.

One of the most important steps was to forgive herself for that far-off Roman life that was so close to all of them still. To recognise that it happened exactly as it was planned to happen, she played her part well, but in doing so she damaged herself by the repression of her emotions – she needed to learn how to handle her sensitivity rather than suppress it and this was a first step in understanding that. The second step was to recognise that her parents' deaths coinciding with her second pregnancy was part of the pre-planning. The toxic womb that resulted from her pain was what her youngest son needed to reseed his unresolved core starvation issues. But, she would also be given the key to help heal that wound. And, one day, she would share all she had learned with a wider public.

As I've said, Elizabeth did not see this reading before coming for a session partly as we did not want to 'contaminate' her own memories but also because I wanted her soul and her advisers to present the material to her in a way they thought appropriate. The scripts below may seem to be somewhat disjointed but that is how a session is, it rarely makes good grammatical sense although it makes perfect sense at a soul level. It also shows how a soul needs to go through an experience, rather than pull back from it, and how the core lifetime can be reframed and healed, which will change the current life for the better. When Elizabeth came for the session, I started by taking her into the lift that would take her up to meet her higher self and then into the planning meeting (see page 23). I asked her who was present at the meeting:

My cousin's there who died from leukaemia when I was about 24-25, he's someone I didn't expect. He's just sitting there looking wise. My aunty is there, my mum's sister and his mum. My mum went to help when my cousin was dying. [Racking sobs]. This feels as though it's all about death, it's horrible.

[Judy]: Ask why it was about death, what was the plan?

[Elizabeth, still sobbing]: It feels like it's cancer, it's really big and everybody wanting to experience that kind of harrowing, slow death and having people to help them through it. But it's more than that, not just that, it's so overwhelming it's really horrible. I can see really clearly that my mum helped my aunty to cope with my cousin's death and then I had to be such a big part of my mum and dad's death. It seems to be about facilitating death, about going – I can't put words to it.

My mum and dad are there and they just look really sorry that I had to go through it all. I feel like I was doing it for them. It was something they needed to do. It wasn't that I wanted to experience death or grief or anything.

[Judy]: So you were helping them?

[Elizabeth]: It was something they needed to do together because they went so close together and knew they were going to go together.
[Pause]
I'm just trying to understand why Mark [her youngest son] had to be involved.

[Judy]: Is Mark there? What does Mark say?

[Elizabeth]: He's really small, he's like the bubbly blonde he was when he was about 3 and 4. He's completely untroubled by it, like a golden child. He's got really bright positive energy and he's not touched by it. He's sitting there trying to be well-behaved and not doing a very good job of it. Like a child.

[Judy]: Ask his higher self why he needed to go through this.

[Elizabeth]: Because he can't stay like that, he's got to grow up and be responsible. He hasn't got the point yet and that's why he still seems quite untouched by it all. His higher self seems so far away from the little boy that's there, it's like he's a very young soul and this is all about him starting to grow.

I feel like I'm the catalyst. I feel like I'm a vehicle that brought him into the world because he had some heavy stuff to go through, like I was the bridge between mum and dad going and him coming.

I feel like I'm still sad and I'm so much more experienced because I've been through so much more. It's really weird, I feel like I'm the oldest person there.

[Moving forward to the present time] Mum and dad are really relaxed and happy now, their energy is really clear. They cleared whatever it was they needed to.

[Back to the planning meeting but also the present time, moving between the two quite easily as appropriate] Jonathan (her oldest son) is there too and he looks upset. It's like he's there calmly just to support me but it was very difficult for him to be born as well. He's saying that he knew he had to do that, he had to be such a difficult child to make me deal with things, to make me stretch and grow and now we can be really close. He says he's really sorry.

[More sobs] I'm still not really understanding why I had to be so unhappy for such a long time.

[Judy]: Ask your higher self to show you. What was it you wanted to learn from that?

[Elizabeth]: I don't know, I just feel like I've been grieving for so long, it goes way back. It's got something to do with children, lots of children. When I was going to the meadow on the way to the house it was full of children. These children seem to be quite happy and ok. Maybe just seeing them so happy helps me, maybe I had a part in their death and I need to know they're ok now.

[Judy]: Ask your higher self if you need to see that or if the information I've got for you will be sufficient.

[Elizabeth]: It's alright just to see them as they are. To know they are ok. Jonathan looks relaxed now, he was really unhappy but now he's calmer and Mark is just Mark. It all seems calmer now.

[Judy]: Ask your higher self what you need to do now.

[Elizabeth]: It's like this is all as it should be now, I don't really feel I've done very much but what I haven't been doing is letting it go. I was kind of carrying it with me and I don't need to do that any more. There isn't any guilt and there isn't any unhappiness or anything now, I can be relaxed. I still feel sad but not as it was. It's like just let it all go and get on with the things you want to do.

[Judy]: Is there any indication what that is?

[Elizabeth, laughs]: They're just saying enjoy yourself and don't go too mad. [More tears] And nothing's really hard because I feel I deserved it.

[Judy]: Can you forgive yourself?

[Elizabeth]: I think so, it just feels so sore inside.

[Judy]: Just hold that Danburite and the Ruby in Zoisite crystal to your heart and take the energy from the stones into your heart. [Danburite is particularly good for forgiveness and Ruby in Zoisite is excellent for releasing 'stuck' grief and old pain].

[Elizabeth]: Oh, it's really warm. [long pause]
They're all sitting there saying 'it's ok, you're fine, just let it go. It's going to take awhile'. The hardest thing is separating Mark from mum and dad because what they're saying is that mum and dad were like a unit and I was in between and it's a shame that it had to happen at once. But Mark isn't held back in any way by their death and I've just got to stop connecting him with it the whole time.

[Judy]: So let's see what we can do with that. Wrap Mark in some pink light [this is a technique I use that Elizabeth was very familiar with] and just go back to the moment of his birth and celebrate his birth.

[Elizabeth, sobbing]: I can't, I can't... [more deep sobs, almost shouts] I can't. It hurts too much because when he comes, they go. I can't be there for him because I'm all wrapped up with them.

[Judy]: So let's just separate them out. Put them in a big bubble of pink light. Say your goodbyes to them, let them go.
[long silence]

[Elizabeth]: I'm going to have to let them go, I know they're ok and I'm going to be ok. It's like it's me that's holding onto them, it's not them that's holding on to me.

This was the break-through insight I'd been waiting for.

[Judy]: Can you let them go with love?

[Elizabeth]: Yes. [long sigh and quiet release]
Mark's such a bright little spirit. He's really raw and bright with great energy. I can see him now. Ah... That's better, I feel I can be me now. It doesn't hurt so much now. It feels like they're all happy now and saying 'come on, just get on with it'. I'm ready, I don't really know what it is but...

[Judy]: Can anyone tell you now what it is?

[Elizabeth]: It's to be discriminating about the people that I'm mixing with and to be proud of what I've done, which is really hard I'm not good at that, to kind of step up to the mark now and I haven't got anything to prove to anybody any more. I've done it and now I can do what I need to do. I can be free to do the books I want, I am really *going to open up now that I've done the hard bit. It's to spread the message and enjoy it. Don't feel guilty. Now they're all going 'yep, we're finished now, it's done'.*

I brought Elizabeth back into the meadow where Gabriel, her twinflame was waiting to meet her.

He's putting his arms round me and saying 'well done' and it's really lovely.

Having had a hug with Gabriel, who had been sitting next to her throughout her regression, she commented how horrible it had been, how black and depressing, how strong and overpowering the emotions had been, especially when she couldn't greet Mark. As Gabriel pointed out, she had been pulled in two directions and was stuck in the middle:

Whichever thing I did, it was going to tear me apart. It was awful. But it was also good, what was really comforting and really lovely was seeing everyone there because once I'd got mum and dad into their pink bubble they were saying 'it's ok, we can go now' and it made me realise I was – while not wanting to – somehow holding onto them. Which released a part of me. I think this is going to take some getting used to.

I remember that I was worried about them long before they were ill, I always had this grief connection with them and used to get terribly upset just thinking about them getting older. It was almost as though I knew – but of course I did know, didn't I? It was like I was grieving in advance because at that stage they weren't even ill. I almost felt like I'd done it before and now I was doing it again for them. I felt absolutely swamped in grief for quite a lot of the way through and I think that's how I've always felt, that's why I cry so easily. The slightest thing sets me off and it's like I'm tapping into the whole of their stuff, it's not just my stuff. The floodgates have got such a fragile lock on them that they get blown open by anything. Weddings and being happy has the same effect in me as being sad. It all wants to pour out like it did then.

As I pointed out to Elizabeth, this is always a sign of unresolved past life business. The trigger is minor but the outpouring is major. The grief, for instance is out of all proportion. At this point Gabriel joined in the discussion saying:

This makes a lot of sense because I'd be watching a film and I'd just suddenly have all this welling up over and above the sentiment of the film. And it was almost because it wasn't close so I could allow something to come through, something bigger. I've always thought I know this is sitting here and I've got to deal with it, I don't know if it's past life things or something else, my mum dying or my first baby dying, I just don't know.

Which was an indication that once we'd finished debriefing Elizabeth, we'd be doing some work with Gabriel too. I gave Elizabeth some Bush Flower essence 'Sturt Desert Pea' for grief and forgiveness and some personal empowerment essence as I find flower essences, like crystals, are a very gentle way of continuing the releasing and healing. While we were waiting for the printer to spit out the soul reading I'd done for Elizabeth she commented:

It's really strange doing that whole thing because part of you thinks: 'is it just my imagination, are those just the people I wanted to be there?' but they look slightly different from how you expect and it's weird because when you start, you think 'this is how I want to see them, this is what I want to imagine' but then something doesn't match up with what you think they're going to say. I wondered why Mark was the pivot because, for me it all seemed to lead to Mark but now after doing that, it doesn't. Mark was caught up in it, he was part of that timing but he's not the cause and he doesn't have the grief connection and I've got to let him go from that – which is what Gabriel has been saying to me all this time. The grief and the guilt and all that is something I've been putting on him because of what I went through and looking at it that way, his higher self was almost going 'oh, gawd'. He's sitting there, this bright bubbly kid and his higher self was behind him going 'this is going to be a tough one' – which I didn't expect.

Elizabeth then read the soul reading I'd already prepared, laughing at how I'd seen seven people and she'd been aware of six which she thought was 'pretty close'. I had seen her ex-husband there as well. She commented that she hadn't been aware of her first husband at the meeting because she felt their connection was more transient rather than being at a soul level (the most surprising people do, however, turn out to be members of our soul group who are around to help us learn some difficult lessons – as she would find out when she'd read the rest of the reading). She commented that a lot of the life I had seen fitted in with what Gabriel had already intuited – of which I hadn't been aware. When she'd finished she said:

> *Wow, that is so accurate. [turning to Gabriel] Have you read it?*

> *[Gabriel]: It's so emotionally powerful and makes sense of such a lot of issues. The characters are all there, the key players. And the guilt.*

> *[Elizabeth]: Yes, I've always felt guilty. I've always felt worried about putting my head above the parapet. Although I've had such strong feelings inside I haven't had the courage to reveal them because I was afraid that I'd get slapped down for it. I'm so glad I didn't have to see all the other stuff, but it just describes exactly how I feel.*
> *[laughs, turning to Gabriel] I bet you can't wait to do one!*

> *[Gabriel]: Well as I mentioned I can relate to so much and it highlights that you recognise instances in your life when things crop up and you see them replayed and realise 'yes, that's probably what was going on with me too' because the symptoms are all there. There was a period when my first baby died, my mother died, my son was born and then I split up with my wife and I never really felt I'd recovered from any of it, it felt like knots in my chest and it's still there. It's not as bad, I used to hyperventilate at one stage. But I still have physical symptoms.*

As we will see, this is yet another instance of a karmic carryover inducing symptoms, but not in quite the way Gabriel was expecting, although he was aware of the connection:

> *I think a lot of the physical issues I get are the result of that rather than any physical problem. It just moves around.*

> *[Judy]: It lands in the body because that's the last place for it to go. There is nowhere else.*

The session with Gabriel naturally followed on from what had been happening. As I said 'half of it is done, so let's do the other half'. I was aware that Elizabeth needed more work but I wanted to give what we had done a chance to work its way through and settle in, and I knew that Gabriel's story was, in any case, closely entwined with hers and suspected that it would naturally lead into the healing and reframing that was required for them both. As with Elizabeth, I took him to the planning meeting and asked who was there:

A lot of it seems to be in shadow. I'm aware that there are people there and I can see Elizabeth and my Uncle Ken, my dad's brother of all people. I don't know quite why he's there. Hmn, he's there in this life to stand at the edge and help me through difficult periods – my dad's not someone you can be close to, he's always been a bit distant and I suppose Ken has been there in some instances. Maybe there's a connection between us at some point further back.

I then asked if Gabriel could see anyone further back in the shadows. Quite often when the planning meeting is 'shadowy' it is because the soul isn't 'all of a piece' and some soul retrieval and integration is required, as proved to be the case. However, he was able to see some of the people gathered there:

My brother and my mum, my sister. I feel my dad's kind of there in spirit but not as a conscious presence if that makes sense. And I get a sense that my son Derek is like that too, kind of partly there and in the background almost.

But, at that stage, Gabriel found it difficult to get any sense of contact with his son or to connect to his own higher self:

I feel like he's there but not as a physical presence.

So I suggested that we see if there was anything he needed to look at first, anything that was relevant:

There's a sense of me going somewhere already, I'm not quite sure where. It feels like it's a long dark tunnel. It's inappropriate to move, I'm with other people, I can't really see them, it's dark, but I'm aware of them around me and I presume we're hiding from something or somebody.

[Judy]: Is it possible to let yourself know what you're hiding from?

[Gabriel]: There are soldiers, an army or something, they're looking for us.

[Judy]: Move around in time until something changes.

[Gabriel]: We've been discovered or somebody's tipped off the Germans and we're being dragged out of the tunnel. I have the sense we're being rounded up and it's like I'm aware of the others' fear but my own concerns are more to do with these people rather than myself.

[Judy]: So do you have some sort of responsibility for them?

[Gabriel]: I get a sense that I could be their priest. I feel more angry than fearful at the way we're being treated and pushed around and so forth.

[Judy]: Do you know what religion you are?

*[Gabriel]: I'm wearing a long smock and a dog collar, full length…
It's a firing squad, they are all lined up and their rifles are aiming at us. They are waiting for the order to fire.*

[Judy]: Which country are you in?

[Gabriel]: I think it's France. It seems like one of those eternal moments when you're standing there and time has been suspended.

[Judy]: Is there a part of you left there, a part that you need to bring back?

[Gabriel]: I feel there is, the strength and dignity that I had there, to stand up and face death, I kind of lost or left behind. I don't feel I have that quality here in this life.

[Judy]: Do you need to help those people move over and pass on?

[Gabriel]: I guess so. Maybe that's why I'm stuck there wanting to make sure they're all ok.

[Judy]: So let yourself move on so you can be ready to meet them the other side of death and direct them to those who can assist them.

[Gabriel]: It's that inner strength and resilience that I'm missing.

[Judy]: Can you bring that part of yourself back now? Or is there anything else you need to do?

[Gabriel]: There's a sense of knots in my chest and solar plexus and

round the urinary area. I'm not quite sure what they indicate but I can feel the three areas quite clearly.

[Judy]: Was this where the bullets hit? Is it a remnant?

[Gabriel]: Yes, it could be. Certainly the one in the chest is.

[Judy]: Let that be healed.

[Gabriel]: That seemed to have eased the chest one.

[Judy]: Move down to the next one.

[Gabriel]: That's been eased as well.

[Judy]: Go on down to the base one.

At this point Gabriel's body began to shudder, twitch and pulsate as the old sensations began to leave his body. He breathed deep and sighed out the feelings. This went on for a long time as the energy released. I knew that he needed time, that there was no point in trying to hurry or cut short the process as deep soul healing was taking place. Eventually I asked him where he was with it:

I've always felt that there was something holding me back and weighing me down inside. There's a lot still coming up from the bladder region but it feels like most of it's out.

At this point I suggested that he breathe in light to help loosen and transmute the remaining energy. Then I asked if he was aware of any other sensations as I suspected that this soul healing needed to go even further back:

Funnily enough my shins feel as though they are on fire. I get a sense of some other life being burned at the stake as though my lower legs up to the knees were burnt.

This seemed to connect to punishment for so-called heresy although it was not relevant to see exactly what it was. I suggested Gabriel move up and out of his body to let the healing flow through. When someone has been burned at the stake their consciousness usually leaves around the time the fire reaches the knees, it's as though all the air is sucked out of their lungs by the heat and it frees the soul. (I have found the Bush Flower essence Mulla Mulla works well in such situations so gave

Gabriel a bottle to take home at the end of the session so that the healing process could continue).

It's still paining my shins, I don't seem to be able to shift that.

[Judy]: Is it a remnant from something earlier?

[Gabriel]: I have a sense of being winded in the stomach as if shins were broken or smashed in some beating.
... [long pause]
I can't seem to shift the shins.

[Judy]: Go back to the core, back to the first time, to before this happened.

[Gabriel]: I want to say that I can't leave my legs behind.

[Judy]: Let's see where you left your legs, where were you separated? Where were your legs taken out from under you?

[Gabriel]: That analogy seems to resonate so deeply, several lifetimes as well as this one. It feels like it's in that gladiatorial ring of Elizabeth's. As if that's what happened there, I was dismembered, I don't know exactly but that's the feeling.

This was the point where the reframing I knew was needed could take place, first for Gabriel and then for Elizabeth.

[Judy]: Go back in that lifetime to the moment when you were standing before the emperor pleading for the lives of all the people in the arena with you. See yourself standing there with courage. Instead of putting his thumb down, the emperor puts his thumb up so that you are all released. He gives clemency.

[Gabriel]: There's huge relief. I am able to walk away. It unwinds the rest of the lives – there's a look of relief on Elizabeth's face too. I want to say that in all my lives it was always my legs, each time it was 'oh no, not again, my legs'.

[Judy]: Well, let's make sure they are healed and that the healing carries forward through all the lives right into the present. No karmic imprint is left, it's all dissolved. Let that split off part of you reintegrate. Now

look at the etheric blueprint from which your body was made this time around and make sure that is healed and whole.

When Gabriel went back to the planning meeting there was far more light and it was less shadowy so he had integrated that part of himself but it seemed clear that another session would be needed before we could really access his soul intention, although he was able to say:

My sense is that I needed to be whole and healed. Elizabeth is beside me and has her arms round me and everybody else seems to have a sense of completion.

I then brought Gabriel into stronger contact with his higher self and left him there while I turned my attention to Elizabeth once more. I took her back to that moment when Gabriel was asking her husband for clemency and to see her husband standing holding his thumb up rather than pointing down. She would then no longer carry that awful burden of guilt, she could put it down and let the lightness move all the way through all her lives up to the present moment and she could be free to express her feelings. She could let go anything that was detrimental to her and move into light.

[Elizabeth]: They're all holding me and telling me it's ok now.

[Gabriel]: I found myself back there with Elizabeth and tears were welling up with relief that what she had been through was now over.

We then put the forgiving energy of Danburite and white light through both of them to help them forgive themselves and everyone involved. Gabriel's comment was that he felt like a weight had been lifted, he felt much calmer on a very deep level. As for Elizabeth:

Even though I hadn't previously been in that life in regression, when you asked me to I could just step straight in, I was absolutely there and in the terror that was inside me at what was happening. When you changed it, I just wanted to give thanks to everything for saving me. It's made a massive difference.

[Gabriel]: It's funny. When you first told me to go back and I couldn't feel my legs, I kept getting a scene of a gladiatorial arena. I kept wondering was I linking into Elizabeth's story and it kept coming and in

the end I thought no it must be that because there's nothing else coming. I suppose I was just resisting because I thought I was tapping into what you'd seen but of course it makes sense, I was there.

It's funny how all these things link in, not just the legs – which I've had problems with in my present life and in many other lives – but the psychological ramifications of being legless or having no legs. The solar plexus and bladder seemed to overlap being related to the legs not just the bullets. The chest thing evaporated straight away because it was a one off, but the other things came from a deeper place. I could feel it unwinding and coming apart as my body moved.

[Elizabeth]: I think it's when you get those bodily reactions, that's what makes you believe. The first time you do it you're really sceptical and scared of failing, but then when you actually get involved and things crop up like my cousin, that's when you start to realise there's something else going on and you have faith in it. Then you've got the courage to move into the scene and realise that it's there with some integrity and it's not just a figment of your imagination. I wasn't that close to my cousin but then I saw that it was a symbol of death and that's when all the death thing started unfurling which I didn't expect. I don't feel at all upset now.

This is a perfect example of how a twinflame appears at just the right moment to facilitate healing; Elizabeth and Gabriel's paths had crossed only relatively recently but they instantly recognised their soul-level connection. When the opportunity arose, they were both ready to reframe and heal their past lives for their mutual benefit and that of their wider soul family.

Karmic consequence or something other?

So, for one last time, let's have a look at options open to a soul in the interlife and explore how something like a failure that may, in most people eyes be a disaster could actually be the soul's way of getting back on its path. Say we have a soul called Matthew who has tried being a very rich man – and who perhaps did not treat his slaves and workers very well. In that life Matthew had a mean spirit that stored up his riches for himself. After death, he'd have been in for something of a shock when he found himself spiritually bankrupt and in no position to give orders or to demand that his needs be met. In the interlife, not yet ready to give up the comfort and trappings of a rich man, Matthew may choose to try another life in which he has considerable wealth but perhaps this time his soulplan will be to develop compassion and generosity of spirit.

So, Matthew might choose to incarnate into a wealthy family with a history of philanthropy. Once in incarnation and having lost the memory of his intention, he would then have to discover whether the soul overlay of holding onto his wealth could be overcome by his soul purpose of learning to be generous. Along the way, Matthew might meet some of those previous life slaves and workers that he treated badly. Perhaps as petitioners for his charity. This is where reparation and recompense could come in. He could make them beneficiaries of a gift of money, food or clothes. But remember the saying that if you give a man a fish, you feed him for one year. Teach him to fish and you feed him for life? This is why wealthy families such as the Frys and Cadburys in England set up communities that had factories and housing to give people work and reasonable conditions in which to live. Our man too could choose to improve the lot of those he had previously treated badly. Or he could not. Matthew might be so stuck in attitudinal karma, arrogance and needing to hold onto his wealth – or to squander it as a rebound from previously hoarding, that he might not learn the lesson that he soul had planned.

Back into the interlife he goes and starts planning for his next incarnation. This time Matthew plans to know what it is like to be without, to experience total lack. He may go into a poor family or into a monastery where he has to give up everything. In the first case, he may experience severe lack but the possibility is open for him to find a way through. In the second case he may have decided to learn humility and his minimal physical needs will be cared for and his soul may receive nourishment but – unless he chose to incarnate during the Reformation when monks were turned out of their monasteries and then learned what real poverty was like – it would be all there was for that life. Matthew may learn that true humility does not come from being scourged and from the constant confession of sin. It is a state of the heart, a way of being. The vow of poverty that he takes in the monastery may tie him to a cycle of lives where lack is all he knows, even if he takes a different path and makes money, he will quickly lose it, or feel guilty and uncomfortable around money and not deal with it well. If Matthew does not progress far enough in the interlife, he could bounce reflexively back into the same conditions over and over again or between the two extremes. He may be pulled between vows made on his deathbed such as 'I'll never know poverty again' and the monkish giving up of all worldly goods.

Eventually, in the interlife, our man will review all these previous lives. Matthew will see how he bounced between extremes, how he tried to learn through lack and how he tried to understand how to handle money. How he intended to learn empathy through sharing the same conditions. How he tried to change his arrogance to humility. And, perhaps, how he learned the tenacity and survival skills that would bring him through eventually into a more balanced place.

So Matthew comes back in recent times, perhaps into a poor family, perhaps not. Perhaps he sees that with education – and with what seems from outside like a bit of luck and good contacts but which may involve careful interlife planning and soul contracts made with members of his soul group – he can build a successful life. But when he gets into incarnation, he forgets everything but that drive towards success. So let's say Matthew takes advantage of the computer revolution and starts up one of those dot com companies that did so well. Maybe his partner is one of those soul contracts he made in the interlife. For a year or two Matthew lives the good life. Then his world crumbles. He finds his partner has taken the profits and run. The dot com dream crashes and failure looms large. His trophy wife leaves, the big house and the fancy car have to be sold.

At this point everything depends on whether Matthew has learned to find inner security, compassion and humility. If he has inner strength, then he may start again. But perhaps this time Matthew will choose another career, one that has a more caring aspect to it. Become an aid worker maybe, or teach computer skills to the disadvantaged. I have met several people who have willingly surrendered the good life to do exactly that. They gave up what they realised wasn't serving their soul. I have met other people who used their money to set up foundations and learning programmes. It all depended on how much they were still caught up in karmic consequences and how much they were living out their soulplan for the present life. In other words, how much they had grown their soul.

Conclusion: Growing your Soul

I am still determined to be cheerful and happy, in whatever situation I may be; for I have also learned from experience that the greater part of our happiness or misery depends upon our dispositions, and not upon our circumstances.

Martha Washington

*O*ne of the most important parts of growing your soul seems to be the compassionate witnessing of your own journey and that of others – that and being able to forgive. The experiences you have may help you to resonate with what someone else is going through – and to be less judgemental of the journey of another or of yourself. It is possible to share your insights gained along the way, sometimes privately and at other times very publicly. I am grateful to author Mario Reading for allowing me to share with you what I consider to be a beautiful example of compassionate witnessing despite what he describes as his moral outrage. This extract also gives us a glimpse of his extraordinary story and of what he has learned from having 'terminal' cancer for the last twenty years. This story is taken, with his willing permission, verbatim from his blog:

> *Very little shocks me in the normal course of events, but today, when I walked into my local newsagent, I was rocked to the core of my being. There, on the racks in front of me, I saw a copy of Britain's* The Sun *newspaper, with a headline, in bold block capitals – JADE'S CRY: I'LL BE DEAD IN A MONTH. Alongside the headline was a photograph of former* Big Brother *and* Celebrity Big Brother *contestant Jade Goody, completely bald from the effects of powerful chemotherapy, and with an expression of such extreme grief on her face, that one could only compare the image she presented with that of Edvard Munch's 1893 painting of* The Scream. *I can only assume that Antonella Lazzeri, who wrote the piece, and Sun editor Rebekah Wade, who presumably okay-ed it, have neither of them suffered the effects of terminal cancer during the course of their lives. I, on the other hand, have. Jade Goody*

[now Mrs Tweed] is, I understand, the mother of two sons. She has terminal cervical cancer which has moved to her liver, bowel and groin. She is 27 years old. I was 38 years old when I received my terminal diagnosis, in 1992, in Toulouse, France, after two years of pretty much unimaginable misery – and I, too, was the father of a young son. Jade Goody will have gone through a similar traumatic period, much truncated – her cancer was confirmed only in August 2008, after two previous scares back in 2004 and 2006 – but equally traumatising.

Without having experienced the utter certainty of imminent death, it is hard for anyone to comprehend the enormity of the situation one is forced, unwillingly, to inhabit. I was lucky enough, following my one month terminal diagnosis, to respond, almost miraculously, to the extreme treatment [surgery, radiotherapy, and chemotherapy] that my French doctors, with little else left in their pharmacological armoury, threw at me. I gather that, in Mrs Tweed's case, such a miracle is unlikely to happen, and that she has just now entered a palliative care hospice, on a two day trial basis, in order to spare her sons the agony of watching their mother go through the process of dying. It is easy to be clever after the event, and to revel in moral outrage. But in this case such moral outrage is, I believe, justified. Confucius wrote that 'To be trustworthy in word is close to being moral in that it enables one's words to be repeated. To be respectful is close to being observant of the rites in that it enables one to stay clear of disgrace and insult'. In the next few weeks, Mrs Tweed must come to terms with the terrible reality which has been thrust upon her. To do that she will need all her strength. Dying is an intensely lonely experience. In my case, I was fortunate enough not to be a celebrity – in other words no one, apart from my closest family, interested themselves in my going. I was thus able to call upon natural reserves I never knew I had – reserves that hadn't been depleted by the forced externalisation of emotion caused by obsessive media interest – in order the better to make my soul. It is, quite frankly, irrelevant, whether or not Mrs Tweed called any or all of this publicity down upon herself – she deserves, just as any person in extremis deserves, our protection. Human beings sometimes behave inappropriately, even self-destructively, and allowance should be made both for Mrs Tweed's age and for her condition – it is impossible to think clearly and rationally when suffering invasive treatment and under an imminent sentence of death.

I was lucky enough to be allowed to go home for one last weekend before my final return to the Institut Claudius Regaud in Toulouse. Unable to walk without a stick, and having lost forty percent of my normal body weight, I was hardly in a position to go walkabout. However something drove me to start down, before dawn, to my favourite meadow below the woods that surrounded my house. I knew that I would never be able to get myself back up the hill again, but I left a note for my still sleeping future wife as to my whereabouts, and departed on what I suspected might be my final adventure. When I reached the lower field, the mist was just rising from the damp grass, and the dawn was breaking. I limped through the knee-high grass, breathing in, for what I felt would be the very last time, the precious scent of meadow sweet. It was at this moment that I felt a presence behind me. For some reason I continued walking, unwilling, or unable, to turn around. Slowly, the presence at my side began to overwhelm me, and I felt a sense of the most unutterably perfect friendship. At that exact moment, stumbling through the sunlit meadow in my dressing gown, my collar turned up against the early morning chill, all fear deserted me, and I realised that I was not alone, and that the presence beside me was that of God. I suddenly knew without knowing that this presence was perfect, and total, and that whatever happened to me, whatever subsequently came to pass, would be all right. I offered myself completely to God at that moment, inexpressibly grateful for the comfort of His presence. I did not need to turn to see Him – He was everywhere, He was everything.

That experience changed my life. On my return to hospital, I slowly recovered from my illness, to the astonishment of my doctors, my family, and myself. I realise now how lucky I was to have been allowed the space and the peace to find these things out about myself – to explore my relationship with God, and to understand that only by total abrogation of the Self – that only by complete submission – is salvation possible. I was quite happy to die by the end. I almost welcomed it. Mrs Tweed must be allowed the same courtesy. I refuse to criticise the people who are benefiting from Mrs Tweed's agony. People do things. It is their nature. But I would like everyone to stop for a moment, and imagine themselves, if they can, in Mrs Tweed's place. To wonder what is appropriate behaviour towards a person who deserves our support. Confucius again [using D. C. Lau's translation, as before]: 'It is only the most intelligent and the most stupid who are not susceptible to change'.[1]

In conversation, Mario, when asked what he had learned from his cancer experience simply said: 'acceptance'. He faces his life with complete equanimity, knowing that he will die, 'most probably sooner rather than later' and determined to do all he came to do. His written output is voracious, he has so much to say and share with the world. A few members of the writers' group to which we both belong were horrified by a passage in his novel based on the genocide of the Mayan race back when the Old World took over the New. The rest of us were totally gripped, it was written as though he was there, with great empathy and understanding of how such a terrible event in the life of one man could have a greater purpose – that of preserving their ancient knowledge. (You'll have to read his book for yourself to learn the rest of the story).

But there was more, not from Mario's point of view but from Jade Goody's. She, or those around her and especially those who are so hungry for 'celebrity culture', may not have given her time for inward reflection but she certainly brought that out in her audience. On Thursday 22nd October 2009 I was looking at my email when I spotted that AOL had another Jade headline:

'Tragic Jade boosts cancer screening'

The article went on to report that Jade Goody's high-profile battle with cervical cancer had boosted cancer screening in the UK especially in young women. The number of women aged 25 to 64 who underwent screening had increased by almost half a million and was still rising according to a report. The first time this percentage had increased since 2002. The British government's Health Secretary, Andy Burnham, said:

'These figures show the remarkable effect that Jade Goody's tragic case has had in reversing a downward trend in the number of young women attending cervical screening. Jade's bravery and openness in her fight against cervical cancer has brought home to young women across the country the importance of regularly going for these checks… which will save the lives of hundreds of women in the years ahead'.

However, just a few months later there was another headline saying that had Jade's cancer been diagnosed a few months earlier, she would have lived. That cannot of course be known but what is known was that the number of young women being screened was falling again. The Director of Jo's Trust,[2] a charity that supports those with cervical cancer and campaigns for earlier diagnosis supported the idea that the sooner the diagnosis, the higher the possibility of survival highlighting the fact that Jade being 'so public and so brave in revealing her diagnosis' had resulted in a 12% increase in young women seeking screening. So this headline and the programme that followed brought the issue back to the public attention. Who knows, the life of an ephemeral so-called-reality T.V. star might have been the vehicle chosen in the interlife by Jade Goody's soul as an act of service to raise awareness amongst women. Her death in the limelight certainly brought home the reality of the cancer epidemic and helped the British public to face something they tend to resolutely avoid: the inevitability of death.

From our earthly perspective I don't think we can ever know the whole breadth of *Why*, either for ourselves and most certainly not for our world. We can, however, gain insights into our personal karma and our soul's purpose for the present life and we may see collective or racial karma played out in front of us or indeed take part in it or oppose it – or find ways of transmuting it. But the vast libraries of the Akashic Record that hold the cosmic memory bank contain all possibilities and who knows whether, in some parallel reality, another part of our soul is asking a different question or living a polar-opposite life. It is by no means certain that our future is fixed and predictable, surprises are always waiting around the corner. Surprises that we can face with equanimity – if we recognise them as triggers to put more of our soulplan into action. Knowing your soulplan does not, of course, mean that you will then have an easy life with no nasty surprises, but it does mean that you will be able to see the purpose that lies behind such events. You will approach them from a calm centre with higher awareness, seeking the gift at their heart as you follow your soul's plan to scour off the karmic encrustations from many lives and grow your soul. I hope that this book has given you an insight into why you are here and what your potential is *in this present moment*.

We are not here just to survive and live long...
We are here to live and know life in its multi-dimensions
to know life in its richness, in all its variety.
And when a man lives multi-dimensionally,
explores all possibilities available,
never shrinks back from any challenge...
then life becomes a flame,
life blooms.

Bhagwan Shree Rajneesh: The Sacred Yes

Notes

Introduction
1. Schwartz, Robert, *Courageous Souls*, Whispering Winds Press, USA, 2007.

Part 1
1. If you are interested in near death experiences, see my book *Psychic Connections* which reviews the evidence and gives case histories.
2. This view was popular in the 1970s in the books of Lobsang Rampa for instance but is found in other authors and stems back to Hindu and Tibetan Buddhist philosophies. (Contrary to what he claimed, Rampa was not a Tibetan monk).
3. Emerson, Ralph Waldo 'The Over-Soul' in *Essays*, 1841.
4. See my books *Good Vibrations* and *Psychic Connections*.
5. Interview in *Reincarnation International*, November 1995, pp.10-15.
6. Hall, Judy *Torn Clouds*, O Books, Alresford.
7. *Plato: The Last Days of Socrates*, translated by Hugh Tredennick, Penguin Classics, London, 1934. p.170ff.
8. Verny quoted in Lipton below, p.143.
9. Lipton, Bruce, *The Biology of Belief*, Hay House, 2008. p.134.
10. For a short summary see Bruce Lipton especially 'Conscious Parenting', p.114ff.
11. Yelverton, Juliet, 'Not enough money – shortage of love?' *South West Connections*, Dec. 2009/March 2010. I am grateful to Juliet for the insights I gained from this and other articles on her website and the researchers to which she pointed the way.
12. See *Good Vibrations* and *Psychic Self Protection*, the most up to date of my psychic protection books.
13. Leboyer, Dr. Frederick, *Birth Without Violence*, 1975, p.30.
14. For details see www.lizroe-french.co.uk and www.psych-k.com
15. *Principles of Past Life Therapy*, long out of print but some of the material has been incorporated into this present book.
16. Ghandi, *Letters to a Disciple*, Harpers, 1950.
17. See Grof, Stanislav, *The Cosmic Game*, State University of New York Press, NY, 1998. I am indebted to James Frazier, who worked with Grof, for several in-depth conversations on the experiences undergone during such work.
18. Haggard, Rider, *She*, Collins, London, 1961 edition, p.158.
19. Cloete, Stuart, 'Introduction' in Haggard, Rider, *She*, Collins, London, 1961 edition, p.12.
20. Addy, Shirley, *Rider Haggard and Egypt*, AL Publications, Accrington, 1998.

Part 2

1. Steiner, p.72.
2. See *Good Vibrations*.
3. The karmic blueprint after Roger Woolger with additional material by Judy Hall.
4. ibid
5. *Bhagavad Gita 2*, Penguin Classics, London, 1962, translated by Juan Mascaro, p.29.
6. Motoyama, p.34.
7. Source: Judy Hall with additional material from Glen Williston and Judith Johnstone, *Discovering your Past Lives*, The Aquarian Press, Wellingborough, 1988, p.86.
8. Quoted in Cerminara, p.123.
9. Steiner, *Manifestations of Karma*, pp.169-209.
10. See Hans Holzer, *Born Again*, Folkestone, Bailey and Swinfern Ltd,1975, for details of this fascinating case.
11. Motoyama, pp.74-75.
12. Steiner, *Manifestations of Karma*, p.81.
13. *Plato: Last Days of Socrates*, Penguin edition, p.179.
14. Information sheet from the Bektash museum, Nevshehir.

Part 3

1. Whitton, Dr Joel, L. and Fisher, Joe, *Life between Life*, Grafton Books, London, 1987, p.106.
2. I do not have a note of the exact Radio 4 programme, but it was most probably *The Call*.
3. *The Call*, 10 August 2009, BBC Radio 4.
4. St James, Jewelle, *Jude: My Reincarnation From Auschwitz*, St James Publishing, Revelstoke, Canada, 2006.
5. *A Stranger in Paradise* is available from http://www.juliechimes.co.uk. For details of Julie's forgiveness and reconciliation work, see http://www.facebook.com/pages/Julie-Chimes-on-Forgiveness/ 119454641419665?ref=sgm
6. See for instance the work of Dr Ian Pierce and other researchers in the field.
7. Morris, Pamela, *I've Had My Dance*, Erica Press, New Zealand.
8. Simonov, Konstantin, *Wait for Me*, trans. Alan Moray Williams, circa 1944.
9. Robert Christofourides in personal correspondence, used with his permission for which I thank him. See my *Hades Moon*, Samuel Weiser, Maine, 1998, for the astrological reading of the synastry between these charts.
10. Hibberd, Dominic, *Owen the Poet*, MacMillan Press, Basingstoke, 1986, p.102. I am indebted to the late Professor Hibberd for his unstinting

assistance and permission to quote from his extensive works on Wilfred Owen.

11. See my *Hades Moon* for further details of Owen's birthchart.
12. Schwartz, Robert, *Courageous Souls*, Whispering Winds Press, USA, 2007, p.36. (Now reissued as *Your Soul's Plan*).
13. This incident was mentioned in a radio programme from an account by Harold Owen some years ago but I have mislaid the reference and the follow-up information I obtained.
14. Owen, Wilfred, *Futility*.
15. See *Good Vibrations* for how to move a soul on and how to speak with them to ascertain their needs – this is work that only experienced therapist and soulworkers should undertake unless an emergency arises.

Conclusion

1. www.marioreading.com This entry was posted on Saturday, February 28th, 2009 at 12:13pm and is filed under Uncategorized. You can follow any responses to this entry through the RSS 2.0 feed.
2. http://www.jotrust.co.uk

Other Books by The Wessex Astrologer

www.wessexastrologer.com

Lightning Source UK Ltd.
Milton Keynes UK
21 September 2010

160154UK00001B/19/P